SPORT AND SOCIETY IN MODERN FRANCE

SPORT AND SOCIETY IN MODERN FRANCE

Richard Holt

Lecturer in History
University of Stirling

ARCHON BOOKS
Hamden, Connecticut

© Richard Holt 1981

First published 1981 in the UK by
THE MACMILLAN PRESS LTD
London and Basingstoke
and in the U.S.A. as an Archon Book
an imprint of
THE SHOE STRING PRESS, INC.
995 Sherman Avenue,
Hamden, Connecticut 06514

Printed in Hong Kong

Library of Congress Cataloging in Publication Data

Holt, Richard, 1948–
  Sport and society in modern France.

  Originally presented as the author's thesis, Oxford,
1979.
  Bibliography: p.
  Includes index.
  1. Sports—Social aspects—France. I. Title.
GV706.5.H64 1980   306'.4   80–18196
ISBN 0–208–01887–5

For Jim Holt and Liz Glass

Contents

List of Plates

The cover photograph and plates 2, 9, 12 and 13 are reproduced by courtesy of *Presse-Sports*; plates 1, 3, 4, 6, 7, 8, 10, 11, 14 and 15 by courtesy of H. Roger-Viollet; and plate 5 by the Mansell Collection.

Acknowledgements

When I applied for a reader's ticket at the Bibliothèque Nationale, I was eventually interviewed by an official of the library who asked me what I wished to do. I replied that I was thinking about writing a thesis on French sport. A mixture of pain and sheer disbelief crossed his face, and I thought I would be told to buy a track suit and sent off to the nearest park. I rather felt as if I were impugning the dignity of French culture by the mere mention of sport in so august an institution, but after careful checking of my letters of recommendation I was given my ticket. After a while I started to like that byzantine institution with its strange indexes and even stranger characters. When a pile of books on football or cycling arrived on my desk I would get the odd bemused look from an elderly scholar sitting nearby. 'What on earth are these foreigners up to?' you could almost hear them saying to themselves. But the porters who delivered the books were less surprised that I should want to read about Georges Carpentier or the Tour de France, and occasionally stopped for a brief chat or to look at a few photographs.

There were a number of people who offered advice and encouragement, and I would like to thank them here. As usual, there are far more than I can mention by name, and I hope those who are not acknowledged here will excuse the omission. Keith Thomas first aroused my interest in social and cultural history when I was an undergraduate. Through his teaching and research he helped me to see that any aspect of the past can be of interest, providing the right questions are asked. I was equally fortunate in my thesis supervisor, Theodore Zeldin. He urged me to do an unusual doctorate and gave me the time and freedom I needed to finish it. He was always encouraging and read various drafts of chapters at a time when he had a great deal of other work to do. The debt I owe to his recent history of France will be evident from the notes at the end of this book. Associate membership of St Antony's College provided access to research facilities and stimulating company from which I gained a great deal in academic and personal terms. Richard Cobb was full of enthusiasm, good humour and fascinating anecdotes. Like so many other students of France, I have reason to be grateful to him. As very few people have written about sport from a serious historical point of view, my other academic acknowledgements are relatively few. However, I would like to single out Professor Eugen Weber, whose excellent work on the cultural and political significance of *fin-de-siècle* French sport provided a starting point for my research. I owe a great deal to his pioneering articles. His advice on archives was also helpful, as was that of Michael Marrus. Roderick Kedward's criticism of the political material was amiable and constructive, and my colleague Iain Hutchison commented on the first two chapters with friendly astringency. I hope I have benefited from their advice, though, of course, I take full responsibility for any short-comings in the finished product.

I would like to thank Nigel and Maggie Pennington for their friendship and generous hospitality in Paris over a number of years. Amongst other friends who helped me at various times I would like to give a special word of thanks to Danièle Troillet, Andy Stelman, Hilary Kemp, Gavin Kitching, Rog and Sandy Baars, Paul Joannides, Jan and Norman Waugh. I also wish to thank the President and Fellows of St John's College, Oxford; the Social Science Research Council; the University of Stirling; and the Carnegie Trust. My colleagues at Stirling have been pleasant and supportive, and I have been exceptionally for-tunate in my typist, Margaret Hendry, who typed and corrected several drafts of what was often a difficult and exasperating manuscript. She has been unfailingly helpful.

Finally, my deepest debt is to Liz Glass, who constantly encouraged me in my early years of research, helped me to settle in France and urged me to complete my work despite the fact that the abrupt and unjust termination of her own research had caused her deep and prolonged despair. Beside the usual sacrifices made by the spouses of those in academic life, hers was very great indeed. I am deeply grateful.

Edinburgh, October 1979   Richard Holt

List of Abbreviations

AD	Archives Départementales
AN	Archives Nationales
Bib. Hist. Coll. Act.	Bibliothèque Historique de la ville de Paris. Collection 'Actualités'
Con. Gen. PV	Conseil Général du département de la Seine: Procès-verbaux
Con. Mun. PV	Conseil Municipal de la ville de Paris: Procès-verbaux
Con. Mun. RD	Conseil Municipal de la ville de Paris: Rapports et Documents
Deb. Parl. Ch. Dep.	Débats Parlementaires: Chambre des Députés
ENSEPS	Ecole Normale Supérieure d'Education Physique et des Sports
FGSPF	Fédération Gymnastique et Sportive des Patronages de France
FSGT	Fédération Sportive et Gymnastique du Travail
USFG	Union des Sociétés Françaises de Gymnastique
USFSA	Union des Sociétés Françaises des Sports Athlétiques
UVF	Union Vélocipédique de France

I Introduction: Sport in its Social Context

As organised sport is now so important an element of modern popular culture, it is perhaps surprising that historians have paid such scant attention to its origins and development. 'Grandfather clocks, balloons and potatoes have benefited from the historical studies that sports and games still lack', comments the author of one of the few pieces of serious historical research on the rise of sport. Other writers on the subject confirm the justification of this remark. An exploratory French work on the sociology of sport published in 1964 complained of the almost complete absence of books dealing with sport from a social or historical perspective. Indeed, until recently the study of leisure as a whole has been virtually ignored by historians. Even in Britain, where so many sports originated, 'the historical coverage of sport has failed to keep up with its increase in social importance in the past century'. The histories of sport which have been written so far are not the work of historians but of popular journalists or important officials in the world of sport itself. In general, they take the form of commentaries on record-breaking performances interspersed with anecdotes evoking the great days of a particular club or a famous sportsman. From such works we learn little of direct relevance to the understanding of sport as a social phenomenon. The interest of large numbers of ordinary people in the achievements of a coterie of great players is taken for granted. But to the social historian it is the involvement of the masses itself which is important. Instead of describing sporting techniques in great detail or moments of outstanding individual achievement, a social history of sport has to show how games move in step with society, explaining the relationship between changing material and cultural circumstances on the one hand and the transformation of physical recreation on the other.[1]

The chief conceptual difficulty in studying sport as a social activity is obvious enough. What are the questions we should be asking about the relationship between recreation and society? What forces influenced the way in which sports developed, and in what respects did these emergent forms of amusement themselves reflect wider social change? If we are to proceed beyond the bare bones of a chronological narrative, proper questions about the role of sport in society have to be formulated, but here we get little assistance from contemporary social theorists. There is no systematic sociological study of sport which provides a widely agreed framework of interpretation. The historian is thrown back on a number of competing, often conflicting, assertions and hypotheses, most of these adding conspicuously little to our knowledge of the evolution of leisure activity; a leading international authority on the sociology of leisure has complained bitterly of the 'ahistorical' quality of most work on the subject. What is missing from sporting theory is an assessment of the primary material factors involved. The changing nature of work – not simply the hours of work but the character and intensity of it – is clearly of great importance. In addition, there are other influences to consider, such as urban development, levels of affluence, education and literacy, mass production, better communications, improvements in diet and public health, greater longevity, the place of the young in society; these are just some of the factors which have a bearing on what we do with our bodies in our spare time.[2]

It is worth stressing at the outset that in looking at the development of sport in France we are not dealing with a minority interest or a passing fad. The subject is by no means as obscure as it sounds to a British or American audience inured to the idea that the French are not a sporting people. In Anglo-Saxon circles the French are not renowned for their prowess in sports. Frenchmen are thought to be good lovers, good talkers and good cooks but not good sportsmen. There is about as much truth in this as there is in the converse French stereotype of the typical Englishman complete with bowler hat or the Yankee with money to burn. In fact, sport is as popular in France as it is almost anywhere else. Strangers to France often confuse a lack of international distinction in a narrow range of activities with a lack of interest in sport at the grass-roots level. This poor competitive reputation is in itself largely undeserved and reflects the tendency of foreigners to discount achievements in sports like cycling and skiing. Variety is the keynote of French sport. While it may be the case that the French spread their talent too thinly, there is no shortage of talent itself. Nor is the rise of sport a recent phenomenon, a product of the New France of the fifties. The roots of the sporting revolution lie in the *belle époque*. It was around the turn of the century that traditional sports assumed their modern forms and during the inter-war years that modern sports won a mass following in France.

To get a rough idea of the pace and scale of recreational change we need only look briefly at the state of sport under the Second Empire. As late as the 1860s physical recreation was divided more or less arbitrarily between the equestrian and venatic diversions of the rich and the traditional village games of the poor. A handbook designed to familiarise the affluent foreign visitor with the sports of Paris in the 1850s restricted itself to a discussion of riding, hunting and shooting, with a brief mention of other forms of exercise tacked on as an after-thought. With the exception of the growth of horse-racing, which became popular under the Second Empire, sport remained overwhelmingly traditional. Despite a few half-hearted attempts at cricket by anglophiles, it was not until the 1880s that English sports began to spread to the upper classes. The leisure activities of the lower classes remained deeply influenced by custom until the end of the nineteenth century, although after 1850 earlier corporate and religious festivals began their irreversible decline, taking with them most of the sports associated with traditional artisan society. Yet, as late as 1880, no less a social observer than Paul Lafargue, the athletic son-in-law of Karl Marx, could still conceive of working-class leisure in terms of 'repos populaires' and 'grandes réjouissances' – collective gatherings, street carnivals, guild feasts and the like. Communal festivities still took place; Carnival on Shrove Tuesday in Paris continued to fill the streets. But the old verve and meaning was disappearing, the *fête* was losing its inner life.

Within the lifespan of a single generation there was a dramatic transformation of leisure activity. A recent survey of French rural life notes that 'whatever indicator we turn to . . . the 1880s and the quarter century that follows them appear as a water-shed'. This is certainly true of sports. Obviously there were important regional differences in the speed at which modern sports replaced old village games, but there can be no doubt that, as a whole, recreation was in the melting pot, as age-old indigenous amusements like skittles and quoits gave way before the allure of the bicycle and team games like rugby and football. Sports lost their casual, communal and regionalised quality and became uniform, national and highly organised. Whereas older traditions of play were essentially spontaneous and unregulated, modern sport was carefully controlled. Rules permitted equality of opportunity for contestants, and emphasis shifted from enjoyment of activity for its own sake to the result of that activity (i.e. winning or losing). The quest for victory is at the heart of modern sport and serves to distinguish it from traditional folk games, which often paid more attention to how the game was played than to who was the winner. Sack-races and leapfrog do not have sophisticated rules and sometimes do not enshrine the concept of competition at all. Traditional football involved hundreds of villagers milling around, pushing and shoving with no particular collective object other than getting the ball into the territory of the neighbouring parish and enjoying themselves at the same time. These matches were often little more than local rituals. There was none of the specialisation of roles found in the modern forms of football. Nor had the game the secularised character it has today. The idea of measuring physical performance with the scientific precision of the stop-watch would have been quite alien, and probably even repugnant, to the forebears of those who timed the stages of the Tour de France or calculated the goal averages of their local football team.[3]

The speed with which traditional patterns of amusement were replaced by new sports in the last decades of the nineteenth century was remarkable, though quite in keeping with the pace of social change as a whole. Within twenty years rugby, which had been the élite preserve of polite Parisian schoolboys, had become the collective winter passion of half the Midi. Football soon ceased to be the prerogative of a few privileged anglophiles and within twenty years had also established itself as a leading participant and spectator sport. Hundreds of small sports clubs of every kind were founded around the turn of the century and a complex network of local, regional and national leagues had been set up by 1914. Sport spawned its own bureaucracy. Cohorts of officials came into existence to organise, administer and adjudicate. At the same time the rise of sport as a form of commercial entertainment saw the creation of a new occupational category: the professional sportsman. This general impression of momentous change is borne out by even the most cursory glance at the membership statistics of the major sporting bodies of the period. The Union des Sociétés Françaises des Sports Athlétiques, which organised rugby, football and athletics, grew from around 200 clubs in the late 1890s to over 1600 on the eve of the First World War. By the 1930s there were over 5000 football clubs in France. Equally dramatic was the rise of the Catholic sports federation, which had a mere handful of teams in 1905 but claimed an active membership of around 180,000 by 1914, and the state-supported gymnastics organisation was even larger. In 1900 around half a million hunting permits were issued and by the 1930s this figure had quadrupled. Sport had become an item of mass consumption.

These are the bare bones of the story, but what lies beneath them? No simple formula can place the development of sports in France in the late nineteenth and early twentieth centuries in its full and proper perspective. The nature of French society is too subtle and complicated to permit, for example, a straightforward correlation between the rate of industrialisation on the one hand and the emergence of a new pattern of physical recreation on the other. It was in the slow-moving towns of the south-west, one of the most economically backward regions of France, that the modern game of rugby had most success. The evolution of sport both as a participant activity and as a spectator activity was influenced not only by economic and environmental change but by a wide range of other cultural and social factors. For instance, the rise of literacy and the growth of the popular press had an important bearing on the spread of interest in new sports and spectacles, whilst the changing attitude of society towards adolescence and a new sense of individualism amongst the young themselves was in part expressed through sporting activity. Changes in the nature and amount of free time available had a crucial role in popularising spectator sport amongst manual workers, whereas middle-class participation in sport was influenced more by factors such as social prestige and fashion. Nor can cultural-cum-political forces like nationalism or Darwinism be overlooked. A study of the history of French sports requires both familiarity with many well-worn themes of French history and an interest in some hitherto neglected aspects of behaviour and opinion.

Perhaps the best starting point for a survey of these diverse influences is traditional recreation itself and the place of sports within it. Under the *ancien régime* popular leisure activities had tended to cluster around the *fête*, which was an integral part of daily life. Festivals and feasts split up the working year into a large number of public holidays, which included official state or religious celebrations and the more popular, spontaneous and profane festivities organised by the local community in accordance with long-standing traditions of public amusement. Beneath the seemingly infinite variety of pre-industrial recreation lay a basic pattern of communal involvement. In fact, it can be argued that leisure as we know it – 'non-obliged' time free from the demands of work, family and social duties not voluntarily chosen – was unknown in traditional French society. The custom of the village, the *quartier* or the guild largely determined the use a person made of his time, whether at work or at play, and no sharp distinctions were drawn between the two. Sports, like other forms of popular entertainment, were intimately linked to a wider pattern of social life in which all were expected to participate in accordance with their place in the community.[4]

Along with singing, dancing and feasting, the playing of sports had a major place in the world of the *fête populaire*. There is almost no end to the number of different activities coming under the general heading of sports which were found in traditional festivities in one part of France or another. Where there were suitable rivers, jousting by teams of boatmen was a favoured spectacle, and long and often violent ball games, sometimes ranging over several miles and usually ending in bloody noses and broken bones, were a frequent accompaniment to festivals, especially at Whitsun. Contests involving the baiting and fighting of animals were commonplace and they also often degenerated into a brutal affray. Other, less violent, sports were popular as well. Athletic events involving lifting, throwing, wrestling or running were often held and it was customary to give a prize in cash or in kind to the winner. Skittles, varieties of bowls, or quoits were played by all ages and by either sex, as were numerous traditional games like blindman's buff and egg-

and-spoon races. Each area had its own unusual sports and pastimes which might be quite unknown outside of the immediate locality. There were no national sports, for France was a nation only in the strictly dynastic sense. Hunting, with its elaborate and costly rituals, was common to the nobility no matter where they lived, but in terms of popular recreation France was a collection of disparate regions, each separate from the other and all internally fragmented by dozens of local traditions and peculiarities.[5]

It is against this background of communal involvement, infinite diversity and a high degree of socially tolerated violence that the subsequent development of sports in France should be considered. In the course of the nineteenth century ancient patterns of amusement were steadily eroded by an amalgam of factors, the most important of which appears to have been the weakening of the commune as a social institution through the development of economic specialisation and the steady secularisation of urban and rural life. In addition to this, the drift to the towns, improved education, and the spread of more humanitarian attitudes towards animals and towards other human beings all played a part in determining how men chose to exercise and amuse themselves. Although the traditions of the *fête* lingered on amongst manual workers until the late nineteenth century and survived in remote peasant communities well into the twentieth, on the whole Frenchmen came to value choice in the games they played and were increasingly guided by individual taste rather than by communal tradition.[6]

The growth of the professional and commercial middle classes had a profound impact on the development of new sports and the modification of old ones. In general, they found traditional festivals distasteful and alien. They sought less brutal and more orderly activities for themselves and their sons, many of whom were required to spend ever longer periods of their youth in secondary and higher education. These influences on games were first apparent in Britain, where the athletic sports of the village were recast in the mould of middle-class values in the public schools of the mid-nineteenth century. The new versions of traditional football (rugby and soccer) restricted play to a specific area and duration. Excessive violence was prohibited through an elaborate set of regulations, which were underpinned by a moral code exhorting the competitor to respect his opponent and 'play the game'. The new sports were designed to train youths for the competitive life and yet contain their individualism within a framework of loyalty to the team. Fair competition, or 'fair play' as it came to be known, was the guiding principle, and it was in this spirit that these sports were adopted by part of the French élite.

Whilst their elders stressed the moral and practical advantages of athletic activities, the younger members of the bourgeoisie for whom the new sports were intended saw them primarily as a liberation from the stern discipline of the *lycée* and the unremitting pressure of the French examination system. The new legion of students took up sport with great enthusiasm. There were as many young men training to be doctors in 1911 (around 10,000) as there had been fully qualified members of the medical profession in 1876, and the numbers in architecture and engineering shot up in similar fashion. To privileged young men such as these, competitive sport came to be seen as a release, a symbol of freedom, a celebration of feeling over intellect. The early popularity of sports with students and *lycéens* encouraged others from less privileged *petit-bourgeois* backgrounds, driven on by similar frustrations and with the added incentive of social emulation, to use their spare money and organisational skills to form sports clubs. Foremost in this category come the young *employés*, the clerks, and the 'reps' or salesmen whose numbers grew so rapidly with the expansion of banking, insurance and retailing services. There were around half a million minor civil servants in France by 1914, whilst the number of primary and secondary teachers had doubled in thirty years and continued to grow. What were these active young men to do with themselves in the years before they married when they were still living at home? They sought respectable substitutes for the fun and games of the *fête*, and to many of them the private sports club, meeting in the backroom of the café and renting playing fields nearby, was the focal point of local society; the club provided a playful outlet for their pent-up energies away from the enervating routine of the office, a place for the companionship of their male peers, and a welcome break from the surveillance of family, employer and fiancée.[7]

The appeal of modern sports also comes in part from an increased awareness of the need to promote actively physical health and from a decline in the traditional fatalism with which illness was accepted. Although folkloric remedies and primitive superstitions still abounded, there was significant progress towards a more rational and scientific understanding of the body. The public gradually began to realise that their limbs were like machines requiring maintenance; the body had to be kept in good order by regular physical exercise, for all too often work, whether at the office desk or the factory bench, did not provide the human frame with the activity it required. Modern sport involved the gratuitous expenditure of energy in the name of exercise, an alien concept to the traditional peasant but an attractive one to the industrial worker increasingly tied to the rhythm of the production line. More and more individuals came to demand open spaces, fresh air and an opportunity to escape the polluted atmosphere of modern urban life. Linked to this was the growing tendency to try to get out of the city and the spread of holidaying on a modest scale. The taking of weekend rail excursions into the countryside or to the new seaside resorts became popular. Sport was an enjoyable way of having a break and taking exercise.

Men probably came increasingly to regard work as 'instrumental', that is as a means to an end rather than as an end in itself; non-work time became 'leisure', when man could express himself more fully than in a job stripped of ritual and sociability. Hours of work fell gradually from around twelve to ten a day during the latter part of the nineteenth century, although the nature of this process often varied greatly from place to place and between one type of job and another. Despite determined efforts by the trade unions, the eight hour day was not won until 1919 and it was only during the twenties that the Saturday half-holiday became fairly widespread. These changes, which culminated in the forty hour week legislation of the Popular Front in 1936, gave an enormous boost to both participant and spectator sport amongst workers whilst leaving the bulk of peasants largely unaffected.

Literacy and the development of the popular press also played a notable role in the spread of sports. About one fifth of all army conscripts were found to be illiterate in the early 1870s but by the end of the century this figure had fallen to one twentieth. The new reading public took a lively interest in exercise. An analysis of the *Annuaire de la presse française* reveals that only 21 newspapers were classed as 'sporting' in 1881 but by 1900 the

number had more than doubled and stood at 219 in 1930. Young
men began to take an interest in new sports by reading about
them as well as by watching others play. For the older man there
was the possibility of subscribing to the *Journal des Chasseurs* or
one of the many other field sports periodicals that sprang up
around this time; here he could learn the rudiments of game-
shooting and find advertisements for land or vacancies in a
nearby club. In 1902 Parisian newspapers devoted only 3·2 per
cent of their space to sport. By the eve of World War One half a
page was about the average and this rose to a full page in the
twenties. By 1958 Paris papers were allotting '14·7 per cent of
their space to sport, as compared with 9·9 per cent to general
news'. Perhaps more significant than these averages is the place
of sport in the new mass press. *Le Petit Journal* and *Le Petit
Parisien* were each selling more than a million copies a day by
1900 and they found in sports, particularly in cycling, just the kind
of apolitical titillation they needed. *Paris Soir*, with 1·8 million
readers in 1939, had a huge sports staff of photographers and
journalists and ran a three-page Monday sports supplement. In
addition, France boasted a highly successful daily sports newspaper, *L'Auto*, which was selling more than forty million copies a
year by 1914 and organised the Tour de France. Commercial
spectator sport and the popular press were inseparably bound
together in the web of mass culture in France. Interest in sport
spread from the papers to the radio. Between 1930 and 1939 the
number of radio sets rose from half a million to five-and-a-half
million, and the reporting of sport figured prominently in the
leisure listening of the nascent electronic age.[8]

The influence of the mass press on the urban working classes
seems to have been primarily directed at increasing the size of
crowds at spectator sports rather than encouraging wider
participation in sporting activity. During the decade preceding
1914 younger workers were beginning to form football teams
and to buy bicycles – some even became professional cyclists –
but, with the exception of gymnastics, the real boom in active
involvement came with the war itself and in the wake of the
eight-hour day in 1919. The early twenties saw a phenomenal
upsurge in lower-class sport. During the *belle époque* it was at the
vélodromes – the cycling tracks – or in the crowds that gathered to
watch major football or rugby matches that the working classes
made their presence felt in sport. During the last quarter of the

nineteenth century real wages may have risen by as much as a third, and other surveys of the value of lower-class possessions in cities like Paris, Lyon, Lille and Toulouse confirm that manual workers were much better off in the early twentieth century than they had been eighty or ninety years earlier. Between 1914 and 1940 inflation eroded savings and assisted those in a position to bargain for higher wages. Growing numbers of working men now had small weekly surpluses to spend on themselves. In their search for alternatives to the dying artisan culture of the past, skilled and unskilled workers turned not only to music and dance halls, and to bigger and more splendid cafés in which to drink, they also began to take a serious interest in commercial sporting entertainment. In the conviviality and sense of group identity engendered at the stadium they found a reassuring substitute for the cheerful tribalism of the *fête populaire*. In the Tour de France urban and rural populations alike found a *fête nationale* which actually coincided with the new Bastille Day celebrations.[9]

There now remains the role of the state to consider. In what sense can it be said that a series of governments promoted the cause of organised sport in France? Despite several reforms including the introduction of 'compulsory' periods of gymnastic exercise in secondary schools, very little real progress was made. The state would not make sufficient funds available for the purpose and there was no proper provision or inspection of facilities or staff. In fact, there were relatively few physical education teachers in schools, and one *lycée* normally had to share the services of a retired army instructor with several other similar establishments in the area. Gym teachers were something of a joke within the rarefied world of the *lycée* and cannot be considered to have given much impetus to the spread of sports. Nor did these unfortunate individuals do much better in the army itself. The large conscript army was the only other national institution in a position to influence physical education on a grand scale but, as a detailed study of the role of sports in the army has recently shown, lively theoretical debates about the physical instruction of the forces had a limited practical effect. School and army encouraged the pupil or recruit to be active, but neither the educational system nor the forces strongly favoured any sport other than gymnastics. It was the First World War, mingling peasant and proletarian in the same regiment, which did most to spread the gospel of modern sport.[10]

The state did give subsidies to such bodies as the Union des Sociétés Françaises des Sports Athlétiques and the Union des Sociétés de Gymnastique de France, and by the immediate post-war period these grants were running at several hundred thousand francs to each of the major organisations. The state did not hinder the cause of sport; on the contrary, it encouraged exercise but it did so indirectly. There was no national sports programme or planned expansion of physical education until the 'Loisirs Populaires' movement of the Popular Front era and the subsequent search of the Vichy regime for new forms of moral and social discipline. Although the state followed rather than led in the development of modern sports, a fair number of politicians lent their support to a wide range of organisations devoted to the regeneration of France through gymnastics and sports. National-ism, so powerful throughout late nineteenth-century Europe, was heightened in France by an enduring resentment against Germany over Alsace-Lorraine. *Revanche* and Darwinism were a potent blend and helped legitimise the cause of sport amongst sceptics and traditionalists. Efforts were made to infuse sports with the dominant militaristic and nationalistic values of the day. 'Il nous faut du muscle' became a shibboleth amongst patriots, as sport took its place in the strident national revival of the *avant-guerre*.

Having outlined the general historical influences on the development of sport, there remain the practical problems of finding the best method to treat so little known a subject and choosing particular sports to study in depth. A selective approach has been used for the simple reason that comprehen-sive coverage of all sporting activities would have been impos-sible. But there are two difficulties arising from the case-study method which require mention here. The first is that this approach concentrates the reader's attention in such a way that it is sometimes hard to see the wood for the trees. By basing each chapter on a particular sport there is a tendency to lose sight of the general evolution of physical recreation and to over-emphasise the special features of individual activities. While it is important to separate the different strands in the story, it is equally important to give full weight to the common social characteristics shared by many sports. Certain themes crop up again and again in the studies of individual sports – democratisation, social conflict, sociability, snobbery, violence, politics – and these common social and ideological aspects are examined separately in the thematic chapters which follow the case-studies. Thus Part I consciously anticipates some of the later social material, whilst Part II seeks to place the major activities in a wider sociological and historical context.

This brings us to the second difficulty: the problem of selection itself. Which sports out of the dozens to choose from should be selected for detailed treatment? The bulk of material in this study has been drawn from the specialist literature on the following sports: hunting and shooting, bullfighting and cock-fighting, gymnastics, rugby, association football, athletics and cycle-racing. In the final analysis no selection can be entirely objective, but an attempt has been made to strike a reasonable balance between the traditional and the modern, the casual and the highly organised, the indigenous and the imported. Cheap and expensive sports attracting correspondingly popular and exclusive followings are included; the balance between individual and team activities, animal and non-animal sports is also reflected in the sample. Special care has been taken to give roughly equal emphasis to participant and spectator sports. Sport is simultaneously exercise for some and entertainment for others, and both aspects deserve equal emphasis. Therefore, the second and third chapters deal with purely participant sports (field sports and gymnastics); the fourth chapter looks at a series of activities which combine both participant and spectator elements (athletics, rugby and football); and the fifth and sixth chapters deal exclusively with commercial spectacles (cycle-racing, bullfighting and cockfighting). The major cross-cutting themes then follow.

A monograph study of so diverse and neglected a range of activities which spans a full century in the history of a large and complex country is naturally vulnerable to errors of omission. Inevitably, some fascinating and important forms of sport have had to be left out. Fishing was a popular sport favoured by lower-class men in middle age, and after 1900 urban youths began to go swimming in the public baths that were being built in the larger cities. Winter sports began in earnest around the turn of the century; mountain-climbing and hill-walking were enjoyed by younger middle-class men, often students, anxious to flee the sprawling cities and 'get back to nature'. Rifle-shooting was an extremely popular activity, almost a patriotic duty in the east of France, and deserves further study, as do traditional games like *pelote*. Even *boule* has had to make do with a far shorter space than its popularity deserved. Tennis, too, one of the few games open to women and a game at which the French excelled, had to be unduly restricted. Finally, horse-racing became very important and its absence is particularly regrettable because of the links it had with popular gambling. The broad canvas chosen for this study has meant that regional variations and technical details have often had to be omitted even from those sports selected for detailed analysis. The Tour de France, for example, could take up many more than the few pages allotted to it here. It would have been possible to produce a full-length study of each sport in its own right, and perhaps one day each will have one. But a precondition of any future research is a broad national survey of the most significant developments. Further research on regional patterns of recreation, articles on the sporting history of major cities, or new biographies of individual sportsmen would then at least have a general outline on which to build. Finally, a brief word on the period covered by the study seems called for. The bulk of the evidence analysed here comes from the late nineteenth and early twentieth centuries. This was when the most important changes took place. Where appropriate, earlier and later developments have been examined, but more attention has been devoted to the emergence of sport as a form of mass leisure during the inter-war years than to the decline of traditional activities during the Second Empire and the early Third Republic.

Part I

Case-studies

2 The Spread of Field Sports

In studying the changes in the way individuals amused and exercised themselves during the Third Republic there is a natural tendency to concentrate on innovations like the bicycle or on new sports at the expense of more traditional activities. Yet in a sense this emphasis is misplaced. Before looking at what was new, it is surely worth sparing some time to examine old-established sports that continued to be popular. Until the early twentieth century the hunting of animals was unquestionably the major sporting preoccupation of the French, and with around two million permits issued annually this arguably remains so today. What could be more appropriate, therefore, than to begin an analysis of sport in France by considering the social changes that were taking place in its most traditional sector? Clearly, no single chapter could do justice to the infinite variety and technical complexity of field sports, which are here taken to mean the varieties of hunting and shooting available. Fishing, as already indicated, is not included in the selection of sports studied in detail, and was not considered to be in the same sporting category as hunting and shooting. As a surprised English visitor remarked, 'a French gentleman seldom wastes his time by the murmuring stream'. The aim here is simply to chart the changing social character of field sports at a crucial period in their history, and to contrast the infiltration of shooting by new social groups with the much more limited penetration of non-noble elements into the world of hunting. How far had the democratisation of field sports gone by 1940 and what factors favoured this process? This is the central question, but in answering it consideration must also be given to the way in which the inhabitants of rural France responded to an unprecedented invasion from the towns.[1]

Wider participation in field sports in the later nineteenth century took place against a background of social exclusivity with its origins in the *ancien régime*. Before the French Revolution the hunting of most animals had been reserved for members of the nobility; Louis XVI permitted commoners to hunt rabbits but sporting access to other game was a jealously guarded feudal prerogative which was not abandoned by the nobility until the famous night of 4 August 1789. The Constituent Assembly proclaimed that 'The Revolution gives to all landowners the right to hunt or shoot on their lands. Each proprietor has the right to kill the game on his possessions or to allow others to do so'. Between 1789 and 1810 field sports were in theory open to anyone. Thereafter, prefectorial permission to carry a sporting gun was obligatory, though it is unclear to what extent this requirement was enforced before the formal introduction of the *permis de chasse* under the July Monarchy. Much of the game on large *emigré* estates was destroyed during the Revolution and packs of valuable hunting dogs were dispersed. In 1804, however, Napoleon made an effort to revive the 'royal' hunt at Rambouillet and ordered some stags from Germany which arrived with a note expressing the hope that they would 'run before your Excellency's dogs and hunting horns as well as the Austrian soldiers ran before His Majesty's armies'. In 1815 there was no restoration of exclusive sporting rights to the hereditary nobility but neither was there any question of abandoning the hunt because of this setback. Instead, many nobles singlemindedly set about reconstructing their *équipages* with no less fervour than Charles X, who insisted that the royal hunt should be restored to its central place in the life of the court. Hunting became, if anything, more popular with the nobility as the reality of their political and military influence was progressively undermined.[2]

Before the introduction of the hunting permit in 1844 there is no precise data on the spread of hunting and shooting, and it is difficult to tell to what extent non-nobles took advantage of the opportunities open to them. Those members of the urban bourgeoisie who had bought noble or church land during the Revolution and the sizeable class of large rural landowners without titles that had grown up during the Napoleonic era probably aped the traditions of the upper-class shooting party, but fewer would have had the equestrian skills required for the hunt. To the townsman the lack of good communications, the cost of arms and ammunition, and the general ignorance and fear of the countryside which lurked in the urban breast formed almost as efficient a deterrent to the spread of field sports as the old feudal laws had been. To peasants the killing of animals was primarily an economic task designed to protect their crops and vary their diet; game shooting was perhaps a more enjoyable way of accomplishing these tasks than trapping, but it was also more expensive and less efficient. The image of the small proprietor beating his fields with his gun over his shoulder in search of something for supper is part of an idealised urban image of rural society cultivated by those who were not in close touch with the realities of peasant life. As we shall see, it was only after the turn of the century that peasants could think of indulging in so gratuitous an activity as shooting for fun.[3]

The control of field sports by the ruling rural élite of old nobles and recently enriched landowners was revealed with the introduction in 1844 of legislation requiring a sportsman to buy a twenty-five franc permit. In that year 125,153 permits were issued, approximately half the number of those persons possessing the vote under the July Monarchy. Clearly, it is premature to speak of a substantial middle-class interest in field sports at this date, but if we look at the sale of permits during the Second Empire, the spread of game-shooting beyond the ranks of the *notables* is undeniable. In 1850 there were approximately 150,000 hunting permits in circulation but by the end of the Second Empire this figure had grown to well over 300,000. It was during the Imperial era that France experienced her most rapid and sustained period of economic growth in the nineteenth century. As far as field sports were concerned the beginnings of large-scale industrialisation had two major consequences. Firstly, a rail network was laid down which henceforth permitted townsmen quick and relatively inexpensive access to the countryside. Admittedly, at this time the rail system was rudimentary, and large sections of the countryside remained isolated until the spread of the secondary network in the 1880s and 1890s. Nevertheless, the rural heart of France was now only a few hours away from Paris and local transport could be arranged from the major stations. Coupled with this advance was the improvement in the manufacture of arms, making guns cheaper, safer and simpler to use. In other words, many of the practical obstacles in the way of the urban sportsman had been removed. Secondly, there were more townsmen than before anxious to escape the polluted, cramped, noisy and sprawling cities and able to afford the recreational and social benefits of rural sports.[4]

A book of sporting lithographs published in 1859 depicts the early spread of shooting to the urban bourgeoisie, and a favourite theme of the sporting cartoons of the period is the inexperience of the newcomer, blasting away at everything in sight more in the hope than in the expectation of hitting anything. Honoré Daumier was fascinated by those who spent their Sundays chasing rabbits, hares and partridges on the outskirts of Paris during the Second Empire. He loved to draw timid city-dwellers running in fear from a deer or shooting a cat in mistake for a rabbit. One caption to a cartoon in which the *petit chasseur* stands ruefully over the dead body of his own dog reads 'They say a dog is a man's best friend, but is a man a dog's?' Daumier's sportsmen are always squabbling over a dead sparrow, snoozing when they should be shooting, or relieving themselves at the moment their dog raises a bird. We see the neophyte swindled by wily peasants who know the social value of a rabbit to a sportsman with an empty bag and a suspicious woman at home. One cartoon shows a wife asking her exhausted husband for the partridge he promised her; 'This time I brought it home as a pâté,' comes the unexpected reply. Improperly cocked guns go off without warning in railway carriages, bemused sportsmen stare at the trunk of a tree to see if a rabbit ran up there, whilst others boast that they never miss a shot as a rabbit runs right under their noses.[5]

The structure of landownership facilitated the spread of shooting to those who did not own land or shooting rights themselves. In Britain, where farming was organised on a large-scale capitalist basis, game-shooting was reserved for the rich who could afford to buy a share in a shooting estate or who were friends with a major landowner. Enclosure had cut back the amount of common land available for sports and the majority of estates were fenced and guarded. This was not so in France where the Revolution had confirmed the peasant in his rights to the land. In the mid-nineteenth century there were still extensive tracts of common land on which game could be found, and the majority of small proprietors did not bother to fence off their property. Peasants were usually prepared to allow strangers to wander over their lands killing small game that they regarded primarily as pests. While many no doubt privately resented the intrusion of outsiders, they rarely put up legal obstacles to game-shooting. English sportsmen were surprised and delighted by the French peasant's lack of a strong proprietory sense about his game. There was 'an almost unlimited liberty in traversing the country', remarked an English visitor to Brittany in the early 1850s. Providing you were considerate you could roam freely in search of hare and partridge, 'with no animated piece of fustian telling you with insolence to "Get off there"'.[6]

By the 1870s game-shooting was no longer the preserve of the rich and privileged, although it had not yet filtered down to the lower middle classes. Hunting remained the sport of the nobility *par excellence*, whilst shooting was now primarily a bourgeois activity. Socially, shooting was poised between the château and the commune. The President of the Republic had game birds bred for him at Rambouillet, but significantly the head of state was not expected to know how to hunt. Shooting, on the other hand, was regarded as an eminently Republican sport. It taught the citizen how to defend his country. The middle-aged, middle-class man taking up shooting with a view to enjoying the countryside and impressing his wife and friends could comfort himself with the additional thought that he was doing the state a service at the same time. Shooting had the great advantage of being easy to learn. In fact, the government provided subsidies for those wishing to take up the sport through the numerous rifle clubs that were founded in the wake of the defeat of 1870. By 1900 there were around 2000 such clubs in France, and the easy access to guns and ammunition they provided probably led many a Frenchman to try his hand at shooting real game, instead of the replicas of wild boar or other animals which were the favourite types of moving target in shooting competitions. The scene was set for an assault on field sports by the lower middle class and the aristocracy of labour.[7]

The rise of this new class of *chasseur* can be followed in the growth in permit sales, although the statistical information provided is of a very rudimentary nature. Whilst the number of permits issued annually probably gives a fairly useful picture of the general level of interest in field sports at any particular moment, the published information gives no indication of the occupation or permanent residence of permit-holders. The

Annuaire statistique admittedly provides a breakdown of permit sales by department but, as some sportsmen bought their permits in their home town and others in the area where they intended to shoot, it is impossible to distinguish the locals from the outsiders in the departmental figures. Statistics of permit sales must be used in conjunction with other references of a more literary kind to the changing composition of the field if they are to be of historical value in illustrating the theme of vulgarisation.

As far as sheer numerical increase is concerned the picture is fairly straightforward. As time passed and enforcement became more effective it was only in really remote areas that it was safe to shoot without a licence. This fact, coupled with the fall in the real cost of the permit as a result of rising living standards and inflation after 1914, meant that the total number of permits issued provides a reasonably accurate record of the actual level of participation in the sport. Within the ninety or so years spanning the mid-nineteenth century to the outbreak of the Second World War the number of Frenchmen taking out shooting permits increased about fifteen-fold. Permit sales doubled during the Second Empire, and between 1870 and 1914 numbers doubled again, rising from around 300,000 to over 600,000, with the bulk of the increase occurring from the mid-1890s onwards. The First World War gave an enormous boost to the sport. Conscription had familiarised the poor with firearms and the war permitted constant practice. The French 'Tommy', the *poilu* or 'hairy face', was allowed to shoot without a permit whilst on leave from the trenches. In the early 1920s there were more than a million licensed guns and by 1930 the pre-war figure of 600,000 had almost tripled. This astounding expansion levelled off in the thirties at around two million, where it has more or less remained since.[8]

Two major points about the nature of this increase are evident. Firstly, there is the general concentration of permit-holders in areas bordering on large urban centres. For instance, between 1895 and 1905 the two departments which issued the highest number of permits were the Gironde (17,909) and the Seine-et-Oise (17,717), clearly reflecting the proximity of Bordeaux and Paris respectively. In fact, all the departments of the Ile-de-France had similarly inflated permit sales. The point is not that the urban centres had a higher per capita level of sales (this was not so), but simply that a large number of the new recruits to the sport must have come from the big cities. The demand from the casual city gun was reflected in the soaring cost of renting sporting land and by the fact that rents varied in almost direct proportion to distance from the capital. Thus the average cost per hectare of sporting land in the early 1880s varied from 9·80 francs in the Seine-et-Marne and 8·41 in the Seine-et-Oise to around 2 francs a hectare in more distant areas like the Orne or the Somme where game was probably about as good. Sporting rents rose rapidly in the Paris area despite the Great Depression and the collapse in agricultural prices and land values. Writing as early as 1882, a contributor to the *Gazette des Sports Illustrés* noted that land near Paris which had been rented at 100 francs 25 years earlier could now fetch as much as 1000. As early as 1880 the state revised its policy of renting sporting land on nine-year leases and replaced them with five-yearly ones, which would reflect rising values more quickly.[9]

By the inter-war period there were so many people looking for shooting within easy reach of the big cities that some departments became completely saturated and game virtually disappeared from unguarded private land. Even before 1914 there was so little game on the common land of the Bouches-du-Rhône that sportsmen from Marseille used to talk of 'the year I'll shoot a hare' in the same way they would speculate about 'the year I'll get married'. Complaints about the general lack of game was one of the staple topics of sporting conversation in such areas, and during the years following the First World War something approaching a national debate on the subject was held. As numbers of enthusiasts rose vertiginously, established sportsmen demanded a substantial increase in the cost of the permit. Politically this was far too unpopular for centrist Republicans to contemplate, especially with the Communists calling for 'free shooting everywhere for everyone'. Conservation became an acute problem and game birds virtually disappeared from public land.[10]

From the turn of the century onwards there was a constant search for unexploited, peripheral sporting land in remoter departments where game was still relatively plentiful and sporting rents moderate. In the Landes, for instance, as early as the decade spanning 1895–1905 there was a decennial increase of 108 per cent in permit applications against a national average of

28 per cent. The hard-pressed sportsmen of the Gironde were spilling over into the sandy plains and pine woods to the south. As a large landowner in that area recalled in his memoirs, the number of casual guns and visiting clubs increased dramatically in the early twentieth century; where there had formerly been 'perhaps fifteen sportsmen visiting the forest once or twice a week . . . devotees of the sport sacrificing lucrative employment for the sake of their passion . . . in the years immediately preceding the First World War in the same area there were fifty sportsmen on weekdays and ten times that number on a Sunday'. Bad as it seemed to the affluent sportsman before 1914, the position in the twenties was far worse. Soon the pre-war years began to assume their now familiar rose-tinted glow as a haven of peace and privilege, a *belle époque* in fact. 'Before [the war]', wrote Henri du Blaisel d'Enquin in 1930, 'with a 28 franc permit field sports were still something of a minor luxury and even amongst the 500,000 sportsmen there was a little game for everyone'. But 'today', he continued in a tone of rising hysteria and indignation, 'field sports are a sacrosanct democratic right; with a permit costing only 7 or 8 gold francs the disappearance of game is imminent unless we fight every inch of the way against this current of demagogy'.[11]

From the preceding analysis of permit sales and distribution it is fairly clear that there were basically two types of twentieth-century sportsman: the most powerful group were the professional, commercial and industrial bourgeoisie, but they alone cannot account for the huge number of permits sold; during the first quarter of this century the group known as the *petits chasseurs*, composed of shopkeepers, skilled craftsmen and richer peasants, became far more numerous and influential. To understand the social complexion of the sport more fully we must examine each of these groups in turn. First comes the bourgeois gun with his upper-class pretensions and ostentatious affluence, measuring the success of the day's sport in the sheer number of pieces shot rather like he might tot up his earnings after a good day at the *Bourse*. The typical bourgeois initiate to game-shooting was the young business or professional man in his late twenties or early thirties who had finished his studies and completed his military service. He was either getting too old for team sports or had not heard of them, but he was still anxious to take active exercise.[12]

This description of the bourgeois gun is confirmed by a social breakdown of the members of the Saint Hubert Club, the leading field sports organisation of the period with a membership of around 50,000 in 1909. The members of the Saint Hubert Club were mostly either landowners, who usually joined because of their interest in hunting, or lawyers, doctors and businessmen, who were primarily concerned with shooting. The Club offered sportsmen legal advice, acted as an agency for the advertising of shooting, and offered concessions on certain items of sporting equipment. An examination of the occupations of Parisians wishing to join the Club in October 1913 reveals twenty-three individuals living off private incomes (*propriétaires-rentiers*), twenty-one businessmen, eight members of the liberal professions, three shopkeepers, two clerks and an artisan. The months of July 1906, August 1907, September 1908 and October 1910 reveal a strikingly similar occupational structure. But in the heavily industrialised areas like the department of the Nord the business element clearly outnumbered all others in the sporting community. In July 1906, forty-three out of a total of seventy-two prospective members of the Saint Hubert Club were businessmen, the rest were made up of seventeen landowners or shareholders, ten professional men, one shopkeeper and one artisan. An examination of several other months chosen at random confirms this picture of the sportsmen of the Nord. In the major cities it was the upper middle classes which dominated the Club, for it was they rather than the lower middle classes who went shooting on a regular basis and had most to gain from membership of a specialised body.[13]

But not all of the new recruits to the Saint Hubert Club came from the big cities. Shooting was popular with the professional people, merchants and officials who formed the élite of the numerous country towns of provincial France. Applications for membership in the department of the Loire in the month of August preceding the opening of the 1907 season included twenty-six from individuals describing themselves as *sans profession*, twenty-four from businessmen and fifteen from the professional and administrative classes; this balance between gentlemen of leisure and the salaried middle class was probably typical. The life of the small town bourgeoisie was itself fairly leisured in the later nineteenth century.

Some went so far as to take a job specifically for the sporting perks it offered. As a tax inspector recalled, the *fin-de-siècle* 'was like the garden of Eden for provincial functionaries; the easy rhythm of work at the office came as a welcome relief from the more serious daily rigours of the Field'. At the dinner given to introduce a new dignitary to his social equals the inspector happened to mention he was fond of shooting and was immediately invited to indulge his inclinations with the solicitor and the court bailiff. At first he reluctantly declined these offers because of the nature and volume of the work he thought he would have to do. 'A gale of laughter greeted this remark', and he was soon persuaded to play a full part in the round of shooting parties organised in the area. He frankly revelled in the opportunities his position afforded for a quiet afternoon's shooting during the week in the company of a handful of similarly leisured acquaintances. The inspector was happy and we may legitimately surmise that his *amis de chasse* cannot have been entirely dissatisfied with the arrangement. According to a local song, with which the inspector soon became familiar, the tax man was not supposed to take his job as seriously as he took his sport, and was expected to confine his researches to the surrounding fields and woods.[14]

Those whose occupations were less favoured from a sporting point of view usually joined a *société de chasse*. By the late nineteenth century most middle-class sortsmen were members of shooting clubs. There were basically two types of club. The first was the commercially run concern where a landowner sold shares in the season's sport; the second, more common arrangement was one where several sportsmen formed themselves into a club with a view to jointly renting sporting land. An authoritative work on field sports published in 1912 categorised clubs according to the rent they paid. For clubs which could pay over 2000 francs per person conditions were perfect, and for 1000 to 2000 francs a small estate of similar quality could be obtained. Below that figure standards varied greatly; some shoots were deceptive and produced very little – the practice of cheating naïve or bombastic townsmen was becoming common – whilst others gave good value for money. Most clubs were dominated by the local members of the upper bourgeoisie. The Société de Chasse de Monthieux-Lapeyrousse in the department of the Ain was probably typical of a fairly prosperous club; here twelve businessmen from Lyon rented 1200 hectares, including five woods and eleven lakes, at a cost of 600 francs each. Shooting took place twice a week. Members took the Lyon–Bourg train, alighting at Villars-les-Dombes and travelling the remaining few kilometres in a cart specially provided for the purpose. The entire business was supervised by Mathieu Gaillard, *négociant à* Lyon. These details are taken from the *Annuaire générale de la chasse*, published in 1912 as a reference work for the sportsman and listing hundreds of similar clubs as well as a number of smaller ones. Indeed, the fact that so thorough a reference work was called for is in itself an indication of the growing number of people with the time and money to take to the field.[15]

Clubs were extremely jealous of their proprietary rights and often became involved in squabbles with their neighbours. Internal politics were also fraught with difficulty. Members who were paying considerable sums of money to shoot expected to see results. Unfortunately, few had any real understanding of the problems of gamekeeping and often put their votes to the wrong use. Presidents were constantly being deposed in those clubs where members had the right to vote. There were frequent arguments over the type of shooting to be practised. In a club of, say, ten members, perhaps only two would be good shots. The skilled shot preferred rough shooting with the help of a trained gun dog, but the majority of the rank and file often refused to consent to the fatigue involved in this and insisted on having the game driven before them. Many good shots despised this form of shooting *en battue*, and were placed in the difficult position of either excluding their friends or adulterating their sport. 'Friendship' usually won the day, for a business deal might be clinched by a well-timed invitation to a day's shooting. Members of clubs made great use of their rights to bring a guest with them. Sometimes one member would bring three or four 'friends', hoping to share them out among other members at the station or on the train, only to be placed in the embarrassing situation of finding that his fellow shareholders had exceeded their quota too. After the war, as game became increasingly scarce, these invitations were all the more sought after and appreciated. Just as the British or American executive might combine business and pleasure on the golf course, so his French counterpart would invite a prospective customer 'to fire off a few rounds on well-stocked and guarded land'.[16]

There was keen competition between members to see who

could shoot the most in a day. Sharing out the bag was a sensitive issue and the expedient usually employed was to give the best shots a small choice before dividing the rest equally. Critics of the *sociétés de chasse* accused members of indulging in petty squabbling over who should have what, and for assessing the success of the day's sport in purely quantitative terms. In effect, it was claimed that the old friendliness of the gentleman's shooting party had given way to the new competitiveness of the bourgeois clubs, where an empty bag was rarely accepted with a good grace. Nobles often claimed that the traditions of good sportsmanship were being undermined by a strident acquisitive individualism, though the extent to which these criticisms were primarily motivated by resentment and distaste is hard to say.[17]

We can now turn our attention to the second group, the *petits chasseurs*, who usually could afford neither the time nor the money to shoot regularly. Increasingly they took up shooting as a holiday sport or as an excuse for the odd Sunday trip into the countryside for an invigorating walk. The lower middle classes were becoming more numerous and were better-off than ever before. The census of 1866 had revealed almost two million one-man businesses; but, remarkably, forty years later the census of 1906 recorded a doubling in this occupational sector to almost four million individual enterprises. Retailing was still organised on a personal basis; no society deserved the scornful Napoleonic epithet for the English – a nation of shopkeepers – more than the French themselves. In addition, education and office work expanded rapidly. Teachers and clerks proved to be some of the keenest of the newcomers to game-shooting. The participation of these groups in what had formerly been an exclusive activity was made possible by rising incomes as well as by improved communications and cheaper arms. Small savers prospered under the early Third Republic. In 1884 the savings banks (*caisses d'épargne*) held around 2000 million francs in deposits, but less than thirty years later in 1913 this figure had tripled to 6000 million francs. Presumably, many a provident family man used a small part of his nest-egg to buy himself a permit, a gun, and to rent a few acres of shooting. He could then behave just like an affluent sportsman, and perhaps might even be mistaken for one. In other words, whilst the *notables* acted as a reference group for the bourgeoisie, the bourgeoisie itself set the standards for those immediately below them in society. There was a definite social pattern behind the apparently random growth of the sport.[18]

The rapid expansion in the number of permit holders from the nineties onwards brought the problems of the *petit chasseur* to the fore. As game became less and less plentiful on common land, poaching was increasingly resented. Whereas the poacher had formerly been seen as something of a social bandit who robbed the rich to feed his family and friends, those who illegally trapped game on common land were seen as robbing ordinary people of their Sunday amusement. The Union des Chasseurs of the Gard complained that 'those who suffer are not the rich and famous . . . but the common clerk, farmer or workman'. Those who were deprived of pleasant and healthy relaxation were not only the local bourgeois: 'armourers, ironmongers, tailors, ribbon-weavers, café-owners and carters' suffered too. In the course of the late nineteenth century an increasing number of clubs were formed to provide cheap shooting for the lower middle classes and skilled urban workers. Take the case of the Société des Chasseurs Libres du Forez founded in 1889:

It was run by a baker from his own shop and had a mixed membership which included a butcher, two wine merchants, a café-owner, two sweet sellers, some local craftsmen and traders, two wholesale merchants, a manufacturer, a land-owner, a *rentier* and the master of a small forge. There was also a foreman from one of the glass factories. Metal craftsmen formed the largest group. There were five turners, four forgers, a general metal worker, a puddler and eleven armourers. We find also three miners and one master ribbon weaver.

Other clubs in the neighbourhood were similarly dominated by shopkeepers and armourers, though the presence of a large munitions industry in the area clearly meant that familiarity with arms was far more common amongst the skilled workers of Saint-Etienne than in the other major industrial cities of France. Elsewhere, shooting was probably less widespread amongst the working class, though by the 1920s workers were beginning to have more time and money to spare for such things.[19]

Advocates of cheaper shooting permits painted a glowing picture of the salutary effects which the spread of the sport to the working classes as a whole would have on the drink and crime problems of the big cities, but this doubtful hypothesis was never really tested. Radicals agitated against the institution of the permit, which they saw as a piece of class legislation, a survival of the bourgeois exclusiveness of the July Monarchy and unworthy of the Republic. In 1881 there was a proposal to abolish the permit altogether; in 1882 a reduction in price was proposed; a 24-hour permit was suggested in 1889, and the introduction of weekly tickets on sale at the *tabac* was added to this list in 1893. With the triumph of radical Republicanism, reformers redoubled their efforts to open up field sports to the lower orders. After five successive annual attempts, the Chamber of Deputies approved a bill to introduce daily permits for twenty-five centimes, but this measure was promptly interred by the more conservative upper house. The Marquis de Beauvoir's horrified prediction that a new kind of club would emerge – 'a shooting club with a twenty centime subscription that would help elect socialists to parliament' – was the product of an over-heated aristocratic imagination and had no firm basis in reality. As better-off sportsmen often pointed out, even if cheap permits were made available, most ordinary working men would still be unable to afford to shoot because of the cost of guns, dogs, ammunition and transport, not to mention the price of land. Shooting became the sport of the *classes moyennes* but was too dear for most urban workers. The permit issue was a good one to use to belabour the privileged, and at bottom it was little more than a radical brickbat.[20]

Nevertheless, from the countryman's point of view the spread of shooting to the lower reaches of the middle classes was bad enough, and he took little comfort from the fact that the proletariat were not yet fully involved. As early as 1889 an indignant sporting landowner from the centre of France wrote to complain of 'the cursed train' which was bringing urban sportsmen in ever increasing numbers into the hitherto undisturbed countryside. Formerly remote or peripheral areas like the Landes or the departments of Brittany were invaded by the more adventurous or impecunious urban sportsmen around the turn of the century. Some small landowners felt the Republic should protect them from these marauding pleasure-seekers, but other, more opportunistic communes and individuals often exploited the gullibility of the newcomer to the countryside. In fact, a veritable 'petite industrie' grew up which was devoted to the milking of ignorant townsmen through the placing of sporting advertisements that always promised far more than they could deliver. A village shoot would be described as full of game – 'une chasse giboyeuse' was the favourite expression – and inquirers would be told that the number of sportsmen would be rigorously limited. Nine times out of ten the shoot turned out to be almost barren, and eventually a court ruling established the principle that where there had been a clear case of misrepresentation the victim had the right to get his money back.[21]

The attitude of peasants towards shooting was closely related to their ability to take part in the sport. The imposition of the shooting permit was deeply resented in many rural areas 'not only because it was for gents against the peasant, but because it suggested that freedoms or privileges achieved within living memory might easily be lost again'. Emile Guillaumin's classic account of the life of a nineteenth-century sharecropper records that there was no question of an ordinary farmer being able to shoot. A landlord would rarely permit such sporting indulgence even if the peasant could afford the permit, which was unlikely. Hence poaching was regarded as a legitimate activity widely connived at by local people. Poaching was carried out on a vast scale and deserves a full study in its own right. Stories of hair-raising escapes from guards or policemen were part and parcel of peasant culture. These tales often involved fleet-footed poachers who, if caught, would take off their clogs so as to outstrip their adversaries, who usually wore heavy boots and spurs. The fleeing poacher would bend back the branches of young trees as he ran so as to impede his pursuers. Poachers frequently got away and a favourite story featured a young poacher who ran so fast he turned round and shouted to the *gendarmes*: 'If you can't do better than that there's no point in taking my shoes off'.[22]

The First World War changed this position considerably. Peasants benefited greatly from the fall in the real cost of the permit, the availability of firearms, and the freedom to shoot enjoyed by troops on leave. Ephraim Grenadou, a young farmer from the Beauce just starting to make his way after the war, recalled 'that shooting was the main amusement [of young married men]. One of my father's neighbours sold me a gun for seventy francs. I made the cartridges myself. I sold the game I shot to pay for the permit. At Saint-Loup there were a dozen guns but no-one ate any game, except perhaps a wild rabbit'. Protected shoots were not within the reach of those who worked the land and they strongly resented 'invasions' of city guns or poachers taking their game. Confrontations sometimes led to violence, although the peasantry's attitude generally tended to oscillate between a determination to capitalise on a scarce resource by renting out their land and a desire to amuse themselves. Villages began to 'communalise' their shooting, either letting out their lands collectively to city clubs or reserving it for themselves. By 1914 there were already thirty-five departments with villages that had organised their shooting in this manner and between the wars the practice became generalised. Communes increasingly tended to confine shooting rights to local residents. Mayors would often ban *battue* shooting altogether and charge outsiders for the right to shoot on village territory. These measures could cause friction, particularly with members of the local bourgeoisie who owned property in a commune but did not reside there. A well-off medal maker from Nimes wrote a furious note of protest to the prefect when the mayor insisted he pay thirty francs for the pleasure of shooting on his own land because he did not live in the commune. But the mayor was within his rights and it seems as if he got his way.[23]

As time passed the nobility ceased to struggle against the usurpation of game-shooting by the middle and lower classes, and took refuge in the complex rules and costly rituals of the hunt. The *chasse à courre*, or 'running hunt' as it was known, remained quite distinct from the *chasse à tir*. The term *chasseur* was applied to the masses who took up game-shooting; those who hunted the boar and the stag were called by the older term *veneur*. Shooting became a sport but hunting was always 'an art'. *L'art de la vénerie* was the expression commonly employed in the many technical works on hunting, most of which drew heavily on the classic treatises of the sixteenth and seventeenth centuries. In fact, modern huntsmen prided themselves on how little had changed since the great days of the *ancien régime*, when commoners were forbidden by law from hunting the stag or the boar and had to content themselves with lesser game.

Despite the theoretical freedom to hunt declared by the Revolution, the element of continuity was far more important than the minor changes that took place. Hunting stayed very much the same. One of the best known figures in the nineteenth-century hunting world was the Marquis de Foudras, son of an *émigré* Burgundian aristocrat who had returned to France determined to recreate the life of the eighteenth-century château in all its splendour. His son tried to maintain this tradition but turned to writing when the family finances collapsed in 1839. Thereafter he wrote around 140 books, many of which were historical romances. His best work, however, was on hunting and culminated with a grand project on the state of the hunt under the Second Empire; he planned thirty-two volumes, of which fourteen were completed at the time of his death in 1872. This seriousness of purpose found an echo in the great huntsmen who followed; the most celebrated *veneur* was, in fact, a woman, the Duchesse d'Uzès, who hunted the forest of Rambouillet with the famous Rallye Bonelles regularly from the death of her husband in 1880 until her own demise fifty-three years later in 1933. She was a stickler for protocol, a formidable *amazone* who, when not engaged in byzantine legitimist machinations (including the secret backing of Boulanger), loved nothing more than to discourse on horn calls or stag droppings.[24]

A survey carried out in 1889 found that almost all of the 73 great hunts (those with more than 40 hounds) belonged to nobles, as did most of the 197 packs of between 10 and 40 dogs. Apart from these there were a large number – estimates varied between 500 and 800 – of smaller packs of mixed ownership but with the nobility again taking a leading role. As a whole, hunting flourished under the Third Republic. Surprisingly, Republican politics were partly responsible for this. 'If politics has any influence over sport', remarked *Le Gazette des Chasseurs*, 'it is because of the boredom and distaste it generates.' After having strenuously fought for a return to monarchy in the 1870s, the nobleman responded to the consolidation of the Republic by a second 'internal emigration'. The high-born closeted themselves in their estates, where there was no need to breathe the democratic and secular air of republican society, and set about creating a private social world in which hunting had a major part to play. After all, what else was there for a man to do during long days on his estate with relatively little business to transact and few calls on his time in the way of public affairs?[25]

A brief examination of the state of hunting in France around 1900 reveals considerable regional differences. The Midi was not a favoured region for hunting because of the lack of good forest land. In Béarn wealthy British expatriates maintained two fox-hunts at Pau and Biarritz, but otherwise hunting was sparse and irregular. Moving north, the central region of France presented a great variety of hunting, especially around Touraine, Berry and Burgundy, but it was not until one reached the west and the Ile de France that hunting on the grand scale became frequent. Here the great hunting nobles like the Duchesse d'Uzès rubbed shoulders with millionaires like the Lebaudy brothers, Paul and Pierre, sugar-refining magnates and backers of Maxim's, who were related to the Schneider family and hunted the forest of Fontainebleau. At Chantilly the Duc d'Aumale, fourth son of Louis-Philippe and former Governor-General of Algeria, hunted his estates until his exile in 1886, whereupon the Duc de Chartres and Prince Murat took over the running of the forest. The best hunts in Normandy were run by Comte Emmanuel de Couteulx de Canteleu, famed for his breeding of pedigree bloodhounds, whilst in the west the Comte de Chambray, the Comte de Fresnaye, the Vicomte de la Rochefoucauld and the Baron de Layre were the most important *veneurs*. The Vendée was full of smaller hunts run personally by the highly traditional local nobility and boasting devices such as 'Vendée quand-meme!'[26]

Hunting certainly helped the upper classes maintain a sense of identity and cohesion at a time when many of them felt their future was in doubt. The hunt with its lavish trappings proclaimed the social supremacy of the nobility and allowed them to retain the illusion of power after they had relinquished it in reality. There were some half-hearted attempts to divest the sport of its aristocratic aura but, in the main, huntsmen revelled in their exclusive status. This was evident in the zeal with which keen huntsmen maintained the traditions of the sport, in particular the *messe de Saint Hubert*, the annual blessing of the hounds and their master in the name of the patron saint of the hunt. A painting of the Duchesse d'Uzès in 1904 by Tenré shows her with the entire pack assembled outside the church with clergy and villagers gathered around in a self-consciously feudal tableau; and every 6 November the Baronne de Rothschild continues the rite today. Whilst the hunt ball never seems to have become the social occasion in France that it was in England, great importance was attached to the dinner which followed a hunt. As a Gascon nobleman recalled, it was common for a neighbour or family friend to be invited for a week's hunting, for 'amongst rural gentlemen hunting stimulated a sense of intimacy which was reinforced by the long evenings spent eating and drinking'. Hospitality was an integral part of hunting.[27]

To what extent was the upper bourgeoisie able to penetrate this apparently closed world? In France there was no equivalent of the subscription pack of hounds kept by the British 'cits' such as the legendary hunting grocer, Jorrocks. Most hunts were the personal property of nobles, who normally hunted with other nobles. In France there was no large class of substantial tenant farmers to be patronised and placated as there was in England. Yet it would be wrong to accept entirely the view that hunting was a caste activity where no social mobility was possible. As in Great Britain the huge costs which the sport incurred necessitated the absorption of new wealth from time to time. Social mobility, however, took place on a carefully controlled individual basis.[28]

Some members of the upper bourgeoisie would do almost anything in order to be invited to ride with a great hunt. If the son of an important industrialist was invited to join a famous hunt it was a public sign that the family as a whole had been accepted into the best society. No expense would be spared to secure such distinction, and certain very rich men, bankers and captains of industry, were prepared to start hunts themselves at enormous personal cost in the hope of attracting influential nobles to hunt with them. A late nineteenth-century estimate of the cost of running a full-scale hunt put the cost at 80,000 francs a year. Only a person in the Rothschild income bracket could afford such a sum; indeed, it was precisely this group of high financiers which made up the most important new social element in hunting. At least, this is the impression critics of the hunt liked to give. The mayor of a small commune in the Seine-et-Marne adjoining the Rothschild estate fulminated against the depredations of the huntsmen at the 'Big House'. 'It is through invitations to hunt that the financial and propertied oligarchy are making close links with the top echelons of French society', complained the mayor, 'and these occasions provide the perfect opportunity for rich speculators to make a clean sweep of our small savings.' Whether it was at the hunt proper or on richly

stocked private shooting estates, there was definitely some
convergence of noble and upper bourgeois elements in field
sports around the end of the nineteenth century. It certainly
seems as if a number of smaller hunts were changing hands after
the turn of the century, although more detailed research is
required.[29]

Even if an invitation to hunt were procured, the elaborate
etiquette of the sport provided a formidable obstacle to the
uninitiated. It was only too easy for the newcomer to make a fool
of himself at the very moment when he had most hoped to make
a good impression. Hunting journals sometimes gave hints on
how to conceal one's ignorance of the finer points of the sport; in
1883 the *Sport Gazette* ran a whole series of articles designed to
give the aspiring huntsman enough knowledge to survive his
first proper meet. Stern warnings against the use of jargon were
issued. All too often its use could rebound on its user; it was
common for beginners to hold forth about the problems of
tracking at great length, only to confuse a boar print with a stag
print when the hunt actually began.[30]

By and large, therefore, hunting remained an activity for the
nobility. As such, it attracted a good deal of hostility from
radical Republican elements like the mayor cited above. Acting
as a spokesman for local interests he attacked the Rothschild's
interference with common rights and the damage to crops
incurred by the hunt. Those peasants who could afford to do so
occasionally harassed the hunt with legal suits, although over-
sensitive or downright reactionary huntsmen tended to exaggerate the effects of litigation on their sport. Consider the
following outraged contribution on the state of the hunt in
France around 1900: 'the division of property renders hunting
more and more difficult, for the law prohibits the presence of
dogs on the propery of anyone if the proprietor chooses to deny
the hunt the right of way . . . it is easy to forsee a time when
hunting will survive only as a memory of the happy past when
France was great and powerful and had no need to struggle
against low and venomous hatreds, stirred up by envy'. In fact,
whilst peasants were undoubtedly more aware of their rights
than before, they rarely exercised them, mainly because the
courts were considered expensive and unreliable. For example,
when the inhabitants of Chaumont-sur-Loire took the Duc de
Broglie to court over extensive damage done to crops by his

stags, they won their case in the local court only to have it over-turned on appeal in Paris. On the whole, it was more the general air of resentment against huntsmen than the damage their enemies could do that most irritated the devotees of the sport. Arguments about the rights and wrongs of hunting were in-extricably bound up with strong class prejudices. A great many huntsmen looked down on their social inferiors with a mixture of pity and contempt, whereas to critics of the hunt 'it was as if one was trying to rebuild the Bastille'. Such, at least, was the observation of the Marquis de l'Aigle, president of the prestigious *Société de la Vénerie*, on the attitude of opponents of hunting. Perhaps the symbol was more appropriate than he realised. For, despite the absorption of the cream of the commoners into the hunt, it remained wedded to an outmoded concept of France. Huntsmen regarded themselves as the true élite of France and used their sport to reinforce their sense of separateness and superiority. Arguably, this is still so. As curious onlookers gather in their cars by the *Carrefour de la Fontaine Roche* at the centre of a star formation of paths designed for French royalty in the Forest of Compiègne, the stag sometimes leaps the path to be followed minutes later by the hunt in its resplendent costumes, sounding its horns just as if the *ancien régime* had never fallen.[31]

To conclude, social change in leisure pursuits in the later nineteenth century was as evident in certain traditional sports as it was in the emergence of new forms of physical activity. The second half of the century saw a profound transformation in field sports involving the spread of shooting to the professional and commercial bourgeoisie and, around the turn of the century, to the lower middle classes. Thereafter the sport was rapidly democratised between the wars. The nobility looked on with a mixture of horror and disbelief as skill with arms, which had formerly been the preserve of the upper classes, became the common property of shopkeepers, office-workers and peasants. Despite this democratisation of shooting there were marked differences in the way in which the various social groups involved practised the sport. Within the bourgeoisie proper a strongly competitive element was often apparent and this class of sportsman sometimes cared more about the total number of pieces shot than the actual challenge which the game presented. The lower middle class, however, were more concerned with finding even a couple of rabbits to fill out their empty bags. For

most of those without access to a private sporting estate the
enjoyment of the countryside and the chance to get away from
the city were as important as the art of shooting itself. By the late
1930s one of the most distinctive features of game-shooting in
France was accessibility. In this sense French sportsmen, like
their American counterparts, were right in thinking that they
lived in a more democratic and open society than the British.

Yet, in another respect field sports in France were even more
exclusive than they were in Britain. Whilst shooting became
steadily more popular in its appeal, almost the reverse is true of
hunting. Here the French nobility raised the drawbridge and
retreated from all but the very richest members of the upper
bourgeoisie into a closed venatic world redolent of the *ancien
régime*. Hunting in France remained a slow aristocratic procession through woodlands in search of the boar or the stag, and it
never acquired that semi-public character of the English fox-
hunt, where the squire, his tenants and a collection of local
businessmen would assemble for a lively gallop across open
country. Formerly, hunting and shooting had been regarded as
closely linked gentlemanly skills, but from the second half of the
nineteenth century onwards the upper classes started to make
invidious distinctions between them. As time passed the two
branches of field sports drew further and further apart and have
not since been reunited. Shooting has several million devotees,
but hunting remains the preserve of a politically disinherited
élite clinging tenaciously to social pre-eminence.

3 The Growth of Gymnastics: Patriotism or Pleasure?

Whilst field sports were outstandingly successful amongst the middle-aged and the middle class, they scarcely touched the young and the urban poor. Lower-class youths in the growing cities had to look beyond traditional country amusements for their exercise in the later nineteenth century, and a good many of them appear to have been attracted by gymnastics. Many of these exercises were almost as old as society itself, and had been advocated by a succession of social thinkers from Aristotle to Rabelais, from Montaigne to the educational reformers of the French Revolution. However, it was not until the nineteenth century that gymnastics developed into an organised popular activity voluntarily undertaken by large numbers of young people in their own time. Social historians in search of the origins of popular participation in organised sport will not find what they are looking for in the early history of football or rugby. On the continent of Europe, unlike the United Kingdom, ball games followed in the wake of more systematic methods of physical training. The subsequent success of the English sports should not blind us to the fact that in the late nineteenth century they were only just beginning to become well known. It follows that if we wish to find out a little more about the early sporting life of the lower classes it is to the practice of gymnastics that we must turn our attention.

A brief glance at the growth in the membership of gymnastic organisations in late nineteenth-century Europe confirms the importance which this form of recreation had assumed in the lives of a great many ordinary young people. In Germany, where gymnastics were more popular than in any other country, the membership of the Deutscheturnband, the largest of several

gymnastic bodies, rose from 170,000 in 1880 to over one-and-a-
quarter million in 1914. In other countries such as Denmark,
Sweden and Switzerland, and in the western parts of the
Habsburg Empire, particularly amongst the Czechs of Bohemia,
gymnastics had a large and enthusiastic following. France was
no exception to the general rule. Although gymnastics came to
France rather later than to some other European countries, by
1900 it was the single most important form of organised lower-
class physical recreation. The first properly constituted gymnastic organisation, the Union des Sociétés Françaises de
Gymnastique (USFG), was formed by a handful of clubs in
1873, but by 1914 it had approximately 350,000 members.
There were also a great many gymnasts in the 1600 Catholic
sports clubs and in the 2000 military preparation societies. In
terms of the numbers affiliated to official bodies, for a time
gymnastics probably had a larger following than any other
sporting activity in France.[1]

How do we set about explaining this dramatic increase in the
popularity of gymnastics during the second half of the nineteenth century? What did gymnastic exercise actually involve
and to whom did it most appeal? To what extent did the
interests of the ordinary club member coincide with those of the
officials who controlled the sport? In particular, the explanation
of the expansion in gymnastic activity offered by those in charge
of the movement needs careful scrutiny. According to the theory
put forward either explicitly or implicitly in many of the
statements of the leadership, the rise of gymnastics was simply
the result of the harnessing of a spontaneous wave of patriotism
which had swept over France after the defeat of 1870. A growing
number of ordinary Frenchmen, it was argued, believed that
there had been a serious deterioration in the racial stock, that
France was becoming enfeebled and that the defeat of 1870 was
partly the result of the greater attention the Germans had paid
to physical fitness. As gymnastics had played a major role in
improving the military prowess of Germany, the French should
learn from their example in order to undo their achievements.
But does this tell the whole story? Can the spread of gymnastics
be understood in purely patriotic and military terms? It will be
argued here that, although nationalism certainly played an
important role in the movement and was the dominant factor as
far as the leaders of the major organisations were concerned,

there were other, half-hidden social and sporting considerations of equal importance. It is only by bringing all the relevant factors together that we can understand why this form of physical activity was so well suited to the later nineteenth century.[2]

Looking briefly at the tradition of gymnastic exercises prior to the advent of the Third Republic, it emerges that there were two quite distinct types of activity: firstly, there were what could be called remedial gymnastics, whereby physical weakness was corrected by a programme of special exercises, and secondly, there was acrobatic display for public entertainment. As we have already noted, various forms of exercise to increase strength and agility and to instill discipline had existed for centuries. It appears, however, that towards the end of the eighteenth century a greater emphasis began to be placed on these aspects of education. This much was true at least in theory. Rousseau was an advocate of fresh air and proper exercise, and it was around this time that Ling developed the Swedish system of carefully monitored exercise designed to improve scientifically the working of the human body. These ideas were taken by the Germans and recast in order to serve a specifically military purpose by the addition of various special-ised pieces of equipment, like high vaulting horses and climbing bars.[3]

Some of these innovations filtered into France during the first half of the nineteenth century. In Paris several large gymnasia were set up, the most famous of which was the one in the rue de Grenelle run by Colonel Francisco Amoros, an exiled Spanish liberal and physical education enthusiast. Amoros exercised considerable influence over those responsible for military train-ing in France under the July Monarchy. The *Journal Militaire Officiel* records that during the year 1843, 48,083 conscripts had followed the basic gymnastic training course. During 1844 this number rose by almost 6000 to 53,942, of whom 1336 became physical training instructors themselves. Although these impres-sive figures conceal serious shortages of equipment and skilled personnel, they nevertheless represent an important initial contribution to physical recreation at the national level. This trend was followed by Napoleon III, who set up an Institut National de Gymnastique at Vincennes in 1852. At that time very few members of the medical profession took an interest in the propagation of general health through proper exercise, and the main impetus undoubtedly came from the military. A few private gymnastic clubs were set up in the 1860s and Victor Duruy, the reforming minister of education under the Liberal Empire, issued a decree in 1869 making gym compulsory in all state schools. However, lack of equipment, shortage of space and the reluctance of teachers to supervise their pupils in what many considered unseemly or degrading activities meant that most official efforts to stimulate gymnastics met with only very limited success.[4]

Gustave Flaubert writing in the mid-seventies caught the slightly cranky character of the early devotees of gym in his celebrated satire of *petit-bourgeois* manners, *Bouvard et Pécuchet*. The central characters are two friends, Parisian clerks who meet on a park bench and later decide to retire to the country after one of them unexpectedly finds he is the beneficiary of a substantial inheritance. Their relative affluence permits them to indulge in every fad of the age, including gymnastics. They buy the standard manual on the subject by Amoros and pore over the illustrations of young men crouching, standing, bending, stretching their arms, lifting weights, crossing beams, climbing ladders and swinging on the trapeze. They duly fell a lime tree and use it as a horizontal beam and fix a long stake in the ground to serve as a vertical bar. Attempts to climb this prove as abortive as most of their other gymnastic efforts. Their only success lies in fixing a thin pole across a ditch at the side of the public highway which they proceed to cross and re-cross constantly; 'the countryside was flat and they were visible for miles. The villagers wondered who these strange creatures were to be seen leaping around in the distance'. As Amoros instructed, they sang marching songs as they beat their chests to exercise their pectoral muscles; they even tried to obtain several school-children to be placed in sacks and carried for marching practice, but the local teacher understandably objected and the plan was abandoned. One of them then took up walking on stilts as prescribed by the handbook, only to come crashing down into a patch of runner beans tied up with string. 'Evidently', Flaubert concludes, 'gym was unsuitable to men of their age.'[5]

Flaubert's early parody of this new interest in more systematic forms of physical exercise is particularly interesting for two reasons. Firstly, he unerringly places gymnastic exercise in its true social context. Apart from a few celebrated politicians and patriotic industrialists, the bulk of the organisers and advocates of gym were drawn from the ranks of the lower middle classes. Clerks, shopkeepers and salesmen of the Bouvard and Pécuchet variety abounded in the numerous *sociétés de gymnastique* founded in the later nineteenth century. These clubs were usually presided over by a local *notable* of some sort, often a doctor, but the real work was done by the club secretary, frequently a self-important local patriot with a *petit-bourgeois* background and outlook. These minor officials loved nothing better than to compose a long-winded letter to the provincial press or an appeal for funds to the sub-prefect full of laboured rhetoric and passionate declarations of disinterested patriotism. The pedantic pomposity with which some of them recorded the minutiae of club life for posterity may have made them the bane of the membership but their records are a boon to the historian. Perhaps we should be a little more grateful for the slightly absurd earnestness with which these Gallic Mr Pooters took up the challenge of gymnastics. The other relevant aspect of Flaubert's early parody of the athletic adventures of office workers concerns the odd mixture of military exercise and festive acrobatics that made up the new sport of gymnastics. Bouvard and Pécuchet spend half their time in crypto-military preparation, clambering over obstacles with packs on their backs, and the rest of their time in carnivalesque antics like learning to walk on stilts.

The acrobatic element in gym easily passes unnoticed if we rely on the accounts of the senior officials of the movement, who wished to stress the martial aspects of the activity. Yet as far as most Frenchmen were concerned the term 'gymnastics', if it meant anything at all, conjured up visions of acrobatic exercise and entertainment. Up until the 1880s at least, the military side of gym was largely ignored. Like Flaubert's bemused villagers, the general public tended to treat serious gymnasts as social oddities. Far from being the preoccupation of a few keep-fit fanatics or outraged nationalists, gymnastics were the traditional preserve of the street acrobat or *saltimbanque*. Acrobatic exercise and feats of strength of a similar, though more flamboyant, variety to those prescribed in the new gymnastic manuals had been a feature of travelling troupes of strongmen and tumblers for centuries. Exhibitions of physical strength and agility had amused and astonished the public long before the growth of the gymnastics movement. The Franconi brothers, for example, the doyens of the circus in France, had been organising acrobatic acts and vast pseudo-military displays since the early nineteenth century. During the Second Empire François Léotard, the original 'daring young man on the flying trapeze', had become a national celebrity. The son of a gymnasium owner, he had intended to be a lawyer but soon abandoned his studies to become an acrobat. Dressed only in the pink body stocking that subsequently bore his name and performing without a net, he enthralled the public in the 1860s and made a fortune from lending his name to a bewildering variety of products, from walking canes to fruit cakes. He spent most of his money on female admirers, of whom he had a prodigious number, and died of the pox in Madrid in 1870.[6]

The successes of Léotard and his many imitators were continued into the 1870s by the Hanlon-Lees brothers, of whom a prominent historian of the circus remarks: 'they were authentic acrobats whose success derived from translating into a popular vaudeville form the skill and discipline of the gymnasium'. Their act partly consisted of conventional gymnastic feats like making human pyramids or performing acrobatic vaults or flips. The rest of the act apparently comprised well-tried routines like chasing a couple of characters dressed as policemen around the stage and belabouring them with large objects. Public fascination for such antics continued unabated but there was an increasing tendency to distinguish between the different elements in the acrobatic tradition. On the whole, the circus became a place where the public went to watch death-defying feats and see wild animals in the flesh; the old acrobatic side of the circus declined in importance, often finding its way into the clown's act. From the late nineteenth century onwards, those who wished to see precision acrobatics turned towards the new gymnastic clubs which held regular outdoor displays. Pure circus in the old sense – equitation and tumbling – died out between the 1860s and 1880s, and sport began to take its place as a popular spectacle. Efforts were made to combine the old and the new; Gaston Desprez took over the Cirque d'Hiver with the express intention of doing so, but such efforts met with only limited success. As a spectacle gymnastics were now firmly in the ambit of the amateur clubs, although the old traditions still survived at the more mundane level of the street performer. There is a charming account of the life of a street acrobat in Paris in the 1920s in a recent biography of Edith Piaf, whose father made his living in this way and used her as part of his act:

> When he found a wide avenue or street, where there was room for passers-by to jostle and crane their necks, Dad rolled out his carpet. It was just a little scrap of threadbare cloth, but they knew at once that this was for real and that they were going to be entertained.
> He would take a swig of wine before launching into his patter. Edith, who had spent six years with him, from eight years old until she was fourteen, imitated him well, and in a raucous shout exactly like his, 'You're in for a treat now, ladies and gentlemen. This isn't a trick, the artist himself is going to work before your very eyes, no safety net, no sawdust, no shit! It's for real. For a hundred centimes we'll begin . . . I am going to perform for you, for my honour and your pleasure, one of the most unique acrobatic feats in the world . . .'
> And Dad gave them their money's worth because he was a good acrobat.[7]

From the outset, therefore, gymnastics were never simply a pedagogical or patriotic device. The sport had firm roots in popular street culture. This point is worth stressing with some force as the organisers of the gymnastic movement in the later nineteenth century refused to recognise the contribution of popular acrobatics, and either ignored or openly condemned the practice of the sport in that form. But, as we shall see, the receptivity of ordinary working-class youths to gymnastics was due in no small measure to its association with time-honoured traditions of public entertainment. Having outlined the chief elements in the gymnastic tradition, we can now concentrate our attention on the process by which a variety of gymnastic exercises were incorporated into a coherent programme during the early Third Republic.

The official impetus behind the gymnastics movement proper came from two related cultural-cum-political sources: Social Darwinism and Germanophobia. Even before the war of 1870 there had been a number of Frenchmen who were disturbed by what they saw as the deterioration of the French race and the increasing feebleness of France in relation to the growing might of Prussia. A few energetic patriots began to form gymnastic clubs in the east of France in the 1860s in the belief that France must either copy German techniques of physical training or suffer the inevitable consequences of national weakness. But, as these individuals were the first to admit, the notion of systematic physical training as practised in Germany had not yet caught on in France. The catastrophic defeat of France in the war of 1870 changed attitudes almost overnight. The Franco-Prussian war was the catalyst which turned casual keep-fit enthusiasts and amateur acrobats into a disciplined national force. The outcome of the war of 1870 was of immense significance for Europe. Up to that date France had been regarded as the strongest continental power with the largest population, the greatest resources and the biggest army. With the formation of the German Empire in 1870 this situation was dramatically transformed. Surrender at Sedan had come as no less a shock to the French than the humiliation of Jena had been to the Prussians sixty-four years earlier. Just as German gymnastics were partly born of the need for a national struggle against the French Empire, so French gymnasts were dedicated to exacting retribution from the new German Reich. Prior to 1870 France had not required the disciplined cohorts of youths working towards the unity of the *Völk* which had been the main purpose of the German gymnasts. Gymnastics had played an important role in the transmission of national feeling in Germany before unification. German gymnasts had thought of themselves as 'a regenerative élite', and after 1870 their French counterparts began to regard themselves in the same light. Like the Germans they raised patriotism to the status of a secular religion. Ceremony was allied to the cause of fitness in their attempt to turn the old festivals into disciplined gatherings of patriots complete with flags, banners, military bands, flaming torches and images of the motherland.[8]

Revanche was the watchword of the movement in its early years and, although this cry became more muted as time passed, the retrieval of Alsace-Lorraine remained a prime objective right up to 1914. Many of the founding fathers of French gymnastics were exiled Alsatians or Lorrainers: men like Jules Sansboeuf, a leading figure in the Ligue des Patriotes for some years, the founder of several Parisian clubs and a president of the USFG. This obsession with the lost provinces and the threat of further

German aggression was reflected in the names of many of the clubs. When the members of a new club formed in Reims in 1882 met to choose a name, they considered various alternatives such as Le Souvenir, La Revanche and L'Alsace-Lorraine (a very common choice) before deciding that La Sentinelle conveyed exactly the sense of readiness and menace they desired. Other names such as La Régénératrice, Le Réveil, La Patriote, France! and Halte-là! were equally self-explanatory.[9]

As its motto the USFG took the words of a soldier, General Chanzy, who had appealed to the patriots of France to school the young in military fashion: 'Faites-moi des hommes, nous en ferons des soldats.' Despite the efforts of moderates to tone down the rampant Germanophobia of much of the patriotic rhetoric of the period, the Germans as a whole, and the Prussians in particular, were frequently reviled in public. 'As far as I'm concerned I detest Prussia', a speaker confided to his audience of gymnasts in 1883, 'I hate this perfidious and cruel hereditary foe.' When, much later, German gymnasts made tentative overtures of friendship, they were quickly reminded of the words of Victor Hugo: 'Repassez le Rhin et puis tendez-nous la main en frères'. Small anti-German outbursts were commonplace. In 1882 Parisian gymnasts led a rowdy demonstration against a German drinking club, and incidents of this kind became more frequent as Germanophobia and chauvinism focused on the person of General Boulanger in the later 1880s. There were several complaints that Germanophobia had spilled over into a more general xenophobia. Foreigners were often forbidden to join gymnastics clubs, and there were several complaints that Belgians had been forced to leave clubs on the grounds of nationality.[10]

As a result of its strong attachment to the nationalist cause the USFG got itself involved in the internecine struggles of the early Third Republic. After his death Gambetta was raised to the status of a national hero by militants seeking an early settlement of accounts with Germany. The gymnasts ran regular trips to his tomb in conjunction with the newly formed Ligue des Patriotes. The more cautious Opportunist politicians of the eighties like Freycinet and Ferry feared that the gymnastics movement was being infiltrated by extra-parliamentary nationalists like the fanatical military propagandist Paul Déroulède, who had been placed at the head of a committee to investigate military training in schools for a few months during Gambetta's 'great ministry' of 1881. Accordingly, they refused to grant the USFG privileged status and substantial subsidies. Conflict eventually broke out over the challenge posed by the ex-minister of war, General Boulanger, to the existing political system. Boulanger was a great favourite with the gymnasts and had cultivated their support by attending rallies and intimating that their clubs would play a prominent role in the 'adult battalions' he proposed to set up on coming to power. Matters came to a head when it was suggested in 1887 that the General be elected an honorary member of the USFG. Loyal Republicans protested against this move and eventually defeated it, though sizeable numbers of gymnasts took part in the rioting of 27 January 1889 which so nearly swept Boulanger into the Elysée. Thereafter, the USFG as a whole took a more moderate line and disowned extreme nationalists, though a good many still remained within the movement.[11]

If they did nothing else, these chauvinistic divisions did at least help gymnastics achieve national recognition as a major recreational activity in the early 1880s. At first most Frenchmen had been either puzzled or amused at the antics of these young men with their caps, blouses, boots and tight-fitting trousers. When, for example, a contingent of gymnasts joined the first Bastille Day parade held under the Third Republic in 1880, 'few onlookers realised that those who were marching past were gymnasts'; some thought that the young marchers were firemen whilst others confidently pronounced them to be sailors on leave. No-one seems to have known their real identity. Yet, within less than five years it would have been much more difficult to have made the same mistake. As a Paris councillor noted in 1885, only a few years earlier he had been accused of wanting to subsidise acrobats when he asked for a grant from municipal funds for gymnastic clubs, whereas now it was standard practice to provide some official financial support. Thanks to their own efforts and to those of the Ligue des Patriotes, everyone now knew who gymnasts were.[12]

During the 1870s and 1880s it would appear that the military threat from across the Rhine was indeed the dominant influence in the growth of gymnastics. Even the exercises which were adopted reflected the twin aims of moral and military re-surgence. German-style exercises which were designed solely to

1. Parisian men playing pétanque on the Champ de Mars.

2. Chayrigues, the top French goalkeeper, in action in 1923. Note the size of the crowd.

3. An early all-Parisian rugby match. Stade Français against the Racing Club in 1907.

4. Perpignan versus Agen in the semi-final of the championship of 1939. Note the advertising around the ground.

5. Traditional bull-running in the streets of a southern town.

6. A Spanish bullfight at Bayonne. A dead horse is removed as the matador
prepares for the kill.

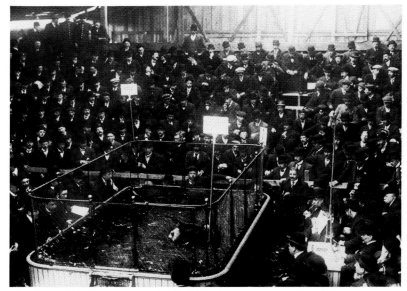

7.   A cockfight in a northern 'gallodrome'.

8.   The annual gathering and parade of Catholic gymnasts (1910).

9.   Jules Ladoumègue, the gifted middle-distance runner (1927).

10. The male sociability of a shooting party.

11. Hunting with the Marquis de L'Aigle.

12. The notorious cobblestones made the Paris-Roubaix 'the hell of the North' for man and machine. An awe-struck child looks on (1902).

13. Crossing Brittany in the 1921 Paris-Brest-Paris. Cycling brought commercial sport to impoverished and remote parts of France.

14. A mountain stage of the Tour de France in 1924. Note the spectators using their newspapers to identify the riders.

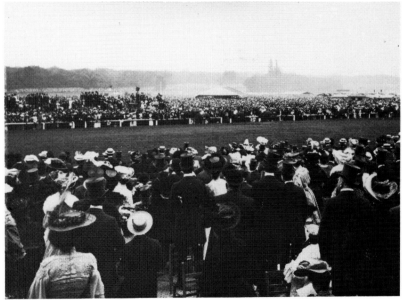

15. Social segregation at the races. A view from the exclusive enclosure across to the bulk of the Parisian crowd in the cheaper part of the course.

increase strength were preferred to the Swedish type of gymnastics which placed greater emphasis on agility, grace and good
posture. The Paris council, for example, spent considerable
sums of money on providing the German-style of gymnastic
equipment for the use of schoolchildren. In general, however,
school gymnastics were relatively unimportant and most schools,
even *lycées*, lacked the basic equipment.[13]

By 1891 there were approximately 900 gymnastic clubs in
France, of which about 300 had joined the USFG. Like the rifle
clubs, with which they were frequently connected, gymnastic
clubs were mainly concentrated in the east of France. In 1882 all
but two departments north of a line from the Seine to the Jura
contained gymnastic clubs, whereas only thirty-six of the sixty-
five departments south of that line were in a similar position. An
inquiry by the prefect of the Hérault into the existence of
gymnastic societies in his department in 1881 failed to uncover a
single one, although ten years later there were at least four, of
which La Cettoise was one of the largest and best-run in France.
As we shall see, the position in the south was complicated by the
fact that some clubs practising gym called themselves dancing
clubs because they combined performing the *farandole* (a
traditional Provençal dance) with modern gymnastics. On the
whole, however, the sport was dominated by the north in its
earlier years. The prime influence here was presumably the need
for national defence and it seems legitimate to concede the point
to the organisers of the movement. Nevertheless, this factor
alone cannot explain the subsequent growth of gymnastics. In
fact, it seems probable that even if the German threat had not
existed there would have been a considerable increase in
gymnastic activity. Obviously, it is dangerous to press such
counter-factual statements too far, but the patriotic aspect on its
own certainly cannot account for the fact that between 1895 and
1910 a further 1029 new clubs joined the USFG. There is no
simple correlation between the vehemence of national feeling
and the growth of the movement.[14]

To understand fully the nature of the appeal which gymnastics made to urban youth we must look more closely at what
it involved. Patriotism aside, why did increasing numbers of
young men wish to take their exercise in this form? First we must
look at their social background. It has already emerged that
during the 1870s and 1880s young men from the lower middle

classes seem to have been drawn to the sport. One gymnastics
paper even ran an employment column for clerks. Shop assistants were also keen on gym. Presumably, the physical tedium of
long hours spent at the counter or the ledger together with the
strongly conformist ethos of such occupations accounts for their
readiness to take up gym as a healthy and patriotic form of
rational recreation. During the 1880s the *petite bourgeoisie* certainly seem to have been the dominant social group, but even at
that date there were a good number of semi-skilled and unskilled
young workers in the movement. The social composition of a
small provincial club chosen more or less at random confirms
this impression. La Gauloise was founded in 1882 at Caudbec-
les-Elbeuf near Rouen, meeting twice a week in the evenings in a
rented hall. Most of the club's officials were respectable lower-
middle-class men: the president was a chemist, the secretary a
bookkeeper, and the treasurer a commercial traveller. The
day-to-day running of the club, however, was left in the hands of
a foreman painter, a carpenter and a plain 'ouvrier'.[15]

During the 1880s many clubs expanded very rapidly. In
Saint-Etienne, for example, a club founded in 1886 with 20
members had 420 members 4 years later; of this number 250
were active members, mostly under 20 years of age. An extensive
survey of the social life of the working class in that region reveals
that most of those joining these clubs came from lower-class
backgrounds: in the Saint-Etienne area 'the gymnastics clubs
were situated chiefly in the mining towns and districts, and
metal workers and small traders joined them'. In fact, a number
of different reports confirm that there seems to have been a
veritable influx of working-class youths into gymnastics in the
1880s. A Paris council survey noted that most of the Parisian
clubs comprised 'de fils d'ouvriers, d'employés, de cultivateurs'.
When a contingent of Parisian gymnasts were invited to attend
an international competition in Geneva, many of them were
unable to go because their manual jobs did not enable them to
afford even the reduced fares they were offered. This impression
of the strong proletarian element in the rank and file of the
movement is further confirmed by a survey of the rooms rented
by provincial workers coming to Paris. This source noted that
among the only decorations regularly found on the walls of their
rooms were citations and medals for gymnastics.[16]

What was the nature of the appeal of these seemingly tedious

forms of exercise to so many young working men? It is difficult
to believe that patriotism alone was the cause. Clearly, even if
the organisers of the movement were reluctant to regard gymnastics as a form of sport, as competitive exercise freely undertaken for its own sake, many of the rank and file had no similar
inhibitions. To the ordinary club member gymnastics were the
cheapest and most convenient form of physical recreation
available in the later nineteenth century. For those who worked
long hours, gym could be enjoyed in the evenings and indoors.
Few clubs had their own gymnasiums but a great many were
able to rent a hall or use school facilities after the children had
gone home. Moreover, the favour with which the government,
the municipalities and affluent private patriots regarded gymnastics meant that subsidies for the purchase of equipment were
often available. This kept down costs, and subscriptions were
rarely more than fifty centimes or so a month. Subsidies to
gymnastics clubs in Paris were usually in the region of 40,000
francs a year in the later nineteenth century, and in addition to
this there were the contributions of associate members to be
taken into account.[17]

In short, there was nothing to stop indigent young workers
from taking up gymnastics on the grounds of lack of time or
money. Gymnastics constituted a form of physical exercise well
suited to the new pattern of the industrial working day. In
addition to this, there can be no doubt that gymnastics could be
of considerable benefit to those tied for long periods to the
factory bench carrying out repetitive and sometimes physically
damaging tasks. A number of factory workers were probably
attracted to gymnastics for health reasons. It seems unlikely,
however, that considerations of improved health and efficiency
played a crucial role in enlisting the majority of new recruits to
gymnastics clubs. It was primarily employers and social
engineers who were interested in this aspect of the rise of sport.
For the ordinary gymnast there must have been more compelling reasons for taking up gymnastics than a sense of national
duty or the desire to repair the damage done to the body by
work.

This is where the festive dimension becomes highly significant. Gymnastics combined public display with private
comradeship in a way which must have appealed strongly to
young people deprived of traditional amusements. It is all too

easy to overlook these features of the popularity of gymnastics as the officials, with their high-flown conception of the purposes of gymnastic exercise, refused to recognise its traditional role as a form of communal entertainment. Yet, the closer we look at the attitudes and behaviour of the mass of participants, the clearer it becomes that the ancient associations between the *fête* and the performing of gymnastic feats were at least partly responsible for the popularity of organised gymnastics in the later nineteenth century. Hence there was a constant tension lurking beneath the surface of the movement: an implicit, though largely unexpressed, conflict between what the organisers wanted the sport to be and what the gymnasts themselves expected of their sport.

The partial indifference of the rank and file to the efforts of the ideologues of the movement to invest gymnastics with special patriotic significance manifested itself in several different ways. Looking first at the purely physical side of the sport, a clear distinction between the values of the official hierarchy and the attitude of many club members is obvious. The middle-aged, middle-class leaders of the movement favoured a programme of exercises that would train the personality to accept orders and instill a sense of civic and national consciousness into the 'recruit'. Gymnastic exercise of a disciplined military kind would replace the decadent village games, the shameful pleasure-seeking revels of country life in which children were corrupted and women abused. The displays of tumbling, which traditionally formed a part of these communal festivities, would be replaced by new exercises designed to improve the race. Useful prizes such as books, maps and geometry sets would replace the drinking and wenching which had formerly been the reward for outstanding displays of prowess.[18]

Men like Frédéric Le Play believed that once the lower classes were given decent, sanitary conditions and taught how to behave in a respectable middle-class fashion the 'social problem' would be solved. Gymnastics were often regarded by officials of the movement as part of a general programme of moral and social reform. Several leading figures in the world of sport attempted to put these ideas into practice, of whom Charles Cazalet was probably the best known and most influential. Cazalet had been born into a wealthy Bordeaux family in which there was a tradition of practical Christianity. Like Pierre de

Coubertin he was influenced by the writings of Le Play and became deeply involved in attempts to improve the material conditions of lower-class life through such organisations as the Société de Bains Douches, Habitations à Bonne Marché and Jardins Ouvriers. It was in the same spirit that he took up the cause of gymnastics. He was the first permanent president of the USFG and guided it along the twin paths of Republican defence and the promotion of social harmony from 1896 to 1931. In typical solidarist fashion, his concern for the physical and moral condition of the lower classes did not go so far as to recommend a reduction in hours of work. Rather he strove to spread the benefits of proper exercise to young workers and encourage them to make better use of the brief periods of free time they had by giving up alcohol and taking up gym.[19]

Most gymnasts clearly regarded the movement in an entirely different light. Not only were they ignorant of, or indifferent to, such social philosophy, they positively rejected the conception of gymnastic exercise held by such individuals. For instance, those who sought to encourage and manipulate gymnastic exercise for ulterior motives were often strongly opposed to the introduction of a competitive element, whereas gymnasts themselves favoured competition and the giving of prizes both in cash and in kind. Unfortunately, the sources are inevitably biased towards those few in control. But in the outraged official reaction to the demands of the ordinary participants we can sometimes catch a glimpse of the real attitudes of the silent majority.

Trapeze work was popular amongst the rank and file but disliked by the rulers of the sport partly because of the danger involved but mainly because of the obvious delight it gave to spectators. *Le Temps* noted, 'the purpose of the USFG is not to entertain the masses'. Gym in their eyes was designed to strengthen the race not to amuse the public. 'Regrettably, one even sees our own clubs follow this stupid trend [towards acrobatic display]', noted the official journal of the USFG, 'a practice which has an unfortunate tendency to attract the applause of spectators.' It appears as if some clubs behaved rather like troupes of itinerant entertainers rejecting the standard military-style uniform of the movement for 'sleeveless vests and trunks which make them look like fairground strongmen'. After all, it was probably a good deal more exciting for the young gymnast to cast himself in the role of a Léotard, with all the dramatic and amorous associations which went with it, than to humbly accept his place as another anonymous and devoted young patriot. Napoleon Laisné, the inspector of gymnastics in the schools of Paris, observed that in the mid-eighties such 'irregularities' were quite common and put this down to the decadent legacy of the Second Empire, which had failed to inspire the young with an austere sense of civic virtue. A recent social history of the Shrove Tuesday Carnival in nineteenth-century Paris has a rather more convincing explanation. 'These new youth groups were involuntary caricatures of the old festive troupes: gymnastics supplanted the dance, traditional costumes were replaced by new uniforms and street farces were turned into military parades.' Gym played its part in the taming of the turbulent world of the *fête*, although a good deal of the earlier rough-and-tumble survived in covert form to infect the movement with a certain mischievousness.[20]

The same was broadly true of the countryside. Despite official censure and complaints about the degeneracy of traditional rural festivals, gymnastic groups regularly took part in them and their displays were often the focus for other entertainments provided by the village band or the firemen. Recent research on the decay of customary life in the French countryside in the later nineteenth century has drawn attention to the decline of communal dancing and its replacement by fashionable imports from Paris. It seems reasonable to suggest that gymnastics played a part in this process by providing a new forum for young men to exhibit their prowess. Traditional dancing had been far from demure and decorous. One historian speaks of country weddings as an occasion for 'the youth to leap and throw themselves about in the peasant gymnastics that passed for dancing'. Dancing was sometimes carried out competitively by teams and it was presumably a small step to move from social institutions of this kind to 'modern' gymnastic clubs. Earlier we noted the interesting example of clubs in the south of France that continued to perform traditional and modern functions side by side. Take the Réveil de Provence from the commune of Langlade in the Gard, for example. They were registered as a group specialising in the typical Provençal dance, the *farandole*. Yet a report from the mayor of the commune in 1910 noted that 'these young people have adopted a kind of costume which is very similar to that of the gymnastic clubs'. In Nimes an organisation called La Jeune

France was founded in 1891 which described itself as a club 'for dancing the *farandole* and performing gymnastics' with 'the principal aim of promoting physical force', and with the motto 'Strength, Agility and Suppleness.'[21]

Local patriotism was immensely important to such groups and often took precedence over considerations of efficiency and regional or national solidarity. Small communes were most reluctant to permit their clubs to amalgamate with others in a similar position in order to save money and share equipment. As far as the local community was concerned, the standard of performance reached was of secondary importance to the know-ledge that they had their own group of village entertainers on hand to lend a carnival atmosphere to public holidays. Such events were an important link between traditional and modern forms of recreation. Officials were deeply worried that the dignity of the sport and the seriousness of its task would be forgotten on such occasions. Many clubs loved nothing more than to join in a local parade wearing medals the size of saucers and hats festooned with ribbons, marching alongside clowns on floats and men dressed up as women. Such antics were the source of great amusement in polite athletic circles, where young sportsmen were advised against democratising their activities lest they turn themselves 'into gymnastic clubs complete with bugles, banners and costumes from the Opéra Comique'.[22]

It would seem as if many young gymnasts preferred occasions of this kind, with the opportunities they provided for dressing up and playing the fool, than they did the more solemn official gatherings. It would be wrong, however, to assume that the great annual celebrations of the gymnastic art organised by the ruling bodies of the sport were poorly attended. At the annual Fête Fédérale of the USFG there were always several thousand active participants and usually a good many more spectators. But it does not follow from the relative popularity of the major national competitions that most of those taking part shared fully the official view of what the sport should entail. In fact, if we are to judge by the behviour of many of the participants, this annual get-together of the faithful had another, quite different significance.

Many youngsters, and others not so young, used these gatherings not only as a means of serving their country and gaining recognition within the movement but also as an excuse for getting away from home, doing a little subsidised travelling and generally having a good time with their friends. Outside the arena a relaxed and hedonistic atmosphere prevailed. Adolescents, free from the surveillance of their families and of the local community, could go on the rampage. Those a little older could get away from their wives and children for a few days, meet up with their old army friends and go out on the town. In fact, it seems as if gymnastics was one of the most common means by which those who had been conscripted kept in touch with their old comrades. It goes almost without saying that severe hangovers and stern official reprimands regularly followed such reunions, but every year more of these 'unfortunate incidents', as the authorities called them, took place. There were similar goings-on in certain private clubs, some of which existed first and foremost as drinking establishments. The mayor of Montpellier reported to the prefect of the Hérault in 1909 that La Revanche, ostensibly a devoted patriotic body for the improvement of local youth, was little more than a dissolute drinking club. It was run by a Monsieur Dinnat, a gym teacher aged thirty-two who had twice been imprisoned, once for wearing medals that were not his and on another occasion for fighting. He ran the club with the aid of his mistress and his nephew, aged eighteen, who had already been convicted of theft. The treasurer and secretary were both plasterers and the president was a tinsmith and drinking pal of Dinnat. Obviously, this is an extreme example, but it serves as a useful corrective to the extravagant claims for the movement by zealots. Critics of musical societies alleged that many 'existed more to encourage drinking than singing', and some of the gymnastic clubs undoubtedly warranted the same criticism.[23]

It was not only the opportunity for antics of this kind which attracted young men into the movement, and perhaps it would be wrong to overemphasise this element. The prospect of subsidised travel to national meetings must also have acted as an inducement to urban youths, many of whom had probably never been outside their home town, let alone had a holiday. What was of marginal importance to the organisers may well have been of great significance to the gymnasts themselves. Here sport spilled over into the general area of recreation and leisure, and we shall never know how many young gymnasts really joined clubs and endured the petty tyrannies of officials primarily in order to get a cheap holiday. What we do know is that some clubs frequently went on excursions, ostensibly to compete in regional competitions or to further their study of topography, where the real purpose was enjoyment pure and simple.

During the decade preceding the outbreak of the First World War, games like football started to infiltrate gymnastics at a grass-roots level, despite all the attempts of the leaders of the movement to stop this. As a form of physical activity gymnastics were capable of meeting the challenge from modern sports only by compromising with them. As we have already noted, gymnastics increasingly resembled athletic sports in their adoption of the competitive ethic. Up until the late 1890s the official hierarchy had been bitterly opposed to the spread to English sports, but soon after that date their attitude mellowed very considerably as football, rugby and cycling began to attract the interest of large numbers of youngsters of all classes. By 1905 the official journal of the USFG had to admit that 'modern sports are increasingly popular in our clubs'. A number of clubs had acquired their own playing fields. In the Catholic gymnastic organisation, which expanded so rapidly after 1905, it was taken for granted that gymnastic exercise and athletic sports should be mixed; in this way church clubs could happily combine patriotic duty with the need to offer the sporting excitement that would bring the athletic youngster into the ambit of the church.[24]

Paradoxically, the gymnastic movement proper was already beginning to decline at the time when membership was at its highest point. Gymnastics had staved off the challenge from modern sports only by incorporating them into a gymnastic programme to the point where it was often hard to tell which activity was the more important. In the long run many gymnastic clubs went over fully to football or rugby. The lower classes had their first taste of organised physical recreation in the gym, but now they were moving on and anxious to try new sports. Whilst gymnastics remained a major sporting activity, it definitely went out of fashion in the inter-war period, despite the fact that it was only then beginning to be widely practised in schools. The official figures of the USFG record that the number of clubs in the union remained static at around 1300 between 1923 and 1939. The Catholic federation maintained its membership at approximately pre-war levels too. Although the Vichy government favoured the practice of gym as a new form of social discipline and a means of regenerating French youth, the actual membership of the USFG fell as a result of the disruption caused by the war and the purging of a large number of officials with Republican sympathies. As in other aspects of its policies, Vichy promised more than it could deliver.[25]

The point of departure for this investigation of gymnastics was to pose the question of the extent to which a particular form of physical activity owed its success to certain militaristic and moral values. There can be no doubt that a good many ideologues and nationalists saw gymnastics primarily as a vehicle for the transmission of their views to the young. However, whereas they certainly had a modicum of success in influencing the outlook of some impressionable youngsters, it is equally clear that much of their propaganda fell on deaf ears. If the complaints of the authorities are anything to go by we can be sure that a fair number of the rank and file responded to the rhetoric of their elders with reassuring indifference. An instructive illustration of this rank-and-file resistance to the moralising efforts of the leadership comes from a recent study of the Republican youth clubs of the twelfth arrondissement of Paris. When the director of the club at 51 rue de Charenton attempted to interfere with the sporting pattern of club activity, 'to continue the work of the school as long as possible by giving our boys a taste for learning', membership declined from 111 in 1900 to 75 in 1909. 'A similar membership trend occurred at 4 rue de Pomard where the Amicale offered gymnastics, riflery and fencing courses for a few years and then replaced them with more frequent lectures and outings: it lost 50 members between 1901, when 131 boys belonged, and 1908, when 81 still participated in its cultural programme.' This sharp downturn in membership at a time when most youth clubs were expanding rapidly can only be attributed to an uncomprehending desire to instruct rather than to amuse on the part of those in charge. The implication for gymnastics is fairly clear. The ordinary gymnast's concern for personal satisfaction – whether expressed in his desire to entertain the public or in his preference for talking, eating and drinking rather than taking exercise – set a practical limit on the extent to which the authorities could use the sport for their own purposes. This mixture of the exhibitionism of some and the epicureanism of others saved gymnastics from becoming an instrument of militarism pure and simple.[26]

According to the official version, the growth of gymnastics had been the result of the efforts of a number of public-spirited citizens, who gave direction to a wave of spontaneous national feeling. A more prosaic but possibly more accurate explanation might well place less emphasis on patriotism and personal initiative, and give more weight to the suitability of gymnastics for young workers whose jobs were incompatible with proper physical expression and development. Gymnastics constituted the first modern sporting activity to be dovetailed into the routine of factory work by concentrating on evening meetings while also attracting youths by offering them the chance to dress up in uniforms, take part in parades and enjoy subsidised travel. These exercises promoted skills which could be useful on the street corner by developing the kind of muscle power which won an adolescent respect amongst his peers. Politics and patriotism aside, to many associate members the sport had a purely social significance. To the younger active gymnasts, swinging around on ropes or standing on each other's shoulders must have been fun in itself, whilst to the older members clubs provided a place to meet and talk.

New research on the social history of leisure in Great Britain has tended to emphasise the importance of 'respectability', with its general overtones of orderliness, sobriety and deference in recreational pursuits. In Britain as in France there was a determined effort to moralise the young through the harnessing of their physical energies to approved civic and patriotic goals. Yet at the same time careful analysis of the evidence makes it clear that the lower classes were quite capable of 'playing the system'. In other words, they would adopt 'respectable' attitudes when it suited them and discard the semblance of 'good behaviour' as easily as they had assumed it. A thorough study of the British Volunteer Force, which was founded at around the same time as the gymnastic and shooting clubs in France with broadly the same functions and social base, offers an illuminating parallel. The Volunteer Force was partly intended to imbue its members with hierarchical values, but in fact it tended to function primarily as a recreational institution, a popular source of seaside holidays and heavy drinking sessions. After a while the more realistic leaders – whether French gymnasts or British volunteers – began to see that direct indoctrination tended to be counter-productive. Gym had to be an enjoyable activity in its own right if it was to survive. It had to turn itself into a 'sport' if it was to compete on equal terms with the new sporting attractions that were developing around the turn of the century. The official rationale of gymnastics remained military, but in fact its true social role was as a source of good fun. Lower-class youths were urged to desist from the company of hard drinkers, gamblers and café habitués and to join a movement that would provide a more enjoyable and fraternal way of life. After 1900 club organisers began to appreciate that if gymnastics were to function as an instrument of military training and civic discipline it would be through the provision of amusement rather than the preaching of patriotic sermons that they would have to operate. Indeed, it was probably this very mixture of immemorial festive tradition with the new spirit of national consciousness that made gymnastics so well suited to the needs of the *belle époque*.[27]

4 The English Sports: Gentlemen and Players

In considering the development of gymnastics in early twentieth-century France, it became clear that this form of physical exercise was steadily losing its appeal in the face of competition from the new athletic activities and team games which came from England. The author of one of the first surveys of the rise of football in France noted that 'association football is taking over almost everywhere from traditional gymnastics'. In comparison to the puerile festive games they replaced, gymnastic exercises had been physically exhilarating. But the routine apparatus work and formation exercises, which made up the core of gymnastic programmes, were too repetitive and inflexible to hold their own against the allure of more complex and less predictable team games like rugby and football. These sports combined to a remarkable degree a sense of the importance and freedom of the individual player with a belief in the value of team work. Very little in the way of equipment was needed, and these games were safe and economical in their use of space and time. Not only did the English sports tend to offer a wider variety of physical and psychological satisfactions to participants, their speed and spontaneity were also more attractive to the spectator than regimented gymnastic displays. Athletics often developed alongside football and rugby, providing summer training for the players and continuity for club social life. In other instances it began independently, building on an old tradition of village running races or throwing contests. When we look at these three forms of modern sport a broadly similar pattern of development emerges. What pioneer anglophiles regarded as instruments of moral education for the élite soon became one of the main sources of a more mindless mass entertainment. From having been the preserve of idealistic amateurs, to a greater or lesser degree all three activities felt the impact of commercialisation and professionalism during the inter-war period.[1]

In the course of the nineteenth century the old game of village football, frequently involving hundreds of players in what was little more than a public affray, gradually died out. As we shall see in a later chapter on changing attitudes to violence in sport, it fell victim to improved standards of public order and a growing official determination to enforce them even if this meant interfering in hitherto unregulated aspects of everyday life. For the present our chief concern is with the new versions of the traditional ball game that had been pioneered in the English public schools and were enthusiastically adopted by the cream of French youth during the *fin-de-siècle*. After generations of regarding street football or *jeu-de-ballon* as distasteful and plebeian, the sons of the Parisian bourgeoisie of the 1880s and 1890s suddenly became ardent *footballeurs* and *rugbymen*. From its former status as a hectic, violent, sprawling village pastime, football had been refined in English public schools such as Rugby; football was now a vigorous and morally uplifting form of exercise designed to prepare a new ruling élite for 'the struggle for life'. Sport would inculcate stability by mixing the sons of the nobility and the bourgeoisie together on the playing field and would create a youthful élite amongst whom instincts of individualism and group loyalty would be nicely balanced. This was part of a wider moral education aimed at encouraging a muscular Christianity that would equip future industrialists and colonial administrators with the strength of character necessary for their task. Through learning the art of 'self-government' they would learn how to govern others.

It was in this spirit that part of the French élite, shocked by the military defeat of 1870, began to look at the English educational system. Just as the gymnasts sought remedies for national weakness in copying the Prussian methods of physical education, so liberal noblemen like the young Pierre de Coubertin or upper-class anglophiles like Georges de Saint-Clair, a former French consul in Edinburgh, turned towards English games. The *lycée* was criticised for its lack of freedom, its failure to encourage moral qualities such as courage, leadership and initiative. For all its academic virtues, the *lycée* turned out puny cerebral youths fit only to pass exams and undertake safe routine tasks, whereas Arnoldian education was thought to imbue boys with a love of adventure, an enjoyment of activity for its own sake tempered by a strict moral code enforced not so much by the masters as by the pupils themselves.[2]

Those who championed the new athletic cause 'believed there was a whole moral and social plan disguised in the form of sports'. Observers of English society were fascinated by the way in which the British managed to combine rapid economic growth with political stability, and most agreed that the educational system played an important part in forging an élite which was apparently capable of combining progress with order, and liberty with hierarchy. Frenchmen marvelled at the amount of time given over to sports in the English public schools, some of which spent almost half their time on the playing fields, and no less emphasis was given to games at the ancient universities. These gentlemen felt that the English educational system taught young men to be good competitors in a world where the competitive principle reigned supreme in business and in political life. By 'good competitors', anglophiles like the Baron de Coubertin did not mean only those who were successful in competition. What he admired in the English system was that it showed men how to compete loyally; boys had to learn to take defeat in good part, for in any competitive system some would lose and others would win. What mattered was to have 'played the game.' Hence the importance attached to participation and, most of all, to amateurism. The entire purpose of sport would be vitiated if the individuals involved were more concerned with financial reward than personal improvement.[3]

These vague moral and social sentiments take on a more practical significance when viewed in the context of the problems of the French upper classes in the later nineteenth century. Coubertin was first drawn to sport as a means of preserving the position of his own social group in a newly democratic world. The young Coubertin's interest in the English sports coincided with the consolidation of the Republican system in France and the collapse of any realistic chance of a return to an idealised *ancien régime*. How would the nobility survive in a competitive environment, and how would France be able to resist the swamping of her traditional institutions by the masses? The answer lay in the formation of a more open élite composed of the sons of the nobility and of the bourgeoisie, an aristocracy of birth and wealth of the kind which those flexible upper class-reformers, the Whigs, had created in Britain. Barriers between the upper and middle classes were broken down at the public schools and particularly on the playing fields. Games like rugby taught the virtues of group cohesion whilst still imbuing the schoolboy with a strong sense of individualism. Sport not only helped to produce practical, resourceful people as opposed to ivory tower intellectuals and time-serving officials, it was also thought to generate group solidarity.[4]

The serious social purpose behind the introduction of the English sports attracted a good deal of public debate, which came to a height in the late 1880s when the first clubs were beginning to establish themselves in Paris and in a few of the major provincial cities like Bordeaux. Coubertin counted no less than seventy-two newspaper articles on the subject of the English sports in France between May and August 1888. The argument about overwork, discipline and sports in the *lycée* was one of the tributaries through which the wider debate on the alleged decadence of French society flowed. Alongside Coubertin in his resistance to the grind of *lycée* examinations, there stood the flamboyant figure of Paschal Grousset, a former liberal journalist under the Second Empire and a delegate for foreign affairs during the Commune. During the 1870s he was exiled from France, living mostly in England where he had a good chance to observe at first hand the British passion for exercise. Amnestied, he returned to France in 1881, working first as a journalist and then from 1893 to his death in 1909 becoming a Radical-Socialist deputy for the twelfth arrondissement of Paris. Grousset was a propagandist of adventure and the outdoor life. In his lifetime he adopted a wide variety of causes ranging from the defence of cyclists against taxation to the defence of Dreyfus from the army. He is said to have collaborated with Robert Louis Stevenson on *Treasure Island* and with Jules Verne. Politically, he was well to the left of Coubertin and the other distinguished advocates of sport who felt that these new activities should be confined to the ranks of the existing élite. Nor did he favour what he saw as the slavish imitation of the English. Sport was to serve the nation as a whole and as such it should have a distinctively French feel about it. All the British had done was to copy games which were originally French like *jeu de paume* (tennis) and *barette, mail* and other ancient ball games.[5]

With a revival of these traditional forms of sport in mind the Ligue Nationale d'Education Physique was formed in 1888 to counter the effects of Coubertin's Union des Sociétés Françaises des Sports Athlétiques (USFSA), founded a year earlier to propagate and regulate the English sports in France. An indication of the urgency and importance attached to this task by those who moulded French opinion and guided French affairs is revealed in the long list of influential persons who joined the Ligue. There were no less than twenty-eight politicians and twenty-three journalists among the seventy-six members of the executive committee. Clemenceau was a prominent supporter of the Ligue and a firm advocate of the cause of sport; so were the world famous chemist and Republican luminary Marcellin Berthelot and the founder of the Ligue d'Enseignement, Jean Macé. For a few years the Ligue made useful contributions both in the field of propaganda and through the organisation of *lycée* competitions, named *lendits* in imitation of medieval student festivals. However, by the mid-1890s the Ligue had collapsed. The revival and modernisation of traditional sports it proposed was not in tune with the interests of schoolboys. Moreover, the important figures on the ruling committee were not prepared to give up the time needed to organise sport on a national level.[6]

Whether it was through the more explicitly nationalist programme of the Ligue or via the efforts of the USFSA, there can be no doubt that it was the *lycéens*, both at school and as old boys, who spearheaded the movement to introduce the English sports into France. The very first club to practice these sports in France, the Le Havre Athletic Club, had been founded in 1872 by expatriate Oxford and Cambridge men. It struggled on for a good while, playing in its dark and light blue colours a game which was a mixture of rugby and football, but it was not until the following decade that there was any indigenous French response. Here the young Parisians came to the fore, founding the Racing Club de France and the Stade Français. The Racing Club was founded by schoolboys from the *lycées* Carnot, Rollin and Condorcet in 1882, and the following year the students of the *lycée* Saint-Louis decided to follow their example and formed the Stade Français. While it appears that the first members of the Racing Club had only the haziest notion of sportsmanship (they wore jockey caps, placed side bets and ran for cash prizes), within a few years the introduction of team games in the winter under the aegis of Georges de Saint-Clair paved the way for a full-blooded emulation of public school games. The ideals of 'fair play', amateurism and disinterested competition were embodied in the statutes of the USFSA and in those of Racing and Stade themselves.[7]

Racing and Stade were extremely selective. Entry was by recommendation only and there were fairly stiff subscriptions to pay in addition to this. Those passers-by who took an interest in the Racing Club in the Bois de Boulogne were quickly removed from contact with the athletes by the erection of a fence around the ground, which the club's illustrious sponsors helped them to obtain from the Paris council at a nominal rent. When a new club-house was opened in 1886 a host of distinguished guests were invited including the minister of war, the famous General Boulanger. The Stade Français was equally smart. After obtaining special prefectorial permission to play on the terrace of the Orangerie it later moved to fine grounds in Saint-Cloud. The members were mostly ex-*lycéens* who had gone into law, medicine or finance. Races were held on Sunday mornings before mass at eleven o'clock. Relations, friends, wives and fiancées mixed easily with the athletes and applauded their efforts. 'What first struck me', remarked a prominent society journalist of these gatherings, 'was the real distinction of these young men, all of whom came from excellent families.'[8]

Racing and Stade played rugby in the winter and organised athletics in the summer. Association football was not thought to be suitable for the well-to-do because of the distinctly popular character it was acquiring in Britain. In fact, the first association football teams formed in France were all British. The employees of Manby and Nicoll, an English firm in Paris, were the first to start a side but this soon collapsed through lack of competition, and it was not until October 1891 that *Les Sports Athlétiques* announced the formation of two new teams which at least could play each other regularly. Both these sides were predominantly British. The White Rovers were begun by Jack Wood, a Scotsman, and the rest of the team was largely made up of his compatriots. A contemporary witness later recalled that 'Sunday games followed too closely on the excesses of Saturday night for many of their players to produce their best form'. Scottish customs of a rather different kind proved an obstacle for another young player called Howatson, whose Presbyterian father would not tolerate his son amusing himself on the Sabbath by playing football. The unfortunate boy did not dare to take his football strip out of the house on a Sunday and had to play under an assumed name in his ordinary clothes. The only rivals of the White Rovers were the Standard Athletic Club founded by a few Englishmen, the Wynn brothers and W. P. Atrill. Several young Frenchmen who had seen the game while at school in Britain then formed their own team in 1892, the Club Français. Led by Eugène Frayasse and Charles Bernat, who had played the game while at Saint Joseph's College in Dumfries, the Club Français joined in a three-sided league, drawing their first game with the Standard Athletic Club on 1 November 1892. Thereafter regular matches were arranged, and Marylebone Football Club were invited to visit Paris the following year to play on the improvised pitch on the north-western fringes of the city at Beçon-les-Bruyères, next to the railway line from Asnières to Courbevoie.[9]

From the start football was a rather less exclusive sport than rugby. Both Racing and Stade rather reluctantly started football sides and organised a competition from the mid-nineties, but their main interests were athletics, rowing and rugby. Whereas Racing and Stade had good facilities, the Standard Athletic Club in its early years had to make do with changing and washing in the shed of a broken-down hotel 'full of all sorts of different bits and pieces: agricultural implements, shovels, picks, rakes, watering cans, packing cases, old scrap iron and piles of wood. In the middle of this chaos there were a few iron chairs . . . you could hang your clothes on the handles of the tools lying around providing you were careful they did not fall into a barrel of water. It was certainly none too warm a place to get changed and there was hardly any light to see what you were doing'. To anyone who has visited its present home in the forest of Meudon and listened to the bar-room gossip of its affluent expatriate membership, the contrast is striking.[10]

During the 1890s athletic sports spread beyond the famous Parisian schools and clubs, taking hold amongst the sons of the provincial bourgeoisie. *Lycée* or university teams were formed as schoolboys and students moved from one institution to another and took their new sporting enthusiasms with them. The USFSA had only a handful of member clubs at the beginning of the 1890s but by 1893 it already numbered some 74 sporting organisations of one kind or another, mostly based on the *lycée*, and only four years later in 1897 there were over 200. Football, rugby and athletics were spreading fast, though clearly at this stage they were still popularly regarded as a bourgeois fad that would soon pass once the initial novelty had worn off. At this time there was no question of commercialising the English sports. The gentleman amateur was the ideal to which sportsmen aspired and the official organ of the USFSA, *Les Sports Athlétiques*, poured scorn on the vainglorious antics of the gymnasts and the crude commercialism of cycle-racing. In the *fin-de-siècle* Parisians flocked to the cycling tracks in their thousands, but few cared enough about rugby or football to watch the early championship matches; nor did the officials of the USFSA encourage them to do so.

It was in the south-west of France that sport was most enthusiastically adopted, and that region has since become the heartland of French rugby. *Lycée* teams sprang up all over Languedoc in the 1890s. Much of the credit for this must go to Phillipe Tissié, a doctor from Bordeaux who dedicated his life to the development of French youth through sports. In 1888 Tissié founded the Ligue Girondine de l'Education Physique, which combined gymnastics and sports to provide a balanced programme of physical training for boys. The Ligue attempted to encourage sports throughout the Bordeaux area and was instrumental in the foundation of the first all-French club outside Paris, Stade Bordelais. The development of rugby in the south-west was assisted by the presence of a sizeable contingent of well-born British families engaged in the wine trade or living in one of the retirement colonies of affluent Britons at Pau or Biarritz. At Pau the local *lycéens* first learned to play rugby through contact with visiting English public schoolboys.[11] Thereafter, French youths quickly learned the game from one another without the need for direct contact with English boys. For instance, the game spread to Bayonne through the son of a local *notaire*, who was a boarder at the *lycée* Montaigne. In 1897 he persuaded the members of a local rowing club to start playing rugby, and that is how the celebrated club Aviron Bayonnais, which later went on to win the French championship, was formed. The doyen of early French rugby, Paul Voivenal, recalled how the sport was first begun at Tarbes in 1895 by a few *lycéens*, who in patriotic style still called the game *barette* and marched off to practice on the parade ground behind a bugle-playing friend. At first the *gratin* (the 'upper crust') refused to join in, preferring their private fencing club, but after a while they formed their own team and the two sets of schoolboys regularly played each other on a pitch overlooked by a huge oak tree, around which would be strewn hats, canes and shirts. These games were starting to spread, as a survey of the English sports in the south-west in 1899 revealed. Out of 112 *lycées* 75 now had sports clubs, and a further 81 out of 229 colleges were similarly provided.[12]

Around the turn of the century football and rugby were both starting to become more familiar. Young men dressed in brightly coloured shirts with hoops or stripes no longer seemed so strange and were beginning to attract the attention of less privileged youngsters. The USFSA catered for the upsurge of enthusiasm by forming regional committees. Between 1898 and 1902 new committees were formed in the Nord, the Beauce, Upper and Lower Normandy, Picardy, Brittany, Champagne and Paris. An analysis of these regional bodies, which had their own buildings and special officers to regulate individual sports, reveals that by 1914 sporting activity was largely concentrated in the Paris conurbation, the south-west and the north. Only four regions had a hundred clubs or more: Upper Normandy, Picardy and the Nord, with Paris way out in front with 217. Proximity to Britain was clearly important in the early years, but looking at those regions with between 50 and 100 clubs, the new importance of sport in the south-west becomes instantly apparent. Of the five areas falling into this category, three were in the south-west and the remaining two centered on Lyon and Marseille. Most of the other regions of France had between thirty and fifty clubs, with the exception of the overwhelmingly rural areas in the centre of France like the Limousin and the Auvergne which had only twelve and nine member clubs respectively. Modern sports were still virtually unknown in the Massif Central before 1914, and in the villages of remote departments like the Ariège traditional village games such as skittles remained predominant until after the Great War.[13]

The spread of the English sports to the French masses came in two stages conveniently separated by the Great War. The first stage covers the period 1900 to 1914 when the number of clubs in the USFSA rose from just over 200 to almost 1600. An eight-fold increase is impressive by any standards, but even more remarkable considering that many new clubs apparently refused to register with the Union on religious grounds or because it refused to officially sanction professionalism. By 1914 the two team games that were to dominate winter sport in France for the rest of the century had already become established. As yet, however, numbers were still fairly limited and there was no significant commercial dimension. It was during the inter-war period that rugby and football were fully integrated into the new world of mass culture. Football and rugby were popularised through makeshift battalion teams, and peasants from the remoter provinces soon picked up some of the new interests of their urban companions in the trenches. In the early twenties the number of rugby clubs shot up to over a thousand, mostly concentrated in the south-west, which has remained the regional stronghold of the sport. There were around a thousand athletics clubs too and this number grew steadily to reach its peak at around two thousand in the mid-thirties. Both these sports were, however, numerically over-shadowed by football, which enjoyed astonishing success just after the war. From about a thousand clubs in 1920 the Fédération Française de Football (FFF) almost quadrupled in size within the next five years. Surely no other participant leisure activity has ever spread so quickly. Thereafter, growth was slower but still steady and by the later 1930s there were almost 6000 clubs, with a licensed membership approaching 200,000. Looking at the regional breakdown for the season 1936/7, the north, the south-east and Paris emerge as the regions where football was most popular. There were 20,274 footballers in the north, 18,752 in the south-east, and 17,238 in the Paris region. Significantly, the areas of France where football was least popular were the centre and the south-west, the strongholds of rugby, where there were less than a quarter of the number of players in the most active areas.[14]

The emergence of football as the dominant sport of the three was evident from as early as 1906, when a popular boys' magazine found that out of 3000 youngsters who answered a questionnaire on their favourite sport, 1500 preferred football and only 400 rugby. As the *Revue Olympique* remarked with a hint of disapproval, 'the most important feature of European sport at the present time is the steady growth of association football'.

The game was perfectly adapted to the conditions of modern urban life. It could be played with almost any number of participants on hard surfaces and in confined spaces without special equipment or much danger of serious injury. Soccer spread rapidly in the ports and industrial towns of northern France in the wake of football-playing British salesmen, engineers and artisans, like the red-haired young Scot who was the star player of the Rouen football club. It became clear in the preceding chapter that during the pre-war decade football was starting to infiltrate the gymnastic clubs, which up to that time had had a virtual monopoly of working-class sport. In 1904 there were already three football clubs in Calais, one of which was called Sport Ouvrier Calaisien. At about that period there were 64 clubs in Paris running 140 football teams. The same craze was sweeping the north. There were so many games of football being played, complained the organisers of an athletics meeting, that 'the athletes and the public are becoming obsessed with the round ball at the expense of other forms of sport'. Picardy, for instance, had sixty-seven teams by 1910, the first of which was the Amiens Athletic Club founded by Frédéric Petit in 1902. Petit came from a bourgeois home and became a textile manufacturer and mayor of Grandvilliers, and his brother, also a footballer, was a graduate of the Ecole de Sciences Politiques in Paris. Football attracted a wide range of social types. Henri Chabrol, an *agrégé* of the Ecole Normale Supérieure, became a great centre-forward and played for FC Nimes, but so too did François Augade, a local baker.[15]

Whilst there can be no doubt that football was the first of the English sports to acquire a really large following, it would be quite misleading to assume that rugby remained a purely middle-class game. By looking at the social composition of two of the first rugby clubs to be set up in Lyon it is possible to form a general impression of the way in which this game began to filter down to the lower classes around the turn of the century. The Football Club de Lyon, founded in 1895, was the first rugby club in the city. A list of club particulars submitted to the prefecture some years later noted that the club was composed of 300 active members paying 4 francs a month and a further 100 schoolboy or student members paying only 50 centimes. The club was run by a committee made up of two merchants, a doctor, a senior civil servant and a clerk. This club, primarily

bourgeois in its social structure, can be instructively compared
with Stade Lyonnais founded five years later in 1900. Here the
lower middle class – the office-worker, skilled artisan and small
shopkeeper groups – were clearly in the ascendancy. Of the
thirty-eight members there were twenty-one clerks, four grocers,
two ironmongers and only one student. The remainder were a
mixture of skilled self-employed men, mostly locksmiths and
engravers. Whereas the Football Club de Lyon had its own
clubhouse and grounds, the Stade Lyonnais met in the backroom of a local café.[16]

This shift in the social basis of rugby towards the *petite
bourgeoisie* and the younger skilled workers is confirmed by
other impressions recorded by several of the early enthusiasts.
In the south-west, where rugby had a head start over football,
the sport developed the kind of popular following it also found in
parts of northern England and south Wales. A Toulouse doctor,
who subsequently became a major figure in rugby in the
Languedoc, recalled that as a young medical student in 1905 he
had been somewhat surprised by the rapid spread of the sport
beyond the confines of the liberal professions to include 'the sons
of salesmen, even of manual workers'. A further illustration of
the democratising of rugby south of the Loire is provided by the
employees of a large drapery firm in Clermont-Ferrand. Some of
these young men had become interested in the sport by watching
the local *lycée* team. When this side became defunct after the best
players had gone off to university in Toulouse, the shop
assistants decided to form their own team. The recollections of
one of the members of this team, the Club Amical Sportif du
Grand Air, gives valuable insight into the impact of the game on
the lives of young working people in that area. Working hours
did not favour the practice of sports, as most of the team
members worked a six-day week and a ten-and-a-half hour day.
But it is important to note that hours of work alone were not the
decisive factor. Sundays were free and games could be played
then. This became and remains standard practice in France. In
some respects a greater obstacle to participation was posed by
the danger of accidents and the family responsibilities of some of
the players. 'I was the eldest of a large family', recalled the
individual in question, 'we had no insurance and I did not like to
risk my salary, which was indispensable to the family budget, in
a rugby accident.' As if to emphasise the risk, the club's full back

was killed whilst making a tackle in 1907. Incidents of this kind, though rare, were a factor to be reckoned with and certainly influenced some players to turn to less dangerous games like football.[17]

Interestingly, athletics was the slowest of the main three Anglo-Saxon sports to find a popular audience. In theory, athletics were the most accessible of activities. They required no special skills or expensive equipment. The early bourgeois devotees of the track had certainly feared that the lower classes would soon take up running in large numbers. Although there were a good number of athletics clubs composed of ordinary working people by 1914, as a whole athletics appears to have been less attractive to the lower classes than football or rugby. However, the degree of popular interest in running is admittedly more difficult to measure than it is with team sports. There may have been a good deal of casual track athletics of the kind that took place in the heart of Paris. The place du Carrousel was a favourite meeting place for athletic young apprentices and clerks, who simply left their jackets by the pavement and offered to race whoever happened to be around at the time. The large square formed a perfect track and impromptu races would sometimes go on until eleven o'clock on summer evenings. Unfortunately, this delightful custom had to be abandoned as the volume of motor traffic increased. But it seems that similar events often took place in the working-class suburbs to the east of Paris: 'on mild summer evenings at dusk you could see lines of runners around the Buttes de Chaumont, in the Place de la Nation and along the Cours de Vincennes. This was sport for the common people which required no club subscriptions to enjoy . . . the cloakroom was the counter of the local café'.[18]

Perhaps one of the reasons that athletics appeared rather less popular with the lower classes than football or rugby was simply that it was less important to form a special club to enjoy this sport than it was for team games. Moreover, athletics were really complementary rather than alternative activities to the ball games. Many clubs organised running races as part of a summer training programme. Thus it is difficult to tell how many clubs trained athletes as well as rugby or football players. There were a few interesting cases of clubs changing over to full-time athletics during the inter-war period because their areas had become saturated with teams playing rugby or football. This was particularly true of the south-west. Before 1914, however, the provinces made less of an impression on Paris in athletics than they did in other sports. Of the fourteen major athletic prizes offered by the USFSA in 1906, only six were won by provincial clubs and this was considered a great improvement on previous performances.[19]

The dramatic increase in the popularity of rugby and football within the space of one generation led to severe problems of administration. Activities which were introduced for the amusement and instruction of the well-to-do had been abruptly annexed by the masses. The sporting gentlemen who found themselves in charge of the various official bodies involved were faced with a dilemma. The logic of mass support led inexorably in the direction of greater professionalism and commercialisation, but this was explicitly contrary to what they considered to be the real spirit of their activities. Disinterested amateurism fought with no-nonsense professionalism. Each side had its advocates and the resulting compromise by which the payment of salaries to players was officially forbidden but effectively permitted was morally unsatisfactory, although it worked reasonably well in practice until the end of the 1920s. Until the thirties crowds were too small to support fully professional leagues in any case.

Rugby developed rather faster as a spectator sport than football. The USFSA had been slow to develop a soccer championship, whereas rugby fixtures had been organised from an early date. During the 1890s there were some memorable encounters between the two great Parisian sides, but the old rivalry between the Racing Club and Stade Français soon gave way to a new one between Paris and Bordeaux. In 1899 Stade Bordelais took the first of the seven championships they were to win between 1899 and 1911. In the decade preceding 1914, clubs at Bayonne, Carcassone, Pau, Béziers and Toulouse all found a substantial local following. But it was in Bordeaux that the largest crowds gathered and where spectator enthusiasm reached its pre-war peak. The final of the French rugby championship in 1911 between Stade Bordelais and the Paris Université Club drew a crowd of 28,000, and for the first time an official representative of the government was present. Touts were selling five-franc tickets for sixty francs in the cafés of Bordeaux.[20]

The authentic atmosphere of French rugby as a spectator sport is to be found in the fanatical support enjoyed by the smaller teams of the Languedoc, Gascony and Aquitaine. When Aviron Bayonnais won the French national championship in 1913 with the aid of a new style of open rugby pioneered by their semi-professional Welsh coach, Owen Roe, the community erupted with delight and excitement. The public of Bayonne followed rugby in the winter as avidly as they watched bull-fighting in the summer. On Sunday evenings after a match large crowds would assemble in the place du Théâtre, where the latest results would be chalked up on a large board as they came in and jeered or applauded as local prejudice and interest required. The large café on the square was owned by a former player, Louis Saubion, who would give public demonstrations of how to heel a ball with the aid of a couple of chairs, and massage the injured whilst feeding them a special cocktail of cinzano and cassis which was famous throughout the region. Like many other small town clubs, Aviron Bayonnais had its own song, the refrain of which was particularly beloved of players and supporters alike: 'Joyeux garçons, enfants de l'Aviron, toujours nous aimerons notre Bayonne. On nous connaît, bons coeurs mais obstinés, comme nos grands aînés. Voilà l'Aviron Bayonnais!' Watching rugby here, as elsewhere in the south-west, became a local passion. The sport was fully integrated in the pattern of festivity, with blue and white colours flying everywhere and huge rugby balls decorating the streets during the *fête*. The small town of Gujan-Mestras, the centre of oyster cultivation near Bordeaux, managed to get its team into the top national league in the 1920s despite a population of only three thousand and having to rely on local players rather than expensive transfers. The team developed an elaborate youth programme and like Aviron Bayonnais had a devoted following. Quillan, which was not much larger, did even better, winning the national championship in 1927, but this was done with the aid of a rich hat manufacturer who lured some of the best players into his team by the offer of sinecure jobs in his factory.[21]

The growth of interest in rugby as a spectator sport is also illustrated on a national level by the success of the early international matches held in France. The first French international fixture was against the New Zealand touring team after their 1905/6 tour of the British Isles, and this was soon followed by internationals against England, Scotland, Ireland and Wales.

The French were defeated 38–8 by the New Zealanders and 35–8 by the English, but they chalked up an international victory against Scotland in Paris in 1911 by the narrow margin of 16–15. French rugby had come of age and thereafter regular matches were arranged with crowds of 40,000 spectators or more until the blatant flouting of the amateur code caused the British rugby unions to break off relations with the French. The atrocious battles to which the British also took strong exception continued through the thirties in the annual struggle for the championship. Clermont-Ferrand, backed by the tyre million-aire Michelin, emerged as a leading contender to break the stranglehold of the south-west on the game, but by this time a new fully professional body had been set up to spread the rugby league game in France. The challenge from the thirteen-a-side game together with the international isolation of French rugby led the governing body to suppress the championship in 1939 and agree to the demands of the British for a full return to amateurism. Since the war French rugby has enjoyed great success, winning the Five Nations Cup for the first time in 1954 under the captaincy of Jean Prat, who also captained the outstanding post-war club side FC Lourdes.[22]

Despite the upsurge of interest in football as a participant sport, especially in the industrial towns of the north, it did not develop quite so dramatically at the spectator level. The average gate of a prominent side would rarely exceed a thousand in the period 1900–1910, and even big cup games would be unlikely to be watched by more than five thousand spectators. As early as 1905 some football clubs had complained that richer clubs were luring high-class players away with cash inducements. A good many players appear to have been able to supplement their income usefully by this means; but only a handful were able to earn a decent living from the sport. The acrobatic goalkeeper of Red Star, Pierre Chayrigues, was one of the fortunate few. He had been persuaded to leave Clichy for Saint-Ouen by an offer of 500 francs, a monthly salary of 400 francs, and a 50-franc bonus for each match the team won. For an ex-apprentice electrician this was a high income. The best teams mostly came from the industrial belt of the north of Paris – Red Star of Saint-Ouen, USA de Clichy and FC Levallois were among the most popular – or from the major industrial centres. The Racing Club de Roubaix and Stade Olympique de Marseille were amongst the first major provincial sides to attract large crowds. In fact, it was in the extreme north and the extreme south that football enjoyed most success as a spectator sport. Obviously, there was some correlation between the presence of a large industrial workforce and the success of football as a popular commercial spectacle, but the relationship did not always hold good. During the inter-war years one of the best sides came from Sète and other prominent teams included Nimes, Antibes and Cannes. The cup-final of 1929 was played in Paris between two neighbouring teams from the Midi, Montpellier and Sète. Gaston Doumergue, the president of the Republic, who came from nearby Aigues-Mortes, took the opportunity to shore up his regional following by attending the match and chatting informally to the players in patois.[23]

Although football was now a thriving sport with far more players than any other game, the lack of conurbations of sufficient size to provide really large crowds on a regular basis inhibited the development of a fully professional national league. Henri de Jooris, a wealthy Lille businessman who ran the northern league, proposed that a single national league replace the existing regional ones, and after a good deal of argument agreement was reached. The first league championship was organised in the season 1932/3. Even in the mid-thirties football was still in a financially precarious position as a form of commercial entertainment. Several clubs misjudged the market and seriously overspent. FC Nimes threw themselves into the international transfer market, buying the Scottish international Andy Wilson in 1933. They secured the services of two more prominent British players and almost succeeded in signing the legendary Newcastle and Scotland centre-forward Hughie Gallacher. Nimes bought players in the expectation that gates would go up as they became more and more successful. They paid the price for their lack of caution and went bankrupt with a debt of over half a million francs despite frantic efforts to get the leader of the city's chamber of commerce to take over the club and pay off the debt. Olympique de Nimes, which replaced them, were more prudent and less ambitious. The rewards for success were certainly considerable – nearly forty thousand spectators paid over half a million francs to watch the cup final in 1937–but a sober calculation of the costs involved in running a professional club amounted to nearly a million francs a year, and few clubs could attract large enough crowds to warrant expenditure of this order.[24]

Problems of commercial viability did not mean standards were low. On the contrary, France produced an excellent international team and performed well in each of the three world cup competitions in the thirties, the last of which was staged successfully in France in 1938. Thépot, the talented goalkeeper of Red Star, Mattler, a full-back, and the captain, Nicholas, who later managed the brilliant French world cup side of 1958, were the leading international players of the thirties. The influx of Poles, especially into the mining districts of northern France, strengthened teams like Lens and eventually produced France's greatest player, Raymond Kopa, the deep-lying centre-forward of the fifties. France also had an important place in the organisation of international football. When the British refused to get involved with the international game around the turn of the century, France offered its established diplomatic and bureaucratic skills in their place. Hence the governing body of world football was born in France and still has a French name, the Fédération Internationale de Football Association (FIFA).

The English sports had come a long way in a comparatively short time. From being a moral and physical antidote to the neuroses of bourgeois youth, they had become an outlet for the frustrations of the lower classes. As spectator sports they no longer attracted the kind of clientele that had been first envisaged for them. As games to play only athletics retained any of the early exclusivity and idealism that had been attached to them by men like the Baron de Coubertin. It is perhaps interesting to note that at the Olympic Games of 1912 only the track athletes were thought to be sufficiently well educated to appreciate the meaning of the Hellenic ideal. Athletes were rather more successful in preserving their early gentlemanly ideals than footballers or rugby players, partly because most of their events were too individualistic to become a vehicle for the strong feelings of local patriotism which became the hallmark of popular team games. The adulation accorded to the great cyclists, backed by the big manufacturers and attracting vast publicity, eclipsed the attention given to the best French athletes like Jean Bouin, who came within an ace of carrying off an Olympic gold medal in 1912.[25]

Even athletics submitted in part to commercial pressures

between the wars. It was a standing joke amongst experienced athletes that 'the white flag of amateurism has a silver lining'. Jules Ladoumègue, who broke the world 1500 metres record in 1930 but was denied a place in the 1932 Olympic Games because he had received money for performing, is a case in point. Ladoumègue had begun life near Bordeaux under tragic circumstances. His father was killed when Jules was four months old while trying to rescue a fellow worker from a collapsing building, and his mother died a few weeks later from burns received while opening a can of petrol. He was brought up by relations and went to work as an assistant gardener at thirteen. He first began running in a Catholic youth club and took part in local 'professional' races for a few francs in prize money. He was trained by a young friend, an apprentice printer, who filched machine oil from his work to use as liniment. Despite these severe handicaps he came second in the French national cross-country competition when he was only eighteen and thereafter was taken under the wing of the famous Stade Bordelais Club, who helped him pay the 500 francs demanded by the authorities for the restitution of his amateur status. He came second in the 1500 metres in the Amsterdam Olympics of 1928 despite complaining that he did not have a proper bed to sleep in. After his success in the 1928 Olympics Ladoumègue became something of a celebrity in France and had to train at dawn to avoid his more enthusiastic fans. He openly admitted that running was a means of social advancement and struggled to dress and to speak correctly so as to avoid seeming uneducated. During the preparations for the Olympics of 1932 he appeared in a special run down the Champs Elysées in front of 200,000 spectators and followed by a motorcade of stars including Georges Carpentier, Maurice Chevalier, Mistinguette, and many more. Ladoumègue was accused of professionalism and lost his amateur status. Instead of taking part in the Olympics he had to content himself with a trip to Los Angeles at the expense of a large newspaper to interview the winner of the 1500 metres (a singularly refined form of mental torture).[26]

Ladoumègue's bad luck is instructive in that it dramatises the peculiar position of amateur sports with widespread public support. Mass audiences for amateur events had not been envisaged by the founders of the English sports in France. Strong commercial pressures on athletes often placed them in a difficult and ambiguous situation. The athletics federation took a firm line with those who received any material reward for the excitement and pleasure they gave to the countless thousands who followed their exploits. The football and rugby authorities, however, were more lax. They often turned a blind eye to infringements of amateur status – backhanders, perks, gifts, phoney jobs and the like – until the later twenties and early thirties, when a more honest and explicit recognition of the professional potential of rugby and football as commercial spectator sports became unavoidable.

The demise of the athletic gentleman is mirrored in the dissolution of the institution formed to uphold the values of the upper-class anglophiles who pioneered these sports in the 1880s. The Union des Sociétés Françaises des Sports Athlétiques, set up jointly in 1888 by the Racing Club and the Stade Français to run all the English sports on an amateur basis, was broken up into autonomous units in 1919, each with responsibility for one sport alone. No common philosophy now bound together those who played the English sports and even the phrase itself went out of fashion. The great majority of sportsmen no longer came from broadly similar middle-class backgrounds or shared the same assumptions about the moral and social purposes ·of games. By 1914 most footballers or athletes, players or spectators, came from the *classes moyennes* or the *classes populaires*. Whilst football and rugby were admittedly not fully absorbed into the wider framework of working-class life until the 1920s, there can be little doubt that their role in the moral training of an élite was over by 1914. The English sports had become the exercise and amusement of the common man rather than an instrument of bourgeois idealism, a source of mass entertainment and monetary gain as opposed to a means of personal improvement and public benefit.

5 Cycling as a Commercial Spectacle

The development of football and rugby in the period between 1890 and 1914 provided evidence not only of the importance of sport in the provision of physical exercise but also of the role of sport as a source of mass entertainment. Many of the factors associated with urbanisation and industrialisation which favoured the growth of participant sports also encouraged the development of commercial spectator sport in its modern form. The modernising societies of Europe and North America required new amusements to replace the communal festivals and religious celebrations of earlier times. Accordingly, a whole range of entertainments from the music hall to modern professional sport arose to cater for the needs of the growing number of people whose brief periods of free time and small amounts of spare money were primarily devoted to seeking excitement or escapism. Quite simply, entertainment became an industry in which money was invested in the sure knowledge that a public existed which desired a temporary diversion from the uniformity of their everyday lives and which could afford to pay for the privilege.

Professional sport had a central place in this world of modern entertainment, and of those sports which first felt the impact of commercialisation cycle-racing was indisputably the most important. Ask any foreigner which sporting spectacle is most typically French and the reply will probably be 'the Tour de France'. In considering the growth of rugby and football in the pre-1914 period it was evident that, despite the existence of certain commercial elements in both of these activities, neither could lay claim to being fully professional at that time. Cycle-racing, however, occupied no such indeterminate position. Professional cyclists openly admitted to being professional; sporting entrepreneurs invested in special cycling stadiums and used every means open to them to draw in the crowds; and cycle manufacturers shamelessly exploited the economic opportunities offered by the rising interest of the public in commercial spectator sport. Lucrative inducements and extensive technical assistance were given to successful riders prepared to advertise a particular make of bicycle. Before long it was essential for any rider who seriously wanted to win one of the major races to ally himself with a leading manufacturer. The popular press fuelled the commercial fire by systematically creating 'stars' for the public to idolise and emulate. By 1914 the cycling season extended from the spring to the early autumn and events were spread over most of the countries of western Europe. France, however, remained the fulcrum of the cycling world. It was in France that the sport was first raised to the status of a national spectacle with the founding of the Tour de France, and it was in France that the richest events were run and the largest crowds gathered.

Why was this so? How can we explain the peculiar hold which this form of spectator sport came to have over the French public? Our object here is not so much to discuss the technical details of the sport itself as to analyse its appeal and the process by which it was 'sold' to the French. At what market was the sport aimed and who financed the major events? Why did the track races, which were so popular in the 1890s, generally decline after 1900 whilst the long distance road races became ever more popular? It is surely odd that so little is known of the nature of the crowds who followed the sport and of the professionals who entertained them when the popular press of the period abounds in detailed accounts of the races at which they were present. Unfortunately, no-one thought of asking a sample of the crowd who they were or why they came, nor do we have a survey of professional riders as an occupational group. It is only by piecing together the many scattered references to these and other related questions that it is possible to give a general account of the commercial and social structure of France's first national spectator sport.

The holding of bicycle races began almost as soon as the bicycle itself had been invented. The penny-farthing was developed in France in the late 1860s and the first major bicycle race was run from Rouen to Paris in 1869. The intervention of the Franco-Prussian War held back the production of bicycles in France and it was not until the late 1870s that races began to be held on a regular basis. As far as the public were concerned such displays were of little more than curiosity value. At this time bicycles were both extremely expensive and risky to ride. As such they primarily attracted the affluent young bourgeois as an item of conspicuous consumption, and it was from this social group that most of the prominent early competitors were drawn.[1]

The leading riders of the 1870s and 1880s generally had private means. For instance, H. O. Duncan, an Englishman who preferred to ride in France, was the grandson of a celebrated fox-hunting squire and had inherited family money. Duncan's ideal was the independent, self-financing gentleman rider, 'a young man of good family in possession of a sizeable income who enjoys participating in races in several countries'. His French rivals of the time generally conformed to this definition. Frédéric Charron, one of the best provincial riders of the 1880s, was the heir to a large grocery business and later became one of the first motor-racing enthusiasts in France. Another celebrated rider of the period, de Civry, had taken up cycling while at school in England and clearly came from a privileged background. Even the most successful competitors could only hope to make a small profit after hotel, travel and technical expenses had been deducted from their winnings. The opportunities for travel, the congenial company and the thrill of novelty and competition were the real attractions for most riders.[2]

At this time cycle races were organised mainly by private clubs and as yet the sport could scarcely be considered a modern commercial spectacle. The most famous of the early clubs was the Véloce Club Bordelais, which was founded in 1879 and had several hundred members by 1885, with the same sprinkling of English influence to be found a little later in the main athletic and rugby clubs of the Gironde. Certainly, English ideals of sportsmanship prevailed within the club and the money raised by charging spectators to watch racing was generally given to charity. The purpose of the many competitions run by this club in the 1880s seems to have been to allow their members to compete against top-class opposition, and little concern was expressed about the comfort or amusement of spectators. This, of course, stands out in striking contrast to the attitude of those who later sought to turn the sport into a form of popular entertainment. In the 1880s cycle-racing was still very much of a minority interest, as the machines themselves were too costly, dangerous and impractical to attract widespread public attention. As an early sports journalist remarked, cyclists remained 'une compagnie, une secte en quelque sorte'.[3]

Nevertheless, the basis for the successful future commercial exploitation of cycling had in part been laid. A rudimentary tournament circuit had been set up and a body of semi-professional competitors existed. In 1882, 328 riders competed in 284 events worth a total of 20,000 francs. By 1885 the number of competitors had risen to 481 and the number of events to 609. The value of prize money now amounted to 67,000 francs, and the prospect of enrichment through sport was beginning to attract a few lower-class riders who could get access to the basic capital required. At this stage racing was more or less confined to short-distance sprinting, and there was no question of manufacturers subsidising riders in the manner that became commonplace later. The cheapest bicycle cost in the region of 400 to 500 francs and, as such, was beyond the reach of all but the rich. As a Rouen councillor said, 'to be a cyclist you require a small fortune'. There was little point in sponsoring professional racing if this would not lead to greater sales. Therefore, manufacturers of the time limited their small advertising drive to promoting the touring rather than the sporting potential of the bicycle.[4]

It was the invention in the later 1880s of the modern bicycle, chain-driven with wheels of equal size and inflatable tyres, which provided the real impetus for the development of cycle-racing as a mass commercial spectacle. Suddenly, the bicycle was no longer the plaything of the daring young *fils de famille*, it was a sensible instrument of private transport which brought to the masses the kind of mobility which had previously been available only to those few who could afford to stable, groom and feed a horse. The new bicycle was safe and easy to ride; it enabled city-dwellers to explore the country and offered peasants the prospect of temporary escape from rural isolation.

Once the initial curiosity evoked by the invention passed, interest in cycling as a spectator sport broadly corresponded to the increase in the number of bicycles in circulation. In the early 1890s bicycles were still extremely expensive items and well beyond the income of ordinary working men. In the course of the decade, however, prices fell dramatically with the advent of mass production and the growth of cut-throat competition between manufacturers. By 1900 a new machine could be bought from as little as 100 francs and the American manufacturers, suffering from a glut of over-production, cut prices even further and offered hire-purchase arrangements to tempt the impecunious apprentice to buy a bicycle. According to taxation figures there were around 130,000 bicycles in 1893, but this figure had risen to over 375,000 by 1898. Thereafter, the number of bicycles officially in circulation rose by approximately one million every five years, so that by 1914 there were about three-and-a-half million bicycles in France. For obvious reasons this figure remained static during the war, but thereafter cycling experienced the same post-war boom as other forms of sporting activity. By 1926 there were over seven million bikes in France. This figure remained roughly constant for the next ten years until the Popular Front era, with its new leisure policy, witnessed a further increase to almost nine million in 1938. Before the early 1920s the bicycle, or at least a good-quality new machine suitable for racing or touring, remained beyond the reach of most unskilled workers. In Lille, for example, it was the skilled artisans who raced their bicycles in the *belle époque*, although a sensitive social historian has noted that by 1914 'the bicycle was starting to become a means of transport for the workers, helping to shift the population away from the city centre and towards the suburbs'.[5]

The relatively small profit margins of manufacturers meant that the volume of sales had to be increased whenever possible. In order to do this producers were prepared to invest large sums of money in cycling as a competitive sport. It was on the cycle track and in the long distance road races that the public assessed the merits and demerits of particular machines. For the manufacturers' success in competition played a vital part in preserving or enhancing the reputation of their products, especially amongst the young, who wanted their bicycles to go as fast as possible and liked to identify themselves with the current champions. Some races, in fact, were little more than advertising stunts for certain firms. In July 1892, for example, a race from Paris to Clermont-Ferrand was organised by Michelin with the express intention of demonstrating the superiority of the tyres they manufactured to those made by Dunlop. Accordingly, nails were scattered on the road at certain pre-arranged places and a Michelin repair team stationed conveniently nearby. Not surprisingly a bicycle equipped with Michelin tyres won the race and the firm proudly announced their product was 'unbeatable'.[6]

Within a few years the sport was thoroughly commercialised. Manufacturers began to sign contracts with the best riders, and a large body of special trainers and managers came into existence to organise works teams and provide technical back-up. As early as 1900, much of the paraphernalia of the professional cycling business was already in existence. The commercial interests of the manufacturers coincided with a genuine enthusiasm on the part of a large number of young men for competitive cycling. The governing body of the sport, the Union Vélocipédique de France (UVF) had been founded in 1881 and had 10,000 members by 1889. With the introduction of the modern bicycle, membership increased to 44,000 by 1893. Henceforth, growth was slower but a steady increase was maintained so that by 1909 the UVF boasted a total of 80,000 members; numbers continued to rise after the Great War reaching around 200,000 by 1939. Naturally, many of those who joined cycling clubs did not do so with the object of truly competitive riding. Nevertheless, the growth of this body is an impressive testimony to the grass-roots popularity of the sport. By 1914 a network of cycling clubs extended throughout France. In most clubs there was a core of keen younger members ready to challenge other clubs to sprints or races round the neighbouring countryside, and the UVF never put the barriers in the way of young riders earning small sums of money that the English with their cult of pure amateurism maintained. The existence of a sizeable rival body, the Fédération Cycliste et Athlétique de France, before 1914 makes it difficult to give accurate overall figures, but it is indisputable that Sunday cycle-racing became a familiar, some might almost say a characteristic, feature of the French roads in the *belle époque*.[7]

The most tangible symbol of the transformation of a middle-class amusement into a means of mass entertainment was the *vélodrome*. These were permanent stadia with proper facilities for paying spectators which replaced the grass tracks and impromptu courses around the city streets typical of the 1880s.

Vélodromes were the new craze and for a brief period the erection of tracks went ahead at a hectic pace. One of the first investors to latch on to this new development in popular entertainment was, not surprisingly, someone with considerable experience in providing the public with what they wanted: Clovis Clerc, the director of the Folies Bergères. He opened a track at Charenton and even held bicycle races in the Folies itself.[8]

It is abundantly clear that there was a strong demand from the public for commercial sporting entertainment of this kind, as a petition presented to the Paris council in 1893 illustrates. This document contained seven thousand signatures, mostly from inhabitants in the eleventh, twelfth and thirteenth arrondissements, requesting the council to build a municipal cycling track. The track was built and in 1895 the council decided to sponsor a Grand Prix de Paris, which subsequently became one of the most coveted sprint trophies in cycling. In the council's deliberations on this question the view emerged that, as the council gave very considerable financial support to horse-racing, it was under some kind of moral obligation to make similar provision for the new sporting interests of the young, the less well-off and the inhabitants of the eastern part of the city (the race-courses at Auteuil and Longchamp being in the west).[9]

Vélodromes were erected in all parts of France in the 1890s. By the turn of the century almost every provincial town of any consequence had a *vélodrome* of some sort, although they were frequently ramshackle affairs which bore little resemblance to the great Parisian tracks. The most famous of the early Parisian *vélodromes* was the 'Buffalo', so called because it was erected on the site of Buffalo Bill's circus. Like the circus, the new *vélodrome* went all out to entertain the public. The Buffalo was more than just a cycle track, 'it was a great outdoor theatre, with tracks for competition, rinks for learners, a place where one could dine and be entertained, where one could buy, rent or repair a bicycle and where the crowds came out on Sunday for the biggest attraction of all, the races'. Significantly, the proprietor of the Buffalo was not much of a sportsman himself. The owner was none other than the rich young socialite and man of letters, Tristan Bernard. A regular patron of the track was his artist friend Toulouse-Lautrec. The latter painted several well-known bicycle posters and clearly took an interest in cycling not only because it was fashionable, but also because it had rapidly found a place in the new world of popular entertainment which fascinated him.[10]

To men like Bernard and Clerc the attraction of cycling lay not so much in the racing itself as in the prospect of creating a new and lucrative form of public entertainment. In the mid-1890s, when track-racing became a craze, substantial profits could be made by the enterprising. The UVF, which had been set up in the early 1880s to regulate the sport and preserve its integrity, was partially infiltrated by those who saw that there were large sums to be made. Just how much money was made is difficult to estimate, as few figures are available, but the following fragments of evidence give some indication of the profitability of commercialised sport. During the season 1893/4 the only indoor stadium in Paris paid 20,000 francs to the council in tax. On this basis (the tax was 6 per cent of the takings) it would appear that receipts were in the region of 330,000 francs. Elsewhere it is recorded that the 15,000 spectators who attended the first Sunday meeting at the Parc des Princes in Paris paid 24,000 francs at the turnstiles. We also know from the accounts of the Grand Prix de Paris that it brought in 45,000 francs in the first year it was run, that this figure had risen to almost 70,000 francs by 1903, and that it surpassed a million francs in 1911, leaving a profit of 348,000 francs which was distributed to the poor by the council. Of course, normally takings were lower. One estimate suggests that around 5000 francs was the usual amount of gate-money for an ordinary meeting and that over the whole season between 150,000 and 200,000 francs might be taken. Clearly, large profits could be made by staging major events, but the financial viability of the week-to-week performances was much more dubious.[11]

Consequently, sporting impresarios with a background in commercial entertainment were anxious to broaden the appeal of cycle-racing and feared (correctly as it turned out) that the public would soon tire of an unadulterated diet of track-racing. Accordingly, those who sunk money into this new branch of the entertainment industry tried to integrate sport more fully into the general pattern of music hall variety performance. Races between scantily clad actresses were devised and there were experiments with cycling acrobats, negro minstrels and animals. None of these circus-like innovations had much success. The crowd certainly wanted to be amused, but the real attraction of the spectacle lay in the element of personal competition and in the speed of the machines and the flamboyance or endurance of the riders.

It was this last element in the sporting equation which the organisers of the new tracks latched on to in the hope of keeping the crowds interested. Endurance events not unlike the marathon dance championships, which were also a feature of popular entertainment in the early twentieth century, became very popular. As far as the organisers were concerned, instant commercial appeal was the sole criterion of what should or should not be offered to the public. They were not worried about the danger of trivialising the sport itself and made a clear distinction between sport as a participant activity and sport as entertainment. Cycling therefore witnessed the curious and occasionally degrading spectacle of races lasting for several days, sometimes for a week, in which riders not infrequently suffered badly from exposure or exhaustion. The new sporting public appeared to be unmoved by such problems and these events were livened up by periodic sprints and sideshows. Commentators were sometimes shocked at the degree to which displays of this kind diverged from the ideals professed by those who advocated sport as a means of national rejuvenation. Even when endurance events did not involve undue suffering on the part of the riders, they frequently brought the sport into disrepute in other respects; most problems stemmed from the blatant materialism of all concerned. Not surprisingly, those who became involved in such races often made private arrangements with other competitors to minimise the effort involved, and on occasions the outcome of a race was determined in advance by private negotiation. This was particularly true of races that attracted the interest of bookmakers, the most famous of which was the Six Jours, with its studied sensationalism and hectic Saturday night sprint.[12]

The first such event to be held in Paris was a non-stop 1500-kilometre race between Charles Terront, France's first professional cycling star, whose career will be examined in more detail later, and a close rival named Corré. The race was held in 1893 at the Vélodrome d'Hiver (the former Salle des Arts Libéraux erected for the exhibition of 1889). The event attracted great publicity, with Terront winning in front of a crowd of thousands with many more, who had been unable to get a ticket, waiting outside for the result. Terront caused a sensation by rigging up a rubber tube to the frame of his bicycle which enabled him to relieve himself without dismounting. Of such ephemeral titillation were sporting sensations made, and incidents of this kind obviously provided marvellous copy for the new mass-circulation popular press, which frequently sponsored racing. These events heralded a new, and to some rather unwelcome, era in spectator sport. Ballyhoo and hyperbole became the stock-in-trade of the sports journalist, who carved out a distinctive and specialised niche in the journalistic world. Sport became the property of market forces and was dominated by material considerations alien to the ideals of amateurism and self-improvement through physical effort. As the organiser of the Terront–Corré match, Paul Meyan, recalled some twenty years later, 'the most important feature of that event was the nature of the crowd it attracted and the effect such spectacles had on the masses. This was the beginning of cycle racing as a popular spectacle'.[13]

It is exceedingly difficult to be precise about who attended professional cycle-racing at the end of the century. All we know for certain is that the sport was extremely popular. All the *vélodromes* of Paris were filled to capacity in the heyday of track-sprinting in the mid-1890s. The Paris council clearly considered cycle-racing a 'democratic' sport and had no doubt that the majority of those who followed it were in the lower income bracket. In the early to mid-1890s, when cycling was still considered chic by elements of the middle class, several incidents took place which reveal something of the new social character of the sport. Complaints were received by the council from bourgeois ladies who had accompanied their sons to race meetings and had come away shocked and indignant after their first brush with proletarian culture. Normally, the classes were separated by the price of their tickets, but at the practice sessions there was no differential pricing policy with the result that 'decent persons could not watch . . . without mixing with ruffians in shabby clothes using coarse or obscene language'. A breakdown of the types of seat sold at the Grand Prix de Paris in 1896 reveals that the great majority of the spectators bought the cheapest seats: 961 spectators paid ten francs for a place in the enclosure, 932 paid five francs for a seat in the stand, but a further 6529 bought the cheapest seats at two francs. A letter to the council made the point that even cheaper seats could easily double the size of the crowd, such was the interest in the race amongst the urban working class.[14]

It is clear that there was a growing gulf between those who bought bicycles for the purpose of touring and casual recreation, and those who formed the bulk of performers and spectators at the new *vélodromes*. The early social homogeneity of the sport had been destroyed by its sudden commercial success. 'At the present time', remarked Maurice Martin as early as 1890, 'cycling is divided into two distinct camps; on the one side there are the racers, and on the other the tourists.' Shortly after this the Touring Club of France was formed to help the middle-class cyclist who sought less demanding exercise from his machine, whilst the Association de la Vélocipédie Amateur was set up in order to provide an opportunity for younger middle-class riders to do some racing without obliging them to come into contact with the lower classes. Membership of the Touring Club grew rapidly in the nineties with a record 3666 applications in the month of June 1896 alone. There were around 125,000 members in 1910 and numbers rose steadily to around a quarter of a million in the middle of the inter-war period, after which a slow lower-class influx began. Apart from the occasional baker or mason, there were virtually no working-class members of the Touring Club. Of the 72,575 individuals in the Club in 1900, 30,722 were either clerks or wholesalers of one kind or another. There were around 5000 lawyers, 6000 doctors and 11,000 shareholders of greater or lesser private means.[15]

The growing gulf between those who followed cycling as a professional spectator sport and sought to emulate the feats of their idols in private clubs devoted to racing, and the well-bred tourist in search of peace and quiet in which to contemplate the countryside is neatly demonstrated by the efforts of the small town of Choisy-le-Roi to start a *vélodrome* in 1895. The municipality thought that because Choisy was a favourite spot for Parisian cyclists to visit for a Sunday excursion it would be an ideal place to build a permanent racing-track. The track was duly built but unfortunately hardly anyone patronised it. The inhabitants of Choisy had miscalculated. Spectator sport and casual recreation were drawing further apart. Those who watched racing in Paris did not always ride themselves. The urban lower classes preferred to have their entertainment near at hand, whereas those who took the trouble to make a Sunday excursion had no desire to watch cycle-racing. They usually wanted to spend a quiet afternoon by the river in the company of their family or a few friends of a similar social background.[16]

Despite the caprice of the crowds and the cupidity of the organisers, there was never any shortage of young men who sought to make their fortune as professional cyclists. In the early 1890s a dramatic change took place in the social composition of competitors; a new breed of competitor came to the fore to oust the affluent amateur rider. The model for the new professional sportsman of the 1890s was provided by Charles Terront, France's first sports 'star'. His life story is fascinating, and seems worth telling in some detail, as his achievement gave inspiration to a whole generation of lower-class youths, who hoped to make a large fortune from professional sport. He was born in Saint-Ouen, an industrial suburb of Paris, in 1857. His father was a semi-skilled mechanic working for a large railway company. He was the eldest of six children and as the family was extremely poor he spent long periods as a *gamin de Paris*, wandering the streets. During the Commune he and his brother collected shrapnel to make into paper clips and table lamps. He became an errand boy for the Agence Havas and began to rent an old wooden bicycle from a local shop to try to win some money in Sunday competitions. He had little success but eventually persuaded his employers to provide him with a proper machine on which to bring news quickly from the *Bourse*. Thus he improved his sporting performance while at work and trained himself for competition at a time when speed and skill were still considered to be natural qualities which could not be significantly improved by practice.[17]

His first major victory came in a local race in 1876, the Paris–Pontoise, and he won the Grand Prix d'Angers in the same year. Later he was invited to compete in England and went with two other French riders to challenge the top three English competitors. The French won, but at first it turned out to be a pyrrhic victory for Terront, who lost his job with the Agence Havas and, unlike the others, had no private means of support. He decided to become a full-time professional, competing in France and in England, where for a while the new industrial concentrations supplied large crowds, which in turn provided the cash for valuable prizes. Competition was intense; brutality and corruption were already common. On one occasion Terront was offered a rose by a pretty young girl just before the start of an important race. His wary trainer snatched it from him and smelt it. The rose had been chloroformed and the trainer almost passed out on the spot.

By the mid 1880s competition was even tougher than it had been in the seventies. All the top riders were now using trainers to improve their performance, especially for the vital final sprint. Terront made a good, though hard, living. In 1885 he rode in 65 races, of which he won 55, and earned 6000 francs. This was enough to enable him to marry the daughter of the widow who owned the hotel in which he stayed when competing in the south-west. In addition, his sporting prestige enabled him to persuade a cycling-mad Russian aristocrat to be the best man at his wedding. Terront stayed in cycling for another ten years, adapting successfully to the moden bicycle and winning the gruelling Paris–Brest–Paris race, which brought him popular acclaim. He became a national celebrity and had a place reserved for him at the Opéra. He was also the first of many sportsmen to publish his life story with the aid of a prominent sports writer, and he retired from cycling a prosperous man with interests in selling, repairing and manufacturing bicycles.

In the hope of emulating the achievements of Terront, thousands of apprentices bought themselves bicycles and trained for competitions. Two of the most famous in the 1890s were Constant Huret and Edmond Jacquelin. Both came from poor homes and had been apprentice bakers before taking up cycling. Huret created a sensation when he knocked four hours off the best previous time for the Bordeaux–Paris race. He arrived in Paris spattered in blood and scarcely conscious, a visible symbol of the fanaticism of the early competitors to better themselves through sport. However, the life of the professional was hard and few managed to stay at the top for long. Jacquelin became the idol of the Parisian tracks after his victory in the Grand Prix de Paris in 1896, and he won again in a neck-and-neck finish with an Italian in 1900. In a surge of patriotic ardour he was carried shoulder-high by the crowds, who found in this humble baker from Ménilmontant, a new hero who had fought his way out of poverty by sporting skill and determination. Jacquelin lived up to their expectations by buying a carriage, always spending liberally on drink for his followers, and even hiring a box at the Comédie Française to acquire a little bourgeois culture. Predictably his fitness suffered, his speculations floundered, and he became a sad, impoverished drifter picking up occasional work unloading coal barges and dreaming of a come-back. In 1929 he was found dead after sleeping rough on the banks of the Seine in icy weather. Jacquelin's was a particularly bitter fate; the celebrated sprinter Georges Sérès looked after himself more carefully, keeping his competitive edge until the remarkable age of forty-one when he won his last title. Yet Sérès, too, had his share of trouble. After a fall early in his career he contracted an illness which left him without a hair on his head, and in 1923 in New York he fell again, this time going into a coma for twenty-two days and sustaining a fracture of the skull, five broken ribs and a perforated lung. He saved some money to purchase a house by the Seine at Suresnes, to which he brought his aunts and cousins from the south-west (near Condom in the Gers), and to educate his two sons, who also became successful cyclists. Such were the small but tangible benefits professional cycling could bring to those who dedicated themselves to it. A survey of fifteen ex-professional cyclists carried out by a Lille paper in 1907 revealed that most of them made a modest but decent living running small cafés and cycle shops.[18]

While the Six Jours joined the Tour de France and one or two other select races as an established sporting institution, on the whole track-racing soon began to lose its following. As early as 1899 *La Vie au Grand Air*, a leading sports paper, had noticed a recession 'after the fantastic and exaggerated passion for cycling spectacles two or three years ago'. The *vélodromes* in Paris and in the largest cities managed to keep going but many of the smaller ones had to close. Why did this happen? How was it that a spectator sport which had given rise to such public interest declined so suddenly? After all, cycling itself had not gone out of fashion. While it is true that the smart young bourgeois was beginning to turn his attention towards the motor car after 1900, the majority of the population were still discovering the joys of the bicycle. Bicycle sales alone testify to this. It was, therefore, not so much the sport of cycling itself which went out of favour as the particular form which that sport had taken in the 1890s. The public were bored with the monotony of track-racing and began to look for new ways in which to explore the sporting possibilities of cycling. Cycling is a sport which is extremely exciting to watch for brief periods but which often begins to pall for all but the most enthusiastic after a while. As such, it was less well suited to the stadium than were the new English ball games, which offered the public a more varied spectacle than the endless passage of riders round a track. Nor could track racing compete with football in terms of its potential for generating group enthusiasm and fostering a sense of local pride and solidarity.[19]

With the exception of the great sprint races like the Grand Prix de Paris and the cumulative frenzy of the Six Jours, the public began to desert the track. Organisers responded by shifting resources from track-racing to road-racing. Road-racing was not only more dramatic and compelling as a spectacle, it had the added advantage as far as the public were concerned of being free. As we shall see when we look more closely at the phenomenal success of the Tour de France, road-racing was also particularly appropriate to a widely dispersed audience and gave those living in the rural areas a chance to see in the flesh the 'géants de la route' that they had read about in the papers. Inhabitants of remote areas often had the chance to combine a general interest in the stars of the race with support for their particular local favourite. They would cheer a modest youngster from their valley with greater fervour than they might applaud the race leader. Local boys with little chance of victory in the overall classification would strain every muscle to achieve momentary glory as they passed through their native heath; it even became the custom in the Tour de France to allow a minor rider to get far enough ahead in a particular stage to permit him to stop briefly and chat to his family before resuming his humble place in the *peloton* (main group of riders).

Whilst track-racing after 1900 was limited to a handful of large *vélodromes* in the big cities, road-racing became the first national spectator sport in France and soon came to be dominated by the twin forces of the press and the manufacturers. The press devoted a good deal of their time to long-distance ₊road-racing and evolved elaborate arrangements for getting the most up-to-date results to their readers before their rival papers; manufacturers, on the other hand, spent enormous sums to ensure that their machines figured amongst the list of those with major victories to their credit during the current year. Profits were made indirectly through increased circulation or sales. The public was not so much asked to pay, it was rather encouraged to buy. A study of cycle-racing published in 1912 stressed the great importance which the major road races had already come to have in French sport: 'You really have to have observed a great road race . . . at close quarters in order to appreciate the intense excitement the passage of the riders generates in the most remote regions and out-of-the-way villages'. The Paris–Roubaix race, winding over the tortuous cobbled roads of northern France, was a great favourite and secularised the Easter Sunday of many of the towns *en route*. 'L'enfer du nord', as it was known, became so popular that on occasion election dates were changed to avoid clashing with it. The Paris–Bruxelles race, founded in 1893, was run annually as a professional race from 1906, emerging as the longest unpaced classic race of the season, and the Paris–Tours, run in the early autumn, became another firm favourite. The oldest established and the longest continuous race, however, was the Bordeaux–Paris, founded in 1891. The riders started from Bordeaux and rode through the night to arrive in Paris late the following day. Frequently the race was decided in the last sprint from Versailles to Paris and huge crowds would gather to watch this section. A host of smaller road races were founded around this time, many of them in conjunction with local newspapers or through the support of an influential industrialist. There is no time here to go into detail concerning these minor events. All of them were to a greater or lesser degree modelled on the major races and, in particular, on the race which came to dominate the cycling year, the Tour de France, in which professionalism and commercialisation reached new levels.[20]

The Tour de France has become one of the great sporting events in the world and it is impossible to do it justice in a few pages. Although a great many books have been devoted to the Tour, those people who do not read French are most fortunate to have one of the best accounts in their own language, that by the British sports writer Geoffrey Nicholson. This work is already well on the way to establishing itself as a minor classic in a genre where fine writing is often hard to come by. As Nicholson reminds us, the Tour was born out of a circulation battle between France's two most popular sporting papers, *L'Auto* and *Le Vélo*. That there should have been two daily papers specialising in cycling at the turn of the century (*L'Auto*, despite its title, was primarily concerned with the bicycle) is in itself remarkable. The enthusiasm of the public for the new sport is undeniable but hardly merited such ample provision. The real reason for the rivalry was more or less political. The Baron de Dion, a staunch nationalist and conservative, was infuriated when *Le Vélo*, a paper in which he as a motor manufacturer and sportsman had substantial interests, criticised an anti-Dreyfusard demonstration that de Dion himself had been involved in. Consequently, *L'Auto* was set up in competition and the Tour emerged as a sensational means of launching the paper and dishing its rival. This it did. Daily sales leapt to 65,000 in 1903, the first year of the Tour. *L'Auto*'s editor, Henri Desgrange, a former notary's clerk and champion sprint rider, who had lost his position because a client had complained that his bare calves were incompatible with the dignity of the law, rapidly became the most influential figure in commercial sport.[21]

The Tour, a sporting by-product of *fin-de-siècle* fanaticism, exerted an instant fascination on the French public and has held its ground ever since. The first Tour de France was run over 2428 kilometres in six stages and was won by Maurice Garin, 'the white bulldog', a tenacious ex-chimney sweep of poor eastern European parents. Garin was a dedicated competitor who had come up the hard way. The caption to a cartoon showing him winning an endurance event in the middle of winter read: 'When you've had to sweep chimneys for a living, 24 hours on the track in 15 degrees of frost doesn't bother you'. Aided by his manager, a tough ex-miner from Lens, Garin won the first prize of 6125 gold francs without much difficulty. The following year, however, Garin and other leading competitors were jostled by motorists backing another rider and were subsequently set upon in a mountain pass at three o'clock in the morning by a large gang of armed ruffians. In despair Desgrange denounced his own creation as a 'race for tricksters, fought out amidst the yells and threats of a bunch of thugs who freely wield knives and sticks to ensure the victory of their favourite'. After months of deliberation the first four riders in the 1904 Tour, including Garin, were disqualified for suspected dishonesty on the night stages, and for a while Desgrange toyed with the idea of abandoning the race altogether. But he was already a prisoner of his own success. Instead of scrapping the race he abolished the night stages and considerably extended the overall length, which now ran to a distance of around two-and-a-half thousand miles over some of the poorest and most inaccessible roads and mountain passes in the whole of France. In 1910 a particularly gruelling 330-kilometre stage over rough Pyrenean tracks was introduced, which provoked the leading rider to hiss at the officials waiting at the summit the single word: 'Murderers!'[22]

The incredible demands made on man and machine meant that success in the Tour became imperative for all ambitious riders and manufacturers. The glamour and glory attached to victory led to furious competition for the top prizes offered by the Tour. Independent competitors, or *touristes-routiers* as they were called, complained bitterly about collusion between teams and drug-taking by individuals even before the First World War. Quite how much doping went on is hard to say, although it was obviously a less serious problem than it became later, when pharmaceutical advances in the manufacture of stimulants made the introduction of urine sampling a necessity. This sombre side to the sport came to the fore with the full commercialisation of the Tour as a mass spectacle during the inter-war years, and led to dishonest riders topping up their sample with another person's urine, which they kept hidden in a small container. This could produce some strange results, as in one case when a 'rider was told his test was negative, but warned that he was pregnant'. Of course, stimulants alone could never give a man the strength to win the Tour and the greatest riders produced truly astonishing feats of endurance. The determination and ingenuity of the top riders was legendary. Eugène Christophe, the Tour leader in 1913, broke a front fork on a fast mountain descent. He picked the bike up, ran over seven miles to the nearest blacksmith's shop, improvised a new fork out of a spare piece of metal and set off again only to be penalised by the officials for allowing a small boy to help him by blowing the bellows. Brambilla, a dedicated competitor of the forties, epitomised the earnestness and devotion to the Tour of the top riders. After his third Tour in 1947, friends visiting his house unannounced found him digging a large hole at the bottom of the garden in which to bury the racing bicycle he no longer considered himself good enough to ride.[23]

The press and the manufacturers exploited interest in the national race with great skill and commercial flair. From the early years up until 1930 the race was dominated by the fierce competition of the major manufacturers, who soon organised their riders into works teams and spent very large sums on promoting their machines. Cautious team managers always locked their bicycles away to avoid sabotage or spying by rivals. When Garrigou, who won in 1911, changed from Peugeot to Alcyon he was paid a retainer of a thousand francs a month, allowed a liberal expense account and provided with free equipment, in addition to any prize money he might win. By the early twenties the communist-controlled *Sport Ouvrier* claimed that special prizes had been created so that each manufacturer could claim to have won something and mediocre competitors did not get too discouraged and drop out of the race. As Nicholson says, 'it's an unlucky rider who can't pick up something. There are prizes for riders who have recently turned professional; for those who show the most *combativité* or who make the longest escapes (breaks from the main group). If all else fails there are daily awards both for elegance and amiability which have gone to some pretty scruffy, disagreeable people'.[24]

By 1919 the wayside crowds had become so numerous – between a quarter and a third of the French population is estimated to watch the Tour from the pavement – that the famous *maillot jaune* or yellow jersey worn by the race leader was introduced. The jersey was yellow because this was the colour of the paper *L'Auto*. The post-war daily sales of *le jaune* climbed to an astonishing 495,000 in July 1923 when Henri Pelissier beat off the challenge of the top Italian rider and won for France. An important change came in 1930 when Desgrange abolished the system of works teams and introduced national teams instead. 'The manufacturer wants to see his man win even if he is not the best', complained Desgrange, 'whereas the organiser wants to see the best man win regardless of the make of bicycle he is riding.' Instead of income from the manufacturers, the Tour turned to other sources of advertising, which formed the now familiar cavalcade of open-topped cars and vans proclaiming the virtues of everything from insect-repellent to banking services and handing out paper hats and packets of crisps by the thousand to the endless lines of roadside spectators.[25]

Critics of the race have mocked the way in which countless small communes have absorbed the Tour into their festive calendar and made it the new focus of their traditional summer celebrations. Successful Tour riders were in great demand for subsequent small town races (*criteriums*) and these events together with all the rest of the ballyhoo led to it being described as little more than 'a well organised masquerade with all the trappings of a carnival procession'. A carnival it certainly was, a masquerade never. The genius of the Tour lay in the ingenious combination of public entertainment with a contest probably unequalled in its physical demands by any other event. The Tour became a national forum where the qualities of the race were put to the test in public. A celebrated literary critic has noted perceptively how the nicknames of riders seemed to derive 'from an earlier age when the nation reverberated to the image of a handful of ethnic heroes: Brankart le Franc, Bobet le Francien, Robic le Celte, Ruiz l'Ibère, Darrigade le Gascon'. The Tour became a three-week epic journey in which the glories of France and the French were celebrated. In a sense, the sporting 'tour' was an adult equivalent of the fictional 'tour de France' by two orphaned Alsatian children which was familiar to most French boys and girls through the famous geography textbook used by state teachers to instill civic virtue and patriotism into the young.[26]

Henri Desgrange was an outspoken nationalist and saw the Tour as an opportunity to display France's new vitality. He wanted to have Metz as a stage on the Tour to symbolise France's right to Alsace-Lorraine and, surprisingly, the Germans agreed to this request in 1906. This concession was quickly withdrawn when the crowds sang the Marseillaise and wept openly. The longest ever Tour was held in 1919, with many of its 5380 kilometres winding round the battlefields, the devastated and conquered provinces, as a testament to French survival. Desgrange justified the Tour on the grounds that it had a nationally unifying function, reinforcing the concept of *la patrie* in concrete geographical terms. Subsequently, it was closely associated in the popular mind with both the beginning of the summer holidays and the celebration of Bastille Day, and it is now an integral part of the traditional French summer along with the flight from Paris and the holiday in the Midi. 'Half Poujadist, half Popular Front, the Tour is embedded in the childhood of the French . . . part of their common secular and republican heritage.'[27]

To a country obsessed with a fear of demographic decline,

economic failure and military defeat, the Tour de France offered
a comforting image of Frenchmen as tenacious, strong and swift.
The name itself conjured up images of the earlier 'tour de
France' by young artisans organised into trade guilds, the
Compagnonnages, whose sturdy independence and violent rituals
had played an important part in working-class life until the later
nineteenth century. Thus the Tour, along with several other
great races, found a place in the national mythology of France
and was followed anxiously by persons not generally interested
in sports as well as by those who were. Once established in this
special position in French life, the great cycle races have had
little difficulty in retaining their place and have been very
successfully adapted to the mass media, especially television.

The success and symbolism of the Tour apart, what reasons
can be advanced to explain the special place which cycling has
come to hold in French sporting life? In France the bicycle
appeared on the scene before any of the other modern spectator
sports were introduced. For most of the 1880s and 1890s cycle-
racing had to itself that section of the sporting public which was
primarily concerned with sport as a form of visual entertainment. With the exception of certain traditional spectacles, it had
no rivals as a summer sport. Moreover, cycle-racing did not
have to rely purely on its own appeal as a spectacle. As we have
seen, racing became inextricably bound up with the business of
selling bicycles and also benefited very considerably from the
growth of the popular press. Newspapers founded races over
which they tried to establish exclusive rights as part of a drive to
increase circulation and bring in greater advertising revenue.
The major manufacturers encouraged newspapers to promote
cycling by offering papers lucrative inducements, and they often
subsidised races themselves.

The suitability of a mobile spectacle for a widely scattered
rural population unable to support other forms of professional
spectator sport helps to explain the special appeal of the classic
road races. To the impecunious communes of provincial France,
cycle-racing offered spectator sport on the cheap. No facilities
were needed save the roads, which they had to maintain in any
case. In country areas young people in search of competitive
sport often turned their attention to cycling rather than to other
sports which needed special facilities. It is perhaps no coincidence that so many champion cyclists have come from villages,

for it is in the country areas rather than in the cities that the success of the sport has been most pronounced. As a recent historian has pointed out, the great road races 'represent a brief, strident compensation as the coloured riders flash by, a sort of royal progress that may give a kingfisher sense of importance to some out-of-the-way dormant commune'.[28]

The tolerant attitude of the authorities, who steadfastly refused to make a clear distinction between amateurs and professionals, also helped the sport. Most of the keen local riders were able to register themselves in an intermediary group, the independents, who were allowed to compete in a range of amateur and professional events. This arrangement enabled promising young riders to get themselves started in the sport and helped to sustain interest in competition at the grass-roots level. In fact, in 1911 the UVF issued only 556 full professional licences as against 7600 to independents.

Many factors helped to promote cycling as a sport but the most important of all was undoubtedly the sheer usefulness of the bicycle in a large country like France with limited public services. Surveying provincial life during the last century, a perceptive social historian, who has carried out exhaustive research on the region of Nevers in central France, has noted that the bicycle was the first of many mechanical inventions to penetrate the countryside. Cycling gave rise to a whole new set of recreational habits which involved the development of new skills and even the wearing of new 'leisure' clothes. Frenchmen became more aware of speed and distance than they had been before, but it was for relaxation rather than for racing that most machines were used. Competitive cycling is a strenuous activity and never appealed as a participant sport to more than a small proportion of cyclists. Cycling became a craze around the turn of the century but its place in popular culture rested primarily on its usefulness in daily life rather than on the active sporting possibilities it opened up for the common man. It was in the realm of mass entertainment that cycle-racing made its unique contribution to French sport. In France, and in most other western European countries, cycle-racing became and remains the foremost summer spectator sport.[29]

In this sense, it is perhaps Britain with its mania for cricket, a game continentals find incomprehensible and which appears to require the experience of British rule to foster it, that is out of step with the rest of European society. Rather than wondering why the Europeans, and the French in particular, like cycle-racing, perhaps we should begin to ask ourselves why the British prefer the long drawn-out conflicts and infinite subtleties of cricket to any other form of summer amusement. In fact, the two sports have far more in common than is often realised. Road-racing involves seemingly endless periods of careful strategy which 'most Frenchmen accept with the stoicism of a Headingley cricket crowd watching the slow construction of an opening stand'. Both road-racing and cricket take time, require patience and provide a pleasant excuse for the onlooker to enjoy the summer sun. For a more profound distinction between British and French sporting habits we should perhaps look in the direction of animal sports like bullfighting and cockfighting, which form the subject of the next chapter.[30]

6 Bullfighting and Cockfighting: The Survival of Regional Culture

The impact of modern sports like football, rugby and cycle-racing in the period 1890 to 1930 was so dramatic that it is all too easy to overlook the continued importance of more traditional forms of spectator sport in the provision of public amusement. Just as the spread of the English ball games tends to overshadow an equally remarkable growth in field sports or gymnastics, so in the case of spectator sports it is difficult to avoid the tendency to concentrate on the new at the expense of the indigenous or old-established. In the case of France this bias is particularly unfortunate because one of the most important and distinctive themes of French physical recreation concerns the survival and successful adaptation of traditional activities. Of those which continued to be popular – skittles, quoits, boating, wrestling and field sports, for example – the two with the greatest spectator appeal were bullfighting and cockfighting. The survival of these animal sports during the modernising phase of the early Third Republic gives a useful indication of both the strength of regional customs and the pragmatism of Republican legislators. Not only did the two activities resist the combined challenge of the rise of rival spectator sports and the efforts of humanitarian reformers to have animal sports banned, but in certain areas these events increased in popularity as time passed. Neither cockfighting nor bullfighting were brutal enough to outrage the sensibility of the average Frenchman, and both were sufficiently well-established to act as a focus for regional identity at a time when the traditions of the French provinces were beginning to be seriously threatened by the growth of mass culture.

Accounts of bullrunning and bullfighting in the Midi go back as far as the late middle ages, and there may well have been a more or less continuous tradition of animal sports dating back to the building of the great arenas of the Roman Empire. Throughout the early modern period, *courses de taureaux* played an important part in the popular culture of Provence and the Landes. Intendants and governors under the Old Regime had frequent cause to complain of 'this powerful and widespread taste for bullfighting'. A letter written by the prefect of the Gard in 1814 noted that the loosing of a Camargue bull on its way to the abattoir was a popular pastime. Since 1811 the arena at Nimes had been restored to its ancient use, drawing crowds of up to twenty thousand to watch festive events which mixed together tumblers and other entertainers with those who wanted to play the bulls. In the small bourgs of the Midi, and particularly around the Camargue and in other areas where cattle kept an important place in the local economy, bullrunning and bullfighting were extremely popular. When Maurice Martin visited the south-west as part of a national survey into the spread of cycling in the later 1890s, he noted with surprise that bullfighting was far more widely appreciated than more modern spectator sports. The *courses de taureaux* were an integral element in the culture of parts of Provence, the Languedoc and Aquitaine. Those who took an active part often wore traditional dress, and Provençal dances and regional music might introduce a contest. Traditional wrestling might also precede the spectacle whilst oranges, grapes and wine were passed round amongst the crowd as was the custom on a *jour de fête*.[1]

Popular sports like the *courses landaises* and the *courses provençales*, as the two main types of bullfight were called, formed part of a wider pattern of festivity characteristic of the Midi as a whole. The traditional southern contest consisted of seizing a cockade worth a certain sum of money from the horns of a young bull or, in the Landes, a cow. Performers were expected to execute a series of daring swerves (in the Landes acrobatic vaults over the animal were common) before taking the cockade and jumping over the barrier at the side of the arena with the beast in hot pursuit. As a deputy from the south pointed out in a parliamentary debate on bullfighting, the *course de taureaux* could not be considered simply as a form of entertainment; bullfighting was intimately linked to long-standing traditions of hospitality and communal amusement. These customs prescribed, for example, that when a candidate won an election or a rich young man got married he should lay on a bullfight as part of the communal celebrations. In some areas bullfighting was virtually a rite of passage. A youth was expected to prove his manhood by executing a daring swerve or jump in front of a dangerous animal until he was 'blooded'. Success in these events shored up a young man's sexual and social prestige within the area and brought him to the attention of the unmarried girls of the surrounding communes. The crowds played on the intense rivalries which sometimes developed and encouraged the bravado of the herdsmen or shepherds who dominated these events. Many a farm boy was seriously injured – some were even killed – in an attempt to establish a local reputation for fearlessness.[2]

Just as the *courses de taureaux* were deeply rooted in the soil of the Midi, so in northern France, and particularly in those regions marked by Flemish influence, cockfighting was an indigenous form of rural entertainment. Cocks were fought in the makeshift cockpits of village *cabarets*, in farmyards and even 'in the courtyards of bourgeois households'. Like other pre-industrial country sports, cockfighting was not restricted to any particular social group within the community. Poor peasants and larger landowners, rural craftsmen and miners from the early industrial villages were mixed together at country cock-fights in the mid-nineteenth century. In some communes the mayor himself would take part. As the prefect of the Nord pointed out to a leading opponent of cockfighting, the sport was not solely the preserve of the lower classes but was enjoyed by 'plenty of people with private means'. Like bullfighting in the south, cockfighting in the north formed part of the general fabric of popular regional culture and proved remarkably resilient to the challenge of new sports and the attacks of reformers.[3]

Whilst cockfighting clearly had its origins in the efforts of countrymen to use domestic animals as a source of amusement and in rural areas was often as much of a participant sport as a spectacle, in the towns it was primarily a form of spectator sport. Information on cockfighting in the cities of the north is very scarce but it seems as if there were a large number of cockfighting clubs in and around Lille in the mid-nineteenth century. Unfortunately, as cockfighting was technically illegal in the Nord after 1852 there is little evidence of its popularity in the departmental archives, and on this basis a major survey of working-class life in Lille under the Second Empire concludes that very little cockfighting took place. This is most improbable. An extremely well-informed folklorist writing less than a generation later claimed that cockfighting was, and continued to be, extremely popular. Concerning the so-called prefectorial ban of 1852 he wrote: 'perhaps no administrative ruling has ever been as little respected as this one'.[4]

Far from declining, both bullfighting and cockfighting flourished in the later nineteenth century. In the 1870s and 1880s the *course provençale* and *course landaise* began to be organised on a more regular and commercial basis. Instead of being confined to small town festivals they spread out to include the larger urban centres. Local councils and shrewd commercial speculators began to exploit the potential of bullfighting as a professional spectacle, and a competition circuit not unlike the early cycling tournament season came into existence. Bull-running through the streets became less common as the public authorities were increasingly unwilling to accept the risk of injury. Wild animals were now placed behind bars in the circus and bulls were confined to hastily erected wooden arenas. Those who had formerly taken part in open village events to show off their prowess and create a reputation for themselves on a local level by winning small sums of money began to be transformed into regional celebrities, competing in front of larger crowds of paying spectators in cities as far afield as Orléans, Limoges, Nantes and Rennes. Towns like Mont-de-Marsan and Dax in the Landes began to sign contracts with the leading *écarteurs* or 'dodgers', as the performers of the *course landaise* were called on account of their great agility. The new urban interest in the traditional spectacles of the Midi culminated in the building of a huge arena in brick and iron in Paris in the rue Pergolèse near the Bois de Boulogne, which had a transparent mobile roof and comfortable seating for 22,000 people. The arena was opened at the same time as the Great Exhibition of 1889. A vast amount of money had been sunk into this unique venture by French and Spanish backers and at first it looked like a good investment with receipts of 70,000 francs for the major contests. All of the most celebrated matadors of the *fin-de-siècle* appeared at the rue Pergolèse during the few years it functioned – Lagartijo, Frascuelo, Mazzantini and Guerrita. The Parisian authorities, however, refused to permit these great bullfighters to carry out a full *corrida*, insisting that the *coup de grâce* be simulated. Parisians soon tired of the indigenous acrobatic displays and the arena was closed at a massive loss after carnivalesque attractions like a circus horsewoman turned bullfighter (Maria Gentis) and bulls jumping through fiery hoops with fireworks tied to their horns failed to draw the crowds.[5]

In the same way that bullfighting began to break away from the village or small town context in which it had existed for centuries and to assume the status of a professional urban entertainment, so too did cockfighting. It became steadily more organised and lost its casual rustic quality. Formerly there had been no general code of conduct, and the running of contests had been determined by local custom, which often varied considerably from place to place. In the late nineteenth century, however, a modern dimension was introduced in the form of a governing body to standardise procedure, regulate contests and arrange competitions. In this sense, the old and the new sports followed a similar bureaucratic path. From being little more than groups of friends or habitués of a particular café, those northerners who fought cocks now began to form themselves into special clubs, read books on the techniques of arming and feeding their birds, and charge an entrance fee to those who wanted to watch the matches they organised.[6]

The discovery of a market for traditional animal sports in the modern city led to the wholesale commercialisation of both bullfighting and cockfighting from the 1880s onwards. In bullfighting, commercial development entailed not only a reorganisation of traditional contests but also the introduction on a large scale of Spanish bullfighting, which previously had been seen only on rare occasions. The success with which the traditional events had been staged in the 1870s tempted ambitious entrepreneurs to go for the large profits associated with the Spanish *corrida*. In the 1880s Spanish bullfights were organised in Béziers and in Bordeaux, and in the ancient arena at Nîmes. In Lyon, Avignon and Marseille, large crowds gathered to watch Spanish bullfights in the 1890s, and some traditionalists began to fear that the dramatic success of the new importation would lead to the demise of the indigenous events which had paved the way for the *corrida* in the larger cities.[7]

Migration may also have had something to do with the

introduction of the *corrida* in the later part of the century, although its subsequent popularity soon spread beyond a narrowly ethnic base. In the second half of the nineteenth century Spanish emigration increased sharply; most went to the Americas but a substantial number of northern peasants, especially Basques and Catalans who had ethnic links with the Languedoc, came to France. In 1876, for instance, 12 per cent of the population of the Bouches-du-Rhône were foreign, and Spaniards played an important part in the replanting of vineyards to the west of the Rhône in the 1880s. A large number of Spanish workers settled in Bordeaux towards the end of the century and similar colonies of Spaniards were to be found in most of the other leading cities of the south-west. It seems probable, although evidence is purely circumstantial, that the presence of significant numbers of Spaniards helped to promote the *corrida* as a popular spectacle between 1880 and 1914.[8]

Unlike most of their urban counterparts in the north, who appeared to be more interested in the achievements of technology than in the qualities of beasts, the new inhabitants of the southern cities were sufficiently imbued with rural values to prefer the solemn rituals and resplendent costumes of the *course de taureaux* to the cult of pure speed celebrated at the cycling track. The growing concentration of population in the larger towns made the organisation of Spanish bullfighting a viable financial proposition and, although there is no proper record of the number of contests held, there can be no doubt that the *corrida* became a staple element in popular entertainment in the cities of the south. In 1896 alone there were 376 actions brought against bullfighters under the provisions of an ineffective law of 1852 forbidding the maltreatment of domestic animals. In 1898 *La Petite Gironde*, a Bordeaux newspaper, published an inexpensive guide to the principles of Spanish bullfighting and sold fifteen thousand copies within a couple of days; between 1887 and 1914 fifty-five different specialist journals were produced to cater for the new French followers of the *corrida*.[9]

The growth of a large and enthusiastic audience for bullfighting in the south was mirrored by the extraordinary success of cockfighting in the north during the same period. A survey of cockfighting in Roubaix in 1892 revealed the existence of twenty-five cockpits, and the number continued to grow throughout the *belle époque* as urban recreational demand

boomed and alternative amusements were only beginning to be
devised. The popularity of cockfighting survived the First World
War. A general survey of popular recreation published in 1924
noted that 'it is very hard to do justice to the enormous
popularity of this spectacle in the Nord'. While it is evident from
these remarks that cockfighting must have remained popular in
the countryside, it is equally clear that the focus of the sport now
shifted to the larger towns. The population of Lille increased
three-fold during the second half of the nineteenth century, with
the bulk of the increase coming from migration from the
surrounding rural departments. These first-generation urban
dwellers from the villages of Flanders presumably retained their
affection for Flemish country sports like cockfighting, and their
arrival may well have given new impetus to the organisation of
contests. Henceforth it was in the major cities that the important
competitions were held and the leading representatives lived.
Throughout the season, which lasted from December to March,
cockfights were held several times a week in all of the larger
towns. 'Not a Sunday or public holiday passes without there
being several major contests in Lille, Tourcoing and Roubaix
and in the other main towns of the Nord and the Pas-de-Calais',
observed a sports journalist in 1892. By the early twentieth
century cockfights were being organised during weekdays at five
or six o'clock in the evening, and afternoon matches were held in
Lille. It was not uncommon for as many as three hundred cocks
to be killed in the course of a week's sport, and on a Sunday in
the height of the season as many as ten contests might be held in
different parts of the Lille area on the same day.[10]

   A brief examination of the followers of these sports confirms
that the pre-industrial tradition of social heterogeneity and
communal involvement was not entirely undermined in the
process of modernisation. As far as cockfighting is concerned,
there seems to be little doubt that a wide variety of social groups
were represented. Photographs of cockfights taken around the
turn of the century depict neat rows of dark-suited men, mostly
wearing bowler hats, sitting around a raised platform fenced off
with iron rails. An account of a typical cockfight written in the
1930s described the crowd as being composed of 'all classes of
society . . . factory workers, commercial travellers, shopkeepers
as well as authentic representatives of the bourgeoisie'. Most
official reports agreed that support for the sport did not come

from the lower classes alone. Although it was amongst the working classes generally that the greatest interest was found, cockfighting was certainly not confined to a brutish proletariat. No doubt unskilled workers formed the largest single element in the crowd, but in proportional terms they were probably not over-represented. Skilled artisans, small shopkeepers and a sprinkling of professional men were also involved. Some indication of the level of middle-class interest can be gauged from the brief biographies of important cock owners which appeared in the specialist newspaper *Le Coqueleur*. It seems that a few northern industrialists fought cocks in the way that the Parisian élite raced horses. Many of the leading owners had a hundred or more birds at any one time. To breed and fight cocks on this scale required substantial funds, so perhaps it should come as no surprise that three of the leading cockfighters, Joseph Josson, Henri Cliquennois and Henri Drumez were respectively the owner of a tannery, an influential shareholder in a brewery and the owner of a flour mill.[11]

Bullfighting attracted spectators from an even wider social range. There appears to have been no major social group that was not represented in the bullfighting crowd. A fair number of the southern nobility attended bullfights during this period, although they showed a marked preference for the *corrida* over the less prestigious and less expensive indigenous events. In Spain it was common for nobles to hire a box at the arena for the season, and in some quarters appearance at a bullfight took on for the provincial nobility a similar significance as attendance at the Opéra might have for the leading Parisian families. In 1889 aristocrats and rich bourgeois from Avignon formed the Frascuelo Club and called themselves 'aficionados' in imitation of the passion of the Spanish nobility for the *corrida*. Hispano-philia is an element in French upper-class thought and behaviour which requires further investigation. In 1894 the first *corrida* held in Lyon attracted 'tout Lyon des premiers'. It is almost as if the upper classes could not resist the occasional public appearance to reassert their social primacy in front of the masses, especially at a contest intimately linked to a reactionary Catholic state. Whether complex aristocratic motives were present, or whether it was that they, like everyone else, had begun to demand properly organised commercial entertainment to replace the old amusements – whatever the reason – for a brief period the *corrida* became positively fashionable, attracting more members of polite southern society than any other popular spectacle except horse-racing. When a 55,000-franc subscription fund to restore the Béziers arena was opened in 1901 a local noble, Castelbon de Beauxhostes, put up 14,000 francs, and of the remaining 26 subscribers most were wealthy landowners.[12]

Moving down the social hierarchy it is noticeable that the French middle classes did not espouse the cause of animal protection with quite the same fervour as many of their Victorian counterparts. Some bullfighting clubs had a distinctly bourgeois flavour. In Bordeaux the committee of the Toro Sport Bordelais was composed of seven office-workers, a doctor, a lawyer, a civil servant and two master-craftsmen. The advertisements for stocks and shares, consumer goods or theatre tickets that appeared in the specialist magazines devoted to the sport were presumably aimed at this sort of person. All the same, it would be misleading to overemphasise the role of the middle classes, for it was from certain sections of this broad stratum (notably Protestants) that the strongest criticism of the brutality and disorder of the *corrida* came. When the local authority in Lunel held a public inquiry to decide whether or not to destroy a tree-lined walkway in the town centre and replace it with a bullring, it was the bourgeoisie who objected most strongly. Similarly, when a herd of bulls were run through the streets of Beaucaire on a quiet Sunday morning in 1868, it was the *notaire* who led a protest to the prefect complaining that women and children had been terrified, a religious procession rudely dispersed and the *curé* thrown into a state of nervous depression.[13]

In other words, bullfighting was primarily, though not exclusively, a popular spectacle. The great majority of seats were bought by ordinary workmen or smallholders. A parliamentary inquiry carried out in the 1890s was shocked by the foul language of the crowd in the cheaper seats. Around the same time a few socialists began to worry that the new popularity of the *corrida* would corrupt and brutalise the proletariat, diverting it from its historic task in the same way that the circuses of the Roman Empire had kept the masses in ignorant contentment. Such fears were greatly exaggerated. The strongest interest in bullfighting came from peasants who had either recently left the land or who had small farms within striking distance of the major cities. Bullfighting was probably the only commercialised sporting spectacle which the peasantry were prepared to pay to watch. The modern bullfight, either the *corrida* or one of the traditional events run on the grand scale, offered the peasant a readily understandable contest with roots deep in rural tradition. Commercialised *courses de taureaux* provided an obvious link between the present and the past and gave an element of continuity to the shift from traditional to modern forms of recreation. Bullfights were still held on customary holidays and were overlaid with the age-old trappings of the *fête populaire*. What could be more natural than that the peasant should use the railway to come to town for a bullfight and perhaps transact some business into the bargain? An article on the success of both the traditional and the Spanish bullfights organised at the great arena at Nimes in the early 1890s noted that the support of the peasantry had been of crucial importance. When the old wooden arena at Béziers burned down, the council debated long and hard over what type of construction should replace it. Eventually, they decided that the degree of interest in bullfighting in the surrounding areas was such that the increased cost of a brick building as opposed to a wooden one was fully justified. Similarly, in Bordeaux the owners of the arena took care to advertise its proximity to the railway station in order to capitalise on the enthusiasm for bullfighting amongst the peasants of the Gironde.[14]

The broad basis of support enjoyed by both bullfighting and cockfighting encouraged those with an interest in popular culture and with experience of the entertainment industry to pour money into the building of special arenas for bullfights, or into the construction of large cockpits or *gallodromes* capable of seating up to several thousand spectators. In the Lille–Roubaix area several such commercial cockpits were built, the most famous of which was owned by a brewery. The importance of these large commercial establishments grew steadily in relation to the smaller ones found in the courtyards or back rooms of cafés which had formerly been the focal point of the cockfighting world. In fact, the decision of one of the biggest of them to hold contests on Sundays as well as throughout the week drew a furious protest from the owners of small premises who relied heavily on cockfighting to boost their Sunday trade. *Gallodromes* ran annual open competitions in which there were often large cash prizes to be won and in which smaller clubs had a chance to compete against famous individual owners as well as against the Belgian clubs. These events usually lasted for several days and coincided with a public holiday. It was not uncommon for the ballroom of a hotel to be hired and a banquet laid on at the end of the competition. Several thousand spectators might pay between two and five francs each to gain admittance, and in a large competition such as that held in Béthune in 1907 there were ninety-six clubs involved with a total of ten thousand spectators attending over a period of a few days.[15]

While there were no doubt sizeable sums of money to be made through the running of cockfights, bullfighting had far greater potential in terms of the cash which could be taken from the public. After all, tens of thousands of spectators could enjoy a bullfight, whereas it is obvious that no such number could watch creatures as small as fighting cocks. There were rich rewards waiting for anyone with the skill and capital required to arrange a series of *corridas*. However, the presentation of a *corrida* was a great deal more difficult and hazardous than the promotion of cockfighting or any other form of spectator sport. Even a traditional *course provençale* could cost as much as 17,000 francs to present, and in the case of the *corrida* a further 10,000 francs had to be added on to pay for the extra cost of Spanish fighting bulls. The high matadors' fees were an additional burden. According to one informed estimate, a proper *corrida* could not be staged for less than 30,000 francs, and this heavy outlay had to be set against an uncertain return. Spanish breeders would fequently withdraw their special fighting bulls at short notice or would send inferior animals in their place in the belief that the French were too ignorant to tell the difference. Matadors were notoriously difficult to handle and frequently failed to turn up or might capriciously demand a much increased fee at the last moment. At Narbonne in 1897 a troupe of bullfighters threatened to walk out as the crowd was filling the arena and the exasperated organiser was forced to increase their fee. He revenged himself by stealing their jewelled capes and swords afterwards, where-upon one of the troupe followed him to a café and tried to stab him. This incident is no doubt more sensational than most, but not unrepresentative of the general atmosphere of distrust prevailing between organisers and performers.[16]

The problems inherent in the organising of such events frightened off the more respectable and cautious figures in the world of commercial entertainment. The town of Lunel, for example, could not find anyone reliable to take over the concession for bullfighting in 1907. This left the way open for unscrupulous and often undercapitalised operators, who were frequently at odds with the municipality over rent and local taxes. In Avignon those who sponsored the holding of *corridas* were usually either music-hall proprietors or café owners hoping to make a small fortune from drink stalls set up around the arena. The latter group stood to gain considerably from the sale of *pastis* which to this day remains an integral part of the ritual of the *corrida*, but they often lacked, or refused to provide, the requisite sums of money to ensure a good contest. Jules Romain, a grocer from Nimes, organised a series of bullfights in the arena during the 1860s on the novel and peculiarly French basis that the cost of season tickets could be recovered in the form of delicacies from a local *pâtisserie* in the event of a cancellation.[17]

A common business arrangement for the financing of bull-fights consisted of a partnership, with one partner taking responsibility for organising the spectacle and the other putting up the capital. It is extremely hard to find out how such partner-ships worked, but the fortuitous survival of a police record on one of these arrangements throws some light on the dangers that could befall the naïve investor. A wealthy businessman from Lyon, Monsieur Walbott, was persuaded by a southerner named Vidal to take part in just such an enterprise. Vidal, a former Marseille hairdresser who at that time was running a seedy café in Toulouse, talked Walbott into putting up 24,000 francs to finance a series of *corridas* and promised that there would be a profit of about 5000 to 6000 francs per contest. In fact, the venture finally cost Walbott around 60,000 francs and he made a loss on each contest. Whether Vidal had been defrauding his partner, as Walbott claimed, or whether there was another explanation for the loss, hardly matters here. What is important is to note the type of person attracted to what was often a murky area between popular entertainment and petty crime.[18]

Given the high costs of putting on a proper *corrida* and the fact that many of those involved were hardly renowned for their integrity, there was a distinct likelihood of malpractice. The most common form of deception involved the substitution of cheap French bulls for expensive Spanish ones, or the hiring of second- or third-rate 'bullfighters' instead of proper Spanish matadors. There were comparatively few good matadors and, as these could command very high fees, hopeful youths were taken on as bullfighters in their stead and given Spanish names and costumes. 'On numerous occasions I have witnessed common orange-sellers and such like pretend to be proper bullfighters simply to earn a few francs', complained a well-informed contemporary. France produced very few decent matadors. Only a handful were ever good enough to fight in Spain. Men like Felix Robert, a poor farm boy who had learned his skills in traditional contests and subsequently married the daughter of a Spanish nobleman, becoming an impresario at the arena in Dax, or Plumenta, the son of a colonial civil servant, who gave up a promising academic career to become a matador, were exceptional. 'Le Pouly' (Provençal for 'handsome') was another performer of the traditional kind who switched to the *corrida* in the late nineteenth century, leaving behind his rather more prosaic surname of Boudin ('Pudding') at the same time. During the inter-war period there were no French matadors in the strict sense of the term – that is, a bullfighter who had received official recognition (the *alternativa*) and passed the stage of *novillada* or apprenticeship. The most famous French figures in the arena at this time were two picadors, a husband and wife: Albert Lescot and Emma 'la Caballera'. Both came from small bourgs of the Camargue and had ridden horses from childhood. They were married in 1930 in true Arlesian fashion; she was dressed in the traditional costume of 'Mireille', and he wore the 'cowboy' clothes of a Camargue horseman. Emma became a very competent performer and achieved a certain notoriety on account of her sex, but these few engaging oddities apart, the Spaniards remained supreme.[19]

Guerrita, Reverte, Bombita and Mazzantini were among the great matadors of the *belle époque* who fought in France. They often pitted themselves against massive creatures sometimes weighing over half a ton. But they did not attempt the balletic cape-play which became the hallmark of a new generation of matadors around the time of the First World War. Joselito and the great Belmonte, who performed a number of times in France, were the leaders of the new movement which substituted smaller bulls for the monsters of old and shifted attention away from the kill and onto the graceful *faena* (the cape-work before the *coup de grâce*). As it happened, the *aficionados* of France were fortunate in seeing some of the finest bullfighting of the 1930s. A combination of the falling value of the peseta in relation to the franc and the disruption of civil war meant that many of the best Spanish bullfighters preferred France to their native country. Manolo Bienvenida achieved a remarkable success in Bordeaux in 1931 with the grace of his *faena*, and Domingo Ortega, the son of a peasant from Toledo, became a firm favourite in the arenas of the south-west; he returned after the war, holding his last *corrida* in 1954. The most frequent performer was the Madrid-born matador Marcial Lalanda, who fought in France on and off for eighteen years in seventy-seven *corridas*. Between 1930 and 1936 he killed around a hundred bulls in France with skill and careful attention to the science of the sport, accomplishing twenty or so memorable *faenas*. Ernest Hemingway had castigated the French crowds in the 1920s for their ignorant applause of 'a killing that was no more than a riskless assassination', but during the 1930s the audience for bullfighting became much more discriminating. This has remained the case, and nowadays the *aficionado* from Nimes or Dax is almost as expert as his counterpart in Seville.[20]

Of course, Spanish bullfighting was, and has remained, a highly controversial activity. The violent nature of the spectacle itself and the turbulent behaviour frequently associated with it have made both bullfighting and cockfighting subject to strong attack from a wide range of sources, including the Protestant churches, animal protection groups and a good many progressive left-wing Republicans and socialists. The theme of violence in sport as a whole will be dealt with separately in the following chapter, and for the present we need only look at the storm of protest evoked by the *corrida* in particular and the means by which it was defended. Interestingly, the controversy over the *corrida* reached its climax at around the same time as the Dreyfus case, and several contemporaries noted that those humanitarians who believed in the innocence of Dreyfus were also outspoken enemies of the *corrida*. Anti-Dreyfusards, on the other hand, tended to see the question in terms of the need to stand out against the insipid doctrines of the Republic and to preserve traditional activities which promoted personal courage and martial values. *Le Torero* wrote that 'apart from the life of a career officer in the army, the art of the bullfighter is the last

refuge of the chivalric tradition'. Support for the *corrida* merged
easily into a wider, sub-Barrèsian cult of heroism, individuality,
'roots' and death. Opponents of the killing of bulls and the
disembowelling of horses were branded as deracinated metro-
politan intellectuals or sentimental socialists with 'unFrench'
internationalist sympathies.[21]

The abolitionists had a maximum and a minimum programme. In the long run many of them would have liked to
abolish all forms of animal sport, including traditional bullfights
and cockfights. In the short term, however, they concentrated on
the more realistic objective of banning the *corrida*, or at least
preventing it from spreading into the north of France in the way
that it had in the south. The government was urged to impose
far stiffer fines on those who contravened the provisions of the
loi Grammont and vigorous efforts were made to disrupt those
corridas held in the north. In France as a whole the lack of a
powerful Protestant middle class weakened the abolitionist
cause considerably, but in Paris there was no shortage of men
and women who were prepared to oppose, with force if necessary, the holding of cockfights and bullfights in the capital. After
having successfully lobbied the council to ban the *corrida* in
Paris – a move which led to the closing down of the arena in the
rue Pergolèse – the abolitionists were determined that it should
not be re-introduced by the simple device of holding the contest
just outside the administrative boundaries of the city. Hence,
when in 1900 a *corrida* was held on the edge of Paris at Enghein,
a powerful contingent of abolitionsts disrupted the contest by
blowing toy trumpets and letting off revolvers with blank
cartridges. The scene was further enlivened by a young woman
who in fury set upon the leader of the Société Protectrice des
Animaux (SPA) and was carried aloft in triumph by the
aficionados. The killing of the bulls was accomplished despite
repeated interruptions from the opponents of the sport, but they
had made their point. The popular Parisian press came out
strongly on the side of the abolitionists and the minister of the
interior instructed the prefect concerned to forbid any other
contests of this nature. Henceforth, Paris was free from animal
sports.[22]

Despite this success in the capital, the opponents of animal
sports had great difficulty in imposing their views elsewhere in
the north of France and had virtually no response from the

south. Interestingly, in those towns where cockfighting was popular, notably Roubaix, there was also a market for Spanish bullfighting. A *taurodrome* was built in Roubaix, and the mayor of Croix, a suburb of Lille, claimed in 1913 that *corridas* had been held in Croix every year since 1900. Public meetings to protest against the introduction of bullfighting into the Nord were poorly attended. 'There were only sixty present, of whom about half were women belonging to the Protestant church', notes one police report on the attendance at a widely publicised anti-*corrida* meeting. It was not until a hundred or so Parisian abolitionists arrived by train accompanied by twenty uniformed inspectors of the SPA to disrupt a *corrida* in 1914 that there was any real threat to animal sports in the Nord.[23]

The militant attitude of the abolitionists and the no less determined defence of their sports which came from the cockfighting and bullfighting clubs of the north and south posed a dilemma for a succession of governments. Marginally, most Republican politicians opposed animal sports and few were openly in favour of the growth of Spanish bullfighting which, despite the protests of its supporters to the contrary, did not have deep roots in the regional traditions of France. Yet no firm action was taken. Those Republican politicians whose constituencies were affected by the controversy preferred the line of least resistance, arguing that whatever their own private views their public duty was to protect the rights of the majority. Deputies pretended to be concerned about the issue, but only 155 actually signed a petition to ban Spanish bullfighting drawn up in 1897 by a socialist representative from the department of the Seine. Similar considerations applied to cockfighting. At the time of the election of 1885 a deputy from the Nord wrote in desperation to the prefect, warning him, 'I assure you that we will lose the election if you go ahead at this moment with your project', the project being the banning of cockfighting. In a confidential letter an outgoing prefect warned his successor against interference in a sensitive local issue. Cockfighting was part of regional culture and best left alone. Besides, such interference could cause all sorts of problems other than purely electoral ones, such as the embarrassing incident involving the sub-prefect of Boulogne who closed down a café holding cockfights only to find out that the indignant proprietor was the leading police informant on the activities of revolutionary socialists in that area. The police had apparently given an assurance to 'this obliging businessman' that his sporting activities were no affair of theirs.[24]

In the south Republican politicians had even more to lose, for there the question of the *corrida* became involved in the revival of Provençal nationalism. When a *corrida* was banned in Nimes in 1894, the celebrated Provençal poet Frédéric Mistral led a march of protest to the arena where the contest was held in defiance of a ministerial ban. The supporters of bullfighting argued their case in terms of the legitimate autonomy of regional traditions in an over-centralised state. The challenge to the *corrida* was interpreted as yet another affront to the identity and integrity of the Midi. This was the line taken by Milliès-Lacroix, mayor of Dax, when the local prefect attempted to ban Spanish contests in the 1890s. When the prefect had a leading matador escorted to the frontier, the council telegraphed the minister of the interior to complain that their way of life was under attack and the matador was duly brought back. Thus Spanish bull-fighting was given an apocryphal place in the regional traditions of Provence and the Landes, and it was defended in the name of the need to take a stand against the forces of uniformity and centralisation which were allegedly destroying French society. The last thing which republican politicians of the 1890s desired was to provoke dissension in the traditionally Republican south by giving fuel to the separatist cause through the intervention of central government in popular regional sports. Local police were reluctant to enforce such prohibitions and troops from outside had to be brought in. This was done in Carmaux on the orders of the local prefect, who was personally opposed to the sport, and caused intense local resentment.[25]

In such circumstances it is hardly surprising that despite the progressive ideals of so many of the Republican ministers, they decided that the whole issue was more trouble than it was worth. As the minister of the interior, Louis Barthou, put it in the parliamentary debate on the subject in 1897, 'recent experience has shown that the use of strong repressive measures and of the armed forces is quite counter-productive; in order to prevent six bulls from being put to death it is necessary to risk the spilling of human blood'. The eminently Republican solution that eventu-ally emerged was that those cities in which there was already a tradition of bullfighting should have the right to continue to hold *corridas*, whereas those which had no such tradition were forbidden the spectacle. A law passed in 1951 finally assured the legal status of the *corrida* and prevented judges from introducing temporary prohibitions in particular areas. After efforts at a legal ban in 1963, cockfighting too was offered the same concessions as the *corrida*. Where these sports were already popular they were permitted, elsewhere they were forbidden.

Whilst the social history of cockfighting and bullfighting ran along parallel lines during the late nineteenth and early twentieth centuries, there has been a marked divergence since the 1930s. The *corrida* as a commercial spectacle has gone from strength to strength and now ranks as a major summer spectator sport. Northerners on holiday often take in a bullfight as part of their annual pilgrimage to the sun. Grander arenas have been built to house the large crowds of locals and visitors, and since the 1950s special bullfighting festivals have become a major tourist attraction. French television broadcasts bullrunning from Aigues-mortes, the ancient walled city of the Camargue, with the same gusto that it transmits the 24-hour motor race from Le Mans. Bullfighting now runs the risk of becoming a deracinated mass spectacle, of losing touch with the old traditions of meridional entertainment.

Nothing of this sort could be said of cockfighting. Recent research has revealed a sharp decline since the height of its success before the Second World War, when there were an estimated two thousand clubs in the Fédération des Coqueleurs du Nord et du Pas-de-Calais. Since then the old *gallodromes* have shut down. The sport persists in smaller mining centres and in the industrial suburbs of Lille, Roubaix and Tourcoing, where clubs meet in the local cafés which underpin older traditions of sociability. The complex jargon, often a Flemish patois, and the peculiar customs surrounding the hatching, rearing and arming of birds draw participants together into close-knit communities with special forms of hospitality. Friendship between cockfighting families has even gone as far as inter-marriage, and the deaths of prominent participants or the birth of a child to one are announced in *Le Coqueleur*. Here the world of cockfighting has much in common with the numerous clubs of the Nord devoted to pigeon-racing or the breeding of song birds for competition. Love of birds, with their speed, softness and warmth, exercises a powerful attraction over men who spend their working lives in rough, claustrophobic conditions underground and live in small communities close to the countryside. Yet there are signs that the breeding of fighting cocks, or of racing pigeons for that matter, is less popular with the youth of today than with their fathers. Young workers increasingly prefer the world of mass consumer culture, of motor-bikes and cars, the juke-box, Coca-cola and television. Cockfighting is for the old and retired, for those who can or still wish to remember the past.[26]

The interplay of strong regional traditions and new recreational needs together with the tolerant attitude of the Republican authorities created the necessary conditions for the remarkable growth of bullfighting and cockfighting in the later nineteenth century. As spectacles they provided an important and neglected bridge between traditional and modern sports, although neither activity can be simply explained in terms of a folkloric survival in a slow-moving peasant society because their success was an essentially urban phenomenon during this period. So-called 'traditional' sports were recast along more commercial lines to suit the needs of a city-dwelling population and both sports lost most of their casual bucolic identity as a consequence. Nevertheless, both activities did retain some of the traditions of social heterogeneity which had been a feature of country sports. On account of its limited spectator potential, cockfighting never became a professional spectator sport like Spanish bullfighting and maintained its intimate amateur atmosphere and intense, introverted sociability. It seems as if the popularity of bullfighting and cockfighting in their respective regional strongholds was closely related to the movement of peasants into the city. 'Brutal' sports in the forms they assumed during this period were popular because they were both customary and innovative, ancient and modern, and as such reflected the ambiguity of an urban culture which still had its roots in popular regional tradition.

Part II

Major Themes

7 The Tradition of Violence: Brutality, Hooliganism and Combativity

Violence in one form or another had a central place in traditional sporting activity until the later nineteenth century. In France games and spectacles which today would be classified as 'brutal' or 'deviant' were widely accepted and enjoyed for the simple excitement and catharsis they offered. In the course of the last century or so, however, there has been a strong reaction against this tradition of violence. As far as sport is concerned, deriving pleasure from watching animals fight or from the display of gratuitous violence in the course of a game is now officially considered improper, and by many barbaric. With few exceptions, civilised middle-class values condemn physically aggressive behaviour beyond the confines of play, and even those sports which legitimise aggression outlaw violence. So much for theory, what about practice? What has been the real impact of this decline in the level of socially tolerated violence on the development of sport? How much of the old remains half-hidden under the mass of new regulations, and in what respects have the various traditional forms of violence been undermined by the general transformation of leisure?

Before we can attempt to answer such questions, the term 'violence' itself requires some preliminary discussion. As a conceptual tool for the analysis of sport it is a most unsatisfactory term which regrettably proves indispensable. Despite the manifest significance of behaviour which is normally termed 'violent' as a factor in daily life, very few historians have attempted to write about it. Part of the reason for this neglect stems from the sheer problem of definition. One of the few social historians to tackle the issue notes that 'it is difficult to generalise about violence in ordinary life, because sensitivity to pain increased very unevenly in this period and the idea of what constituted violence must have changed'. Clearly, an assessment of the general place of violence in modern French society goes far beyond the scope of the present study. However, in order to give a measure of precision to the history of violence as a theme in French sport, three constituent elements have been isolated: brutality, hooliganism and combativity. By disentangling these different strands of sporting violence it may be possible to show how certain forms of behaviour or types of contest have been substantially changed, whilst other violent aspects of sport have remained more or less as they were. These apparently clear-cut divisions have their disadvantages in that they require us to look separately at aspects of human conduct which in reality are closely related. This cannot be helped. The subject is so important, though as yet so under-researched, that even arbitrary and approximate categories such as these may offer some clarification where little or none existed before.[1]

BRUTALITY

The strict definition of the term 'brutality' restricts it to 'the condition of the brutes', i.e. the behaviour of animals to each other and, by extension, the repetition of such 'inhuman' behaviour by humans. 'Brutal' sports, therefore, are commonly understood to involve animals in some form of violent contest organised for human enjoyment. Until the middle years of the nineteenth century it seems clear that activities of this kind were commonplace. Under the *ancien régime* sports like bull-baiting, bear-baiting, badger-baiting or even donkey-baiting evoked only occasional protest, usually on the grounds of disorder rather than cruelty. The public took a simple delight in the natural propensity of certain creatures to attack and to kill other species or rivals, and all sorts of ways were devised by which such instincts could be provoked, exaggerated and fortified for the purposes of providing the people with sport.

Dog-fights were a particularly vicious spectacle and these were organised with considerable success in Paris at the notorious *barrière du combat* between Belleville and La Villette. Arenas of this type were the favourite haunt of butchers and members of other 'violent trades' examined in Louis Chevalier's famous study of crime and poverty in Paris during the July Monarchy. The *barrière du combat*, which was patronised in its time by such celebrated literary figures as Jules Janin and Théophile Gautier, was shut down in 1845 in the course of urban renewal. This arena, where tough workers gathered to enjoy a cheap drink beyond the reach of the city's tax collectors, mounted a wide variety of brutal sports other than the dog-fights already mentioned. It advertised its programme on yellow posters throughout Paris. Up until its closure donkey-baiting (a great favourite because of the peculiar ferocity of the creatures when roused and the kicking power of their hind legs) and wolf-fights were amongst the most popular entertainments put on there. Gautier was particularly fascinated by the bull-baiting in which a 'young and vigorous Spanish bull tossed in the air half a dozen disembowelled dogs whose guts flew around the ring in graceful arcs and whose blood rained down in black drops as long as a man's thumb; their handlers, roughly dressed in peasant fashion, . . . caught them tenderly in their arms or snatched them in mid-flight'.[2]

However, the civilised bourgeois conscience increasingly began to make itself felt around the middle of the century. As we have already seen in the preceding chapter, there were serious efforts to stamp out bullfighting and cockfighting in the second half of the nineteenth century. While these efforts met with only partial success, animal protectionists did manage to outlaw other forms of animal-baiting fairly effectively. Whether the decline of these activities was primarily the result of pressure from reformers or whether it stemmed from a change in public taste in the middle years of the century still remains unclear and awaits further research. All that can be said within the confines of the present study is that brutal spectacles where beasts were pitted against each other did become increasingly rare, and that the provisions of the *loi Grammont* of 1851 probably had some influence on this process. Nevertheless, the power of the Protestant middle class was a great deal weaker in France than in Britain and the weight of custom considerably stronger. Old habits die hard and there is some evidence that these kinds of amusement still took place from time to time, although they were no longer regular events. As late as 1896 a man in Beaucaire was sent to prison for organising a fight in which a bear killed several bulls; in 1899 a public contest between a lion and a bull was held in Roubaix and a special train from Paris was laid on to transport spectators. However, such incidents were the exceptions that proved the rule. Nineteenth-century France saw the demise of the most bloody of animal sports and their replacement by more organised, 'legitimate' contests in which there was an attempt to place definite limits on the degree of brutality involved. Bullfighting, as we saw, provided a classic example of this ambiguous response to violence in sport. Attempts were made by those directly involved to put a stop to most of the bloody, unregulated contests, but at the same time bullfights to the death in the Spanish manner were successfully introduced into the Midi. As far as reformers were concerned this was a perfect instance of the innate adaptability of brutal sports. Only the worst excesses had been prohibited; the form had changed but the substance remained more or less intact.[3]

All too often bullfights degenerated into a violent farce not dissimilar in many respects to the more openly cruel sports of earlier generations. Frightened young bulls bred in France were used instead of the more expensive, specially trained Spanish fighting bulls. These pathetic creatures would be chased around the makeshift ring by inexperienced young 'matadors' until they were cornered and clumsily killed. In 1898 two incidents of this kind took place within a fortnight of each other, one in Marseille and the other in Bordeaux. In each case the two 'matadors' concerned were under twenty years of age and both missed the bull completely the first time they tried to make the kill. The points that require emphasis here are not so much the ignorance of the public as their enjoyment of the sight of blood for its own sake and the similarities between some modern bullfights and older animal sports. The crude attitude of certain spectators sometimes shocked those who knew more about the sport. A good instance of this is the use of *les banderilles à feu*, flaming rags attached to the animal's back as a last resort if he showed himself unwilling to fight. In the later nineteenth century crowds frequently called for the use of this painful device even when there was strictly speaking no justification for it. They simply liked the increased savagery it lent to the spectacle.[4]

Similarly, cockfighting often led to scenes of cruelty and near hysteria on a rather smaller scale. The nature of the spectacle tended to envenom many spectators, who were no doubt willing enough to let themselves go. As the cocks tore at each other those seated around the cockpit were occasionally drenched with blood, and the victorious cocks were sometimes so furious that they lashed out at their handlers and at anyone else nearby. As early as 1852 there had been a prefectorial ban in the department of the Nord on the ground that 'these contests are often the cause of serious arguments and bloody brawling'. In a letter to the prefect of the Pas-de-Calais, a man who had lived amongst the mining communities of that region for twenty years remarked, 'Wherever there is a cockfight there is likely to be a fist fight too'. The most barbaric scenes were reserved for the losing cock and its angry owner. If the creature was not killed outright its demented breeder would often destroy the half-dead bird on the spot. Some owners behaved so brutally that their antics gave rise to criticism in sporting journals hardly renowned for their sentimental attitude towards animals. *Le Petit Chasseur*, a popular field sports magazine, complained about furious scenes where a man would dash out a losing cock's brains with the nearest thing to hand. On one occasion an owner lost all control of himself and roasted his creature alive while threatening those around him with a dagger when they tried to intervene.[5]

Animal protectionists usually blamed scenes of this sort on the innate cruelty of the spectacle and the sadistic impulses it generated in those involved. No doubt there is a good deal of truth in this. In essence, what we are saying is that the process by which the most bloodthirsty animal sports were regulated was only a partial success. Elements of the old co-existed with the new codification of these sports designed to make them less violent and more acceptable to educated public opinion. There is a further dimension to the question which requires consideration at this point. Both cockfighting and bullfighting were commercialised in such a fashion that new reasons for violent behaviour were added to the old. No careful study of the violent element in these animal sports can ignore the fact that the calculated malpractice of those organising bullfights and the amount of gambling involved in cockfighting greatly contributed to the problem.

Deliberate deception of the paying public aggravated the traditional inclination to join in and take to the streets as far as bullfighting was concerned. Spanish bullfights were notoriously corrupt. The preceding case-study showed how often proper matadors were replaced by incompetent locals, and French bulls substituted for Spanish ones. Evening *corridas* were particularly prone to malpractice. Presumably the organisers felt they could get away with more in artificial light or fading daylight than was possible in the full glare of the afternoon sun. The evening *corridas* at Bayonne ended in disaster in 1886 when the crowd destroyed the stands. A similar incident took place in Montpellier in 1893 when police and troops were called in to clear out angry spectators who had surrounded the cash desk to demand their money back after a disappointing contest. Spectators who might have spent the equivalent of two or three days' wages on a ticket reacted with predictable vehemence when they felt they had been duped. Their suppressed traditions of violent protest quickly came to the surface, eliciting equally predictable denunciations from the ranks of animal protectionists and middle-class intellectuals. Commenting on the disorder and destruction which followed in the wake of a *corrida* held in Villeurbanne near Lyon in 1905, the police commissioner noted that 'the spectacle actually presented in no way corresponded with the programme advertised in advance . . . the crowd protested vehemently demanding their money back . . . hurling chairs into the arena and risking the safety of women and children'.[6]

Cockfights, too, sometimes promised more than they could deliver, but the real problem in this case was the level of gambling involved. The giving and taking of bets was traditional to the sport, but it seems as if this side of the sport became far more highly organised in the late nineteenth century. Men sometimes wagered far more than they could afford and went berserk when their cock was defeated. Maxence van der Meersch's prize-winning novel, *L'Empreinte du Dieu*, first published in 1935, contains some magnificent passages on cockfighting in the Nord in the 1930s which leave us in little doubt about the role of betting in sustaining cockfighting and nourishing the ancient frenzy and violence of the spectacle. The following extract seems worth quoting at some length:

. . . Everyone was shouting, waving their arms, making signs, exchanging bets and challenges. Mautret, the fat flax merchant, seated in the front row, showed off a stomach bedecked with gold and had an ecstatic, crimson expression on his face. He was betting in lots of one thousand francs. Next to him in a yellow coloured outfit, with arms naked and elbow-length gloves, was his mistress, 'Moucheronne', a fanatical gambler who would stake her all on a bet, lashing out like the cocks themselves, carried away at violent moments such as these with the brutal memories of the tough childhood she had never quite left behind. Others joined in too – Flemish women in brightly coloured dresses of red, blue, yellow and green; they were even louder than the men shouting their odds in sharp piercing voices, moving without any apparent discomfort amid all the dirt, the dust and the brutality . . . Into this mob, this dense mass, from the high windows fell shafts of golden sunlight heightening the clash of colours and setting in sharp relief the tortured and excited faces, the contorted, avid expression of a gambler and the grinning, purply, bloated features of a drunkard.[7]

Even allowing for a certain poetic licence (and this novelist was generally praised for his sense of realism), the fetid, rowdy atmosphere of the modern cockfight with its mingling of naked materialism and half-remembered rites of violence comes across powerfully.

Investigations of cockfighting since the war report a general decline in the level of fanaticism and aggression displayed by all concerned. Since the Second World War the old culture of the café has been eroded by the affluence of the nuclear family, with its televisions and private cars. The young now prefer the new spectator sports. Whilst bullfighting and cockfighting still continue the old traditions (and in this sense France is much closer to the Iberian countries than to Great Britain), they lack their former gusto. The 'New France' of the fifties and sixties found such brutality increasingly incompatible with its ultra-modern image. Where the state has been unable to prohibit violent behaviour by legal means, the growth of tourism has succeeded in weakening it. Painted on a wall in Nimes is the following epitaph to the *feria*, the rowdy Whitsun festival of bullrunning: 'La feria se meurt, les flics et les touristes l'achèvent.' (The *feria* is dying, the cops and the tourists are killing it.) Bullfighting today is a pale reflection of its former gory self. It has become a self-consciously folkloric aspect of regional culture. The frank celebration of brutality is no longer generally acceptable.

HOOLIGANISM

The second feature of pre-industrial play relevant to an analysis of the place of violence in modern sport is hooliganism, or the enjoyment of fighting for its own sake. Van Gennep's classic work on custom in French society abounds in examples of organised fighting. Faction-fighting was virtually an adolescent rite of passage. To be allowed to fight by the adults of a community was a step on the road towards acceptance into full male society. It carried with it connotations of admission to 'the tribe'. The quasi-formal exchange of insults that usually preceded a fight, the special times and places where faction-fighting was permitted all contributed towards transforming the gang rivalries of adolescent village peer groups into full-blown rituals of rural society.

The popularity of this kind of violence stemmed from the fact that it had a clear function within traditional communities; it formed 'part of a coherent set of understandings and part of normal life', a means 'of righting wrongs and redressing injuries, indeed even for containing quarrels and letting off steam'. In eighteenth-century France 'inter-village fights were ubiquitous' and 'young agricultural workers were prepared to spend their *fête* days slanging those of a neighbouring commune; they would beat them up, tearing their clothes, having set forth and walked five or ten miles with such aggression in mind'. In other words fighting was a 'sport', and tolerated as such. Conflicts of this type were rarely random or casual. They were often carefully organised by municipal 'bands' or 'abbeys', the semi-official juvenile institutions with responsibility for courtship and sociability analysed by Maurice Agulhon in his work on late eighteenth-century Provence. Fights followed 'a set pattern where rules permitted the young to beat each other insensible until at the crucial juncture authority in the shape of the *maréchaussée*, the *archers* [town watch], village elders or officials of the *milice* would intervene'.[8]

These fights continued long into the nineteenth century. For example, there was a 'frightful struggle' involving the inhabitants of two villages in Finistère on the day of the annual draft lottery in March 1866. The lads from one commune insisted on marching around a monument in the centre of the village where the lottery was being held. This was a traditional challenge to the native inhabitants and was bound to be resisted on their behalf by the able-bodied young men of that commune. The prefect, like so many other civilised nineteenth-century officials, could not comprehend such primitive behaviour. The incident gave rise to a lengthy correspondence in which the mayor of Plogastel urged him to 'try to understand the ways of our peasant young and their need for violent contrasts to their agricultural labours'.[9]

In the later nineteenth century the tradition of fighting declined, although the pace at which this happened varied considerably from one place to another. Thabault notes in his famous study of Mazières-en-Gâtine in western France that as late as 1880 'veritable set battles took place from which the combatants came away with black-eyes, broken noses and torn clothes'. But, he adds, 'twenty years later all this had stopped'. The *belle époque* seems to have marked a turning point in faction-fighting as it did in so many other traditional activities. By the inter-war period Van Gennep noted that what fighting there was took place from time to time within the village itself rather than at customarily designated dates and on special fields or at crossroads, as had formerly been the practice. A recent study of the Berry region observes that 'rivalry between communes is now . . . non-existent. There was a time when the "Turquin", as the youth of Déols were known, would not let the boys of Châteauroux cross the bridge and there were regular Sunday fights'.[10]

Fighting ceased to be a regulated social ritual and became a casual private amusement, participation in which largely depended on individual temperament and drinking habits. It survived into the twentieth century in the most remote regions but even in these places brawling began to go out of fashion. No history of modern sport should neglect these changes in the behaviour of the young and their rites of violence. This is because modern sport often proved to be both a means by which play was civilised *and* an occasional outlet for atavistic ferocity. In principle, the newly codified games of the late nineteenth century prohibited gratuitous aggression in the name of skill and stamina; but in practice, twentieth-century sport has frequently generated openly violent and provocative behaviour from players and spectators. To imagine that rowdyism in sport is somehow an abnormal, or even a pathological, form of behaviour, shows how short our memories have become and how completely the traces of traditional culture have been expunged from official thinking. New games and contests with their elaborate rules concerning non-violence and fair competition provided a useful framework for physical recreation in an increasingly urbanised and technocratic society, but innovations such as these could hardly transform immemorial traditions of play at a stroke. A good deal of the old wine found its way into the new bottles.

An examination of the relationship between the old game of village football and the new sport of rugby is a case in point. Before the onset of modernisation village football was played in most areas of France in one form or another. Often, football and fighting were virtually two sides of the same coin. 'The primitive form of village football played in Brittany in the seventeenth and eighteenth centuries had been little more than ritualised battle between two parishes', comments a recent historian of the rural community in the late eighteenth century. The same was true of early nineteenth-century Brittany where, according to Souvestre, *soule* 'is not an ordinary amusement but a heated and dramatic game in which the players fight, strangle each other and smash each other's heads . . . a sort of frenetic drunkenness seizes the players, the instincts of wild beasts seem to be aroused in the hearts of men'. Recalling a game of *soule* played in 1855, a bewildered observer remarked that 'it was hard to discern more than a confused mass of players who seemed to want nothing more than to destroy each other; those at the edge of the scrum tearing at those in the centre; a huge shifting mass, a heap of bodies moving first to the right and then to the left. Every now and then a head disappears beneath a mound of flesh only to reappear pale and bloodied as the scrum moves on after trampling him into the ground'. The authorities increasingly refused to tolerate such mayhem as the century advanced, and it seems as if the participants, too, began to lose the taste for so undiluted a diet of festive violence. Charles Tilly has claimed that the middle years of the century saw the modernisation of collective violence in the economic and political spheres, as bread riots gave way to organised strikes and the street riot or *journée* lost ground to the ballot box. Perhaps the same was true of popular recreation.[11]

At first sight there can certainly be little doubt that the furious rowdyism of football in its traditional form, with the pig's bladder blessed by the priest and hurled into the crowd by the lord of the manor, was far removed from the modern game of rugby, with its elaborate rules and code of conduct. The trouble is that the obvious differences have tended to obscure the hidden similarities. It is not enough to argue that sport has been adjusted to suit contemporary norms of violence and order, that it has been modernised *tout court*. If rugby had in fact been played according to the rules and in the spirit of disinterested amateur competition laid down by Coubertin, there would indeed have been an unbridgeable gulf between the old and the new. But even the most cursory glance at the history of French rugby in the twentieth century reveals that this was not so.

Take the behaviour of spectators, for instance. Traditional games or contests often made little distinction between participants and onlookers. Everyone tended to find themselves caught up in the collective frenzy of the moment, and this turbulent legacy was bequeathed as much to rugby spectators as it was to the players themselves. Predictably, violence amongst the crowd was common from the start of the modern game. As early as 1905 the supporters of Toulouse stoned a tram carrying the rival Stade Bordelais home from a cup game. At the final of the 1909 rugby championship held in Bordeaux posters were plastered around the ground and the surrounding streets urging spectators 'to avoid turbulent demonstrations', but they took place all the same.[12]

Perhaps the most dramatic instance of pre-war crowd violence happened at the international rugby match between France and Scotland in Paris in 1913. Two years earlier the French national side had celebrated its first major victory by beating the Scots 16–15 in a magnificent game. The crowd assembled on New Year's Day 1913 in a spirit of chauvinistic fervour, hoping for a repeat performance and an excuse to prolong the seasonal festivities. In the event, the Scots came well prepared, and the frustrated French players began to lose their tempers and foul their opponents. When the English referee, a Mr Baxter, gave a series of decisions against the French, the crowd began to scream abuse and accuse him of taking bribes. With splendid *sang-froid* and economy of gesture the referee left the crowd in no doubt about what he thought of their behaviour. At the end of the game hundreds of fans invaded the pitch and attacked

Baxter, who had to be escorted from the field by policemen and players and later smuggled out of the ground to avoid groups of angry French supporters baying for his blood. Some of them later made their way to the offices of the daily sports paper, *L'Auto*, blocking the rue Montmartre for several hours until they were finally dispersed by mounted police and soldiers with fixed bayonets.[13]

No doubt part of the blame for what came to be known as 'l'affaire Baxter' can be laid at the door of the ultra-nationalism of the pre-war years. This was a new phenomenon that had no direct equivalent in earlier forms of spectator sport. All the same, the French and the British were virtually allies and on fairly good terms by this time. If it had been the Germans who had been involved, an explanation cast purely in terms of the affront to national pride would have been more convincing. Leaving the new nationalism of the *avant-guerre* out of the discussion for the moment, what are we left with? The interpretation which any student of popular protest under the *ancien régime* would be tempted to give is obvious: an *émeute* – a spontaneous uprising or outburst of popular anger. These events, so familiar until the middle of the nineteenth century, could be sparked off by an insult to local pride as well as by a shortage of bread. Faction-fighting institutionalised the *émeute* and regulated popular violence to some degree. Is it really too far-fetched to suggest that in taking to the streets to show their anger many of these spectators were simply working off their aggression in the traditional tumultuous fashion?

Violent behaviour was by no means confined to the crowd. The 1920s witnessed a rapid increase in flagrant fouling and viciousness on the field of play itself. Fierce competition amongst the clubs of the south-west was aggravated by age-old ethnic animosities and local rivalries. In the Languedoc the battles of the Basques and Catalans, the Gascons and the Aquitainians were re-enacted in rugby. To take one instance out of many, when Carcassonne played Toulouse in a crucial semi-final match in the early 1920s, the referee was punched in the face and knocked to the ground when he tried to stop a fight on the pitch. As he left the field the Carcassonne crowd tried to tear him limb from limb, only to be dissuaded by some of their own team with the comforting words, 'Don't hit him here, we'll be disqualified. Wait till he gets outside.' Things soon got even worse. Commenting on a key cup game between Perpignan and Carcassonne in 1925, an experienced sports journalist less given to exaggeration than most of his colleagues wrote that 'this was a match for brutes . . . there were fights on the terraces, fights on the field . . . scenes of unprecedented vindictiveness as players openly kicked and punched each other whenever the ball went into touch'. The inevitable and tragic consequences of this type of behaviour came a year later when Perpignan played the small town of Quillan, a team sponsored by a rich hat manufacturer who had cynically strengthened his side by luring away the best Perpignan players with offers of jobs and illicit cash. From the outset Perpignan were determined to teach the 'traitors' a lesson, and violence escalated until the Quillan hooker, Gaston Rivière, fractured a vertebra and died forty-eight hours later.[14]

'Rugby de *muerte*' and 'ambiance de *corrida*' were two of the Spanish terms used to describe the character of the game in Languedoc at this time. The clear analogy with an acknowledged violent sport is instructive. Alphonse Jauréguy, a brilliant Toulouse three-quarter deeply imbued with the ideals of fair play, deplored the path taken by the sport. In his memoirs he recalled the sense of shame he felt when the British rugby authorities finally broke off formal relations with the French on the twin issues of violence and professionalism. 'The crowd gesticulate like the damned and yell themselves hoarse', he declared, and when his friend, a laconic Scots expatriate, compared such behaviour with the apes in Kipling's *Jungle Book*, he was forced to agree. There was no sensible explanation for such strange behaviour. The thoughtful periodical, *La Nouvelle Revue du Midi*, had a similar reaction. 'There is a new phenomenon in France: the "supporter". He will endure wind, rain and freezing temperatures to see his team. Capable of sudden and dramatic changes of mood, he abandons all critical or common sense and identifies himself with his side by wearing its colours, bawling out its songs and beating up the supporters of rival teams when the opportunity presents itself.' The horrified author conveniently forgot about the earlier forms such activities had taken. For him, football hooliganism was nothing but an obnoxious novelty, just another instance of mindless modernity. He did not bother to look any further.[15]

Brutality on the field and hooliganism off it were put down almost entirely to the rapid commercialisation of the sport which, it was alleged, fostered a spirit of competition that frequently got out of hand. No doubt there is some truth in this, but it is only part of the story. Traditional rites of violence and modern commercial influences should not be regarded as alternative explanations when in fact they are complementary. What seems to have happened is this: violent local patriotism shifted from the declining *fête patronale* and fixed itself on new phenomena, notably the growing sport of rugby introduced around the turn of the century and extremely popular by the 1920s. In town and country, youths who had formerly faced each other in open combat in the fields and market places began to congregate in the local stadium with broadly similar ends in view. The author of a useful account of the history of sport in Anjou points out that in many instances the rivalries of new sports clubs based in particular towns or villages were conterminous with more ancient traditions of local antagonism. Did modern sportsmen realise, he wondered, that as they took to the field they were re-enacting the use made of 'football' by their ancestors in the endless struggle for territoriality?[16]

On a conscious level perhaps not, but in their response to the imperatives of local pride, in their stubborn particularism, they may well have half-consciously realised their role in continuing immemorial customs. To such as these the partisan frenzy which sometimes led to fighting was an integral part of the whole experience – as was drinking, singing and even dancing. As a perceptive Toulouse doctor remarked, 'le rugby est une fête'. Streaming in or out of the ground with banners waving and sporting the emblems of their team, there was ample opportunity for the familiar, almost friendly, insult to the pride or parentage of the supporters of the other team. Obviously, not all spectators indulged in this kind of behaviour. Probably only a minority did so, and fewer still came to blows. As a whole, spectator sports were less violent than former collective rituals. The point here is that for a significant minority – very often those youths who no longer had faction-fights and charivaris to amuse them – some spectator sports continued to fulfil a useful and traditional function.

It would be quite wrong to suggest that such antics were confined to the game of rugby. It is simply that the evidence is particularly plentiful for this sport. Broadly speaking, the same observations applied to football. When the football team from the *lycée* Charlemagne in Roubaix met the *lycée* de Tourcoing in the final of the school competition in 1905, pairs of knuckle-dusters had to be taken from several of the players before the game could commence; in the same year football referees in the Nord threatened to go on strike because of the violence and insubordination of the players and spectators. Middle-class norms of good behaviour were only gradually transmitted and were never fully assimilated.[17]

Even the Union des Sociétés Françaises de Gymnastique, which took as axiomatic the need to rid French youth of its tumultuous traditions and to discipline adolescents in the interests of national patriotism, had publicly to concede defeat on occasions. For example, at Lyon in 1894 there were complaints that some of the young men attending the annual gymnastic festival had spent half the night fighting, causing a good deal of damage and keeping neighbours awake. At the annual festival held in Nice in 1901 groups of youths had roamed the streets half-drunk, tunics unbuttoned, chanting, propositioning innocent women who passed and waking the town's elderly inhabitants with ear-splitting bugle calls. In fact, abuse of the bugles issued to gymnasts as part of their military training was a regular cause for complaint. According to *Le Figaro*, a favourite trick of mischievous youngsters was to creep up on ageing bystanders and scare them out of their wits with sudden piercing blasts on their bugles. If we remember that gymnastic clubs were often linked to shooting clubs and that many members were involved in both activities, the similarities between rowdy incidents of this type and the ritual salvoes of gunfire, parades and farces formerly organised by the *guet* (village militia) are quite striking.[18]

Even cycle-racing, which at first sight might appear unlikely to give rise to such boisterous behaviour, had its share. Crowds at the *vélodromes* of the *fin-de-siècle* yelled, stamped and swore almost as furiously as rugby fans from the Midi. Cycling could be an exhausting and brutal spectacle on occasions. The marathon races so popular with the Parisian crowds have already been examined in the case study of cycling and the fickle and fiercely partisan response of spectators mentioned. Take, for instance, the case of a black American cyclist called Major Taylor, or 'le nègre volant', as the crowd christened him. During a two-man race between Taylor and a French track star, Lucien

Dubois, the 'flying nigger' was knocked off his machine four times and ended the race badly cut and in a state of shock. The crowd merely roared their approval and jeered Taylor off the track.[19]

It became only too evident that despite the modernising of sport, crowds were still willing to react in an ancient brutal fashion to rival groups, to provocation by promoters or to ferocity on the pitch. Both those who wished to use sport as a form of social engineering and those who merely sought to profit from it deplored this response. They wanted to isolate the positive elements in sport – energy, enthusiasm, loyalty, patriotism – from the more violent characteristics of sports crowds – swearing, chanting, pushing, fighting and so on. Older spectators conformed well to the new stereotype, but others, notably the young, wanted to be more than just passive onlookers observing a skilful activity with detached expertise. They were unwilling to become mere consumers of sporting entertainment. They wanted to participate themselves and in this sense they were harking back to older forms of sporting activity which made no clear distinctions between active and passive involvement. By seeing who could chant the loudest or who could insult and manhandle the opposition's support most effectively, 'spectators' sometimes extended the struggle for superiority beyond the confines set by formal regulations. The gangs of rival supporters on the terraces persisted in regarding 'the game' not as a series of isolated manoeuvres on the field of play but as a complete social event which called for their active, sometimes violent, participation. At moments such as these, 'hooliganism' was in the eye of the beholder.[20]

COMBATIVITY

The coexistence of ancient traditions of aggression and modern commercial practices reached its apotheosis in two sports specifically concerned with human combat: wrestling and boxing. Both wrestling and boxing were refined and reformed in the course of the nineteenth century and have been successfully sold to the masses in the twentieth. In France, at least, wrestling was much the older and more popular sport before 1914. Wrestling contests had been a regular accompaniment to village festivals, and styles varied from one region to another. Wrestling seems to have been especially popular in Brittany and in Provence. Paul Pons, the doyen of French wrestling around the turn of the century, was born in Sorgues in the Vaucluse, where the sport was so popular that local dignitaries frequently attended contests which thereby acquired a semi-official status. Jacques Hélias recalled watching Breton wrestling at the time of the First World War in his native commune, though he notes that football was becoming more popular as a spectator sport. In fact, traditional wrestling steadily declined in popularity during the second half of the nineteenth century and was replaced by travelling wrestling booths run by sporting impresarios, the most famous of whom was a man called Rossignol-Rollin. He was the first major promoter of the modern kind. He used his background in the circus to play skilfully on the turbulent passions of his audience, and it was he who began the fashion for terrifying soubriquets that has since become part and parcel of the wrestling game. On his books he had 'The Wild Beast of the Jungles', 'The Hercules of the Midi', 'The Untameable', 'The Man of Iron'. Tacked on intriguingly to this fearsome list was 'Alfred, the Elegant Parisian Model', who could vault over six chairs placed in line from a stationary position. Most famous of all was 'Arpin, the Terrible Savoyard'. Arpin's strength, viciousness and ill-temper were second to none, and his reputation as a *salaud* was carefully cultivated by his publicity-conscious manager. Having remained undefeated in numerous contests, he finally succumbed to a more phlegmatic fighter, whereupon his humiliated mistress, 'an irascible and vindictive orangeseller' from Marseille, tried to cut off his head with a circus sword.[21]

These wrestling booths became popular in the 1860s and 1870s as a supplement to traditional country sports. Most of the suffering such wrestlers inflicted on each other was either faked or grossly exaggerated. Still, it was a tough and dangerous job. Even in Rossignol-Rollin's comparatively well-run operation several wrestlers were killed, notably a former butcher, 'Edward, the Jura Bear'. After this misfortune the diplomatic promoter closed down for a few days in mourning for the dead and in the hope the authorities would overlook the matter.

A major rift in the wrestling world opened up in the 1890s over the twin issues of dissimulation and histrionics. Those who took wrestling seriously as a competitive amateur sport insisted that a detailed set of rules be drawn up based on the athletic traditions of village wrestling. But promoters knew that the wrestling public, drawn chiefly from the working-class districts of the big cities, were more interested in the pseudo-sadistic rituals organised from time to time at places like the Folies Bergères, the Eldorado and the Casino. Around the turn of the century the modern division in wrestling emerged, with the essentially amateur Graeco-Roman school on the one side and the supporters of 'free' commercial wrestling on the other. Despite the fact that the French won several medals in Graeco-Roman wrestling in the inter-war Olympics, it was 'free' wrestling that captured public interest.[22]

Wrestling, therefore, has remained popular this century less as a sport than as a spectacle. Watching wrestling in the early 1950s, Roland Barthes noted that it takes the form of a morality play in which good engages in physical combat with evil. According to the conventions of the bout, suffering is first inflicted on the 'good' wrestler, the decent and fair competitor with whom the spectators identify. When he has had enough he then turns on the evil one, the treacherous and ugly contestant who bends the 'rules' and then pleads for them to be enforced when it suits him. Each hold is accompanied by elaborate and exaggerated gestures of cruelty or affliction to which the spectators respond by shouting support or abuse. The entire spectacle is in essence a kind of theatre, where the audience finds cathartic release from its violent emotions within an instantly comprehensible moral framework. Simulated frenzy is integral to the spectacle and the best contests 'are crowned by a final *charivari*, a sort of unrestrained fantasia where the rules . . . and the limits of the ring are swept away by a triumphant disorder which overflows into the hall and carries off pell-mell wrestlers, seconds, referee and spectators' [my italic].[23]

A comparison of wrestling and boxing is instructive here. In commercial wrestling it is the simulation of violence which lies at the core of the contest, whereas in boxing the pain inflicted is more palpable. During the nineteenth century efforts had been made to refine the savage fighting techniques of Parisian workmen (*savate*) and produce a new sport, *la boxe française*, which permitted the use of fists as well as the feet. French-style boxing was quite popular in the later nineteenth century but it was overtaken by international developments. Boxing in Britain and the United States had become a highly organised mass spectator sport. Heavyweight bouts between men like John Sullivan, the first fighter to make a million dollars, and 'Gentleman' Jim Corbett, a former bank clerk, brought new levels of skill and professionalism to the sport in the 1890s. The wide publicity given to the world championship fought under the Queensberry rules and the avid following these contests found amongst the Anglo-Saxon working classes began to attract attention in France around the turn of the century. In particular, those who had invested heavily in the bicycle boom of the nineties began to explore the possibilities of British boxing as a means of reviving their flagging fortunes. Paul Rousseau, a former speculator in track-racing during the *fin-de-siècle*, founded the Fédération Française de Boxe in 1903 and Victor Breyer, another ex-cycling promoter, opened the first purpose-built boxing hall in 1907, called 'Wonderland' in honour of the famous ring of the same name in London's Whitechapel Road. Louis Hémon, a popular French novelist living in England, caught nicely the amazed Anglo-Saxon response with its ill-concealed contempt in his novel *Battling Malone*, written about 1909: 'One fine day they [the French] had suddenly grown tired of kicking each other in the face and had determined to learn the art of using their fists like men – of boxing, in short. All England had roared. A boxing Frenchman! It was the absurdest of paradoxes, a challenge to reason and common sense!' But, as the novel went on to show, the French learned very quickly, too quickly for English tastes, and a consortium of wealthy sportsmen was formed to put up the money to train a champion who would restore British self-respect by beating the French.[24]

There was a good deal of Gallic wish-fulfilment in Hémon's novel, though, as we shall see, the career of Georges Carpentier was soon to put French boxing on the world map. At the outset, however, French promoters were a little worried that a Parisian audience would be rather less receptive to the spectacle of one human being pounding another than were the English or the American public. But this was not so. The 'east end' Parisian crowd were fairly similar to their cockney counterparts in their preference for strength rather than science. What Hémon said of the British also applied to the French crowd: 'What they want to see is the realistic semblance of a street fight, the combative ardour of two strongly built men who see red, exchange savage thumps, fall, get up, fall again and get up once more with a sullen magnificent obstinacy as long as a vestige of strength is left in them'. In 1909, shortly before the international rules were amended' two American negroes, Sam MacVea and Joe Jeanette, slugged at each other for an astonishing forty-nine rounds to the obvious delight of the Parisian crowd. Remarking on the rapid growth of the sport around 1908–9, the editor of a newly founded boxing weekly noted that 'a few months ago a man, who might have been put off by the sight of a few drops of blood at a fight, now follows all the big bouts like a fanatic, leaving the Wonderland, the Tivoli or the Cirque after an evening's fighting hoarse with yelling at the boxers'. Here again we come across the complex, often paradoxical place of violence in modern sport. In theory, boxing was carefully regulated to avoid excessive injury. In practice, it was often an unashamedly ferocious spectacle.[25]

Professional boxing enjoyed meteoric success with the wider French public in the years that followed. The career of Georges Carpentier undoubtedly had a lot to do with this. Born in 1894, the son of a miner from the Nord, the 'gosse lensois' first learned to box in a local gymnastic club. At the age of fourteen he had his first professional fight against a twenty-six year old jockey in Paris and won. Within three years he had captured the European light-middleweight and middleweight championships, and he went on to beat 'Bombardier' Billy Wells for the light-heavy-weight championship of the world in 1913. When Carpentier had twice defeated Wells, once in front of his own supporters and once in London despite giving away 2 stones in weight, the French felt understandably that they had proved themselves in what was generally accepted as the toughest and most violent of modern sports. In total, Carpentier boxed at all eight professional weights, winning European titles in four divisions. Distinguished war service and a spell as a three-quarter in the French services' rugby side along with his natural charm and good looks turned him into a national hero. For the first time women became interested in top-class professional boxing. Carpentier was no brute. He was an elegant and skilful fighter but one who could also take punishment. The papers elevated him into a symbol of the resurgence of the French spirit. When he fought Jack Dempsey, the ferocious heavyweight champion of the world, in Jersey City on 2 June 1921, the match was watched by a crowd of 112,000 who paid nearly two million dollars for the privilege. In France public interest in boxing reached new and unprecedented levels. People who knew next to nothing about the sport were suddenly caught up in the special mystique of the heavyweight championship – what one writer on male culture has termed 'the dramaturgical predominance' of the biggest and the strongest. The young Simone de Beauvoir inadvertently observed the popular hysteria surrounding the contest when she recalled in her memoirs: 'There was one quite extraordinary evening when we were drinking hot chocolate on the terrace of the café Prévost, near the offices of *Le Matin*. An electric sign on top of the building was giving the progress of the fight between Dempsey and Carpentier in New York. The street corners were black with people. When Carpentier was knocked out men and women burst into tears.'[26]

Unfortunately, Carpentier lost his European title rather feebly to a naturalised Frenchman from Senegal, 'Battling Siki', and, predictably, his once adoring public suddenly rejected and reviled him. Siki was an incredible character in his own right. A mediocre boxer who had benefited from Carpentier's over-confidence, he had been 'discovered' by a rich Dutch woman who had seen him as a boy diving for silver coins thrown into the sea by tourists. She brought him back to Marseille, sent him to a *lycée* and soon after died leaving him a little money which he soon spent. He drifted into the boxing booths around Toulouse and was then conscripted into the French forces when the Great War broke out. After the war he went back to boxing, attracting a good deal of publicity by his bizarre dress and behaviour. He wore a white hat, a white suit and often carried around a white goat in his arms. On one occasion he borrowed three lion cubs and with a friend took them to a café, where he proceeded to order five Pernods, one for each of the young lions and one each for himself and his companion. He even kept a full-grown lion in his flat in Montrouge until he was forced to sell it by the other residents. Sadly, 'Battling Siki' quickly went the way of so many other ill-educated fighters. He spent money like water, soon lost his fitness and surrendered his title. He got mixed up with organised crime and was mysteriously murdered in New York. The regulated violence of the ring became too closely involved with the calculated and vicious activities of the underworld during the inter-war years and began to attract adverse publicity.[27]

Nevertheless, although France failed to produce another boxer of the calibre of Carpentier during the inter-war years, boxing remained fairly popular as a spectator sport. It was not until the late thirties that the public found a new fighting idol, Marcel Cerdan, the son of a French tripe-seller from Casablanca. By 1939 Cerdan, a slightly diffident individual who was also a good footballer, had won all twenty-three of his professional fights. He had several big matches during the Vichy period, culminating in a defence of the European middleweight title in 1946 which drew receipts of four million old francs. His good manners, gentleness and, above all, his well-publicised relationship with Édith Piaf made him a legend. He died tragically in an air crash while the affair was still going on. With Piaf's recording of *Hymne à l'Amour*, a love song in his memory, he became a part of popular mythology during the post-war years. Cerdan's mixture of sentiment and aggression appealed to the feelings of a new public, a public still deeply fascinated by the spectacle of human violence but which had begun to demand that boxers behave like full human beings. Their blows were henceforth to be softened by the display of a certain sensitivity, even sentimentality, out of the ring.

CONCLUSION

Although it is clearly naïve to assume that codification and the imposition of ideals of skill and fair play had effectively pacified sport, it is equally simplistic to assume that sport was isolated from the conflicting currents of opinion working against the open and explicit celebration of violence. The overall picture is an intriguing patchwork of continuity and change. Concentrating on the first of the three forms of violence in sport isolated here, the most obvious example of pacification is the disappearance of really brutal sports like bull-baiting and dog-fighting. Bullfighting and cockfighting clearly provide an important link with the past, but even they had to tolerate official interference designed to limit the degree of violence involved. Moreover, both of these sports have been fairly effectively confined to their regional strongholds. This mixture of reform and continuity is typical of the ambiguous attitude to traditional animal sports which still survives in France. Take the case of field sports, which were examined in depth in an earlier chapter. The old hunting instincts survive but huntsmen themselves appear to have become a good deal more self-conscious about admitting to deriving pleasure from the act of killing itself. Sportsmen no longer talk freely about their feelings, and yet a good many would probably still silently agree with Maupassant's huntsman who confessed, 'I passionately love to hunt; the bleeding creature, the pure blood on its feathers, on my hands, moves me so much that I feel momentarily weak'. Perhaps the real difference between the nineteenth-century lover of animal sports and his twentieth-century counterpart lies in the frankness of the former when set against the self-consciousness of the latter. Even many *aficionados* now feel the need to justify their obsession primarily in terms of maintaining local traditions and attracting tourism.[28]

Looking next at the hooligan or rowdy element, a similar mingling of innovation and survival emerges. Obviously, a game like football became less violent than it had been. Judging by the comments of contemporaries it is hard to imagine how any ball game could have been more savage than *soule*. And yet, as we saw, the ostensible pursuit of skill and strategy in the new forms of football clearly failed to suppress fighting and group aggression on the field and off. Nor was this violence haphazard. As in traditional football, violent behaviour was part of the real atmosphere of the modern game. Despite the alarmist attitude of some contemporary 'experts', it seems probable that in the course of the twentieth century the overall level of rowdyism has declined as new generations have progressively lost touch with older traditions. Sometimes rioting was the result of fraudulent claims by promoters, but more often these seem to have served as irritants which brought into play half-forgotten habits of turbulent revelry. Again, most spectators are probably more self-conscious about this sort of thing than they used to be. Psychologists now diagnose such playful aggression in adults as 'behavioural regression'. Only those too young to take offence remain effectively isolated from public disapproval. Twentieth-century adolescents still fight and chant at football matches, though less violently than their forebears, and the young 'hooligans' of this century seem almost as unconcerned about

their behaviour as the *compagnons* were about theirs. In each case
the implicit assumption behind their allegedly 'meaningless'
misconduct remains the same. A piece of graffiti found recently
on the wall of a London football ground puts their case perfectly:
'A little bit of violence never did anyone any harm.'[29]

When we come to look closely at changes in the pattern of
human combativity, the picture is again more complex than it
might appear. Violent human combat remained popular,
though it became steadily less dangerous and better controlled.
'Boxing rules function to depersonalise conflict and maintain
ultimate amity between contestants', comments an expert on
male behaviour, though he is quick to point out that as a
professional sport boxing still remains pretty tough: 'The
element of sanctioned brutality is increased in professional
boxing where smaller gloves are worn which . . . increases the
possibility of one inflicting on another the minor brain con-
cussion called a knock-out.' In practice, this restricted diet of
violence is accepted by most and enjoyed by many in France as
it is in Britain or America. Wrestling continues to attract a large
following even though most of the crowd are aware that a good
deal of the suffering is simulated. In fact, it is for this very reason
that the sport is still acceptable in the later twentieth century.
The regulations of the boxing ring and the showmanship of the
wrestling business permit the modern spectator to enjoy the
experience of violence whilst keeping the reality of it at a safe
distance.[30]

At present there is no overall consensus amongst historians
about the development of violence in modern society. Most of
the received ideas about violence often turn out to be half-truths
and are sometimes quite false. For example, a careful statistical
study of violent crime in France and Germany between 1830 and
1914 dismisses the common view that life in the new cities was
more violent than it was in the countryside; 'in the long run', the
author concludes, 'traditions of violence appear to have been a
more important determinant than the degree of urbanism'. The
same was broadly true of sport. The urban centres attracted the
big boxing matches and the rowdy finals of rugby or football
championships, but it was in the industrial villages of the Nord
and the small bourgs of the Midi that bullfighting and cockfighting found their staunchest support. Similarly, it was in some of
the smaller towns that rugby and football were most disorderly.

But, if there was no clear-cut distinction between the town and the country with regard to the degree of violence in sports, there was nonetheless a marked change in the general degree of violence over time. While it is certainly true to point out that 'attitudes to violence were complex in this period and the common, optimistic view that men were beginning to treat each other more gently, was not entirely accurate', it remains the case that brutal sports did become less brutal and that stricter controls were placed on the right of one individual to destroy another in human combat. Even hooliganism, the most resilient of the elements of violence isolated here, had become rather half-hearted and less explicit than before. Despite important survivals, sport in the mid-twentieth century was less violent than it had been a hundred years earlier.[31]

8 Sport and Sociability

For a good many 'sportsmen' physical exertion was manifestly less important than the social advantages conferred by sport. Perusing the statutes of a wide range of clubs, it is evident from the declared objectives of numerous sporting bodies, as well as from the way in which members spent their time and money, that eating, drinking and the art of conversation were integral aspects of the sporting life. For some, especially the older members, such social possibilities might well provide the prime reason for joining a club or for staying on as a member after the desire or the ability to engage in strenuous physical exercise had long passed. In the privacy of their clubs, which often met in the back room of a local café, men sought to cultivate the timeless art of conviviality and reaffirm the bonds of masculine society. Even the younger and fitter men were often as anxious to make use of sport in the cause of friendship as they were to build up their muscles or to win the next match. For the young and old alike, going to 'the club' – be it a choral society, a political organisation, a trade union or a rugby, cycling or hunting club – could offer a new and valuable form of male association. The rise of the sports club must be located in the wider context of the collapse of traditional culture and the emergence of new forms of social life. In other words, modern sport has an important place in the intricate history of sociability which historians of nineteenth-century France have begun to piece together in the last decade. Before examining the ways in which modern sport fulfilled sociable functions, therefore, we must give an analytical outline of the nature and history of sociability itself.

Sociability may be defined in terms of the aptitude of individuals within a community to form and sustain social groups primarily devoted to companionship and conviviality outside of the framework of the family. A good deal of research has been done on the tendency of mediterranean France, notably Provence, to cultivate a wide range of sociable institutions through which the population of the small wine-growing country towns, or *bourgs*, conducted their public life. *Sociabilité* has come to be regarded as a meridional characteristic, which has helped mould the radical-democratic consciousness of the south. In the course of the careful investigation of this phenomenon in Provence, pioneered by Maurice Agulhon, an important new area of social and historical research has emerged which is of relevance to the whole of France and, indeed, to western society in general. Sociability has a major bearing on the history of all types of private association (including sports clubs) in the nineteenth and twentieth centuries. In effect, an approach of this kind offers a new ethnographical perspective on the evolution of a wide range of modern specialist voluntary associations formerly considered only in terms of their official policy and function. Put more simply, this means that we may have taken the declared objectives of many professional bodies or private organisations too literally. This is exactly what emerged when we looked closely at the organisation of gymnastic clubs in an earlier chapter. The propaganda put out by the governing body had obscured the social functions of the sport at the grass-roots. The old traditions of the village militia found new expression in gymnastic activity. Whether private associations were formed to promote sport or political or occupational solidarity, their day-to-day life usually laid as much emphasis on eating, drinking and conversation as on the ostensible aims of the club. In some cases eating actually became the official *raison d'être*, and business or politics officially took second place to sociability and the joys of the table.[1]

The nineteenth century saw the emergence and diffusion of a wide variety of clubs (referred to as *sociétés*, *cercles*, or *chambrées*, depending on the region and the social class involved). Clubs, in the general sense of formally constituted groups of free individuals meeting regularly for the furtherance of common interests, are an essentially modern phenomenon. Sociability has its phases; it has its own history wherein we can trace through time the various ways that men have found to fulfil their need to enjoy each other's company. Restricting ourselves to the case of Provence for the moment, there appear to have been several general stages in the development of sociability. Until the later eighteenth century social life was regulated by distinctions based on the traditional separation of social orders. The nobility still exchanged visits or met in the *salon* of an important host or hostess who invited suitable guests. Such gatherings were typical of the cultured world of the Enlightenment. The Third Estate, largely excluded from such élite gatherings, pursued a social life as rich and varied as the diverse components of that vast group itself. Artisans met in guilds to celebrate the feast of their patron saints; those in smaller towns or villages joined the *guet*, or local militia, which had ceased to have any real military significance and existed primarily to run the annual festivities and provide an outlet for the horseplay of the young. Similar in function, though quite separate in principle, were the *confréries de pénitents*; these small groups had responsibility for looking after the church, but seemed to spend most of their time planning parades or holding banquets. Under the supervision of a captain of youth annually elected by the village bachelors, these groups would collect money for feasts, organise courtship and arrange dances. Sport played an integral part in these festivities. Competition was fierce and great honour was attached to the winning of one of the traditional prizes (called 'joyes') – 'silk scarves, bridles or harnesses for the winners of the horse or mule races, and sickles, ropes, or tools . . . for the winners of the jumping, greasy pole, or singing contests'.[2]

Although the activities associated with these bodies have continued to exist in a modified form, the old militia and groups of penitents themselves gave way during the first half of the nineteenth century to new social institutions. Just as the upperclass *salon* was replaced by the carefully regulated private bourgeois club from which women were excluded (the *cercle*), so on the popular level there was also an increasing formalisation of social life along the lines of sexually segregated clubs. In the 1830s and 1840s Agulhon has observed 'a huge increase in popular sociability' measured in terms of the number of new associations that were founded specifically for sociable purposes. A police report on the department of the Var listed 707 clubs or *chambrées*, 657 of which served drink, in the year 1836. The old religious groupings had been secularised and transformed into private clubs meeting in hired rooms and supplying drink, cards and conversation for the twenty or so men comprising the average membership. In similar fashion to the *cercle*, women were rigorously excluded from the *chambrées*; so too were outsiders. One of the favourite activities of the *chambrée* was to plan a shooting trip into the mountains and then hold a feast with the game that they brought back. Though private, these clubs played an active part in the public revels of the community, with the village youth, organised in their own *chambrées*, still taking the lead. The *chambrée* seems to have provided a half-way house between the world of traditional social life, which involved the entire village in one way or another, and the modern pattern of private amusement based on individual preference. In his *chambrée* a man could enjoy the closed society of his male friends and neighbours without fear of intrusion whilst at the same time benefiting from the superior resources and comforts offered by a permanent club freed from customary religious duties or restrictions.[3]

By the end of the nineteenth century the *chambrée* in its turn was going into decline. A recent study of socialism in Provence points out that between 1850 and 1880 increased mobility and the drift of the young to the towns, together with the emergence of sharper political antagonisms, worked against the solidarity of the neighbourhood group and therefore against the *chambrée*. In Provence, as in those parts of the centre and the south-west of France studied by Eugen Weber, the forces of modernisation were eroding customary pursuits. 'Despite evidence of a considerable element of traditional activity still informing local pastimes and leisure, the old festivals were in decline at this time . . . in the Var as elsewhere, the patronal, religious and corporate holidays of the last decades of the century were fewer in number, poorly attended and lacking in spirit.' In all but the most remote communities the formerly ubiquitous features of village life – the carnivals and neighbourly evening gatherings or *veillées* – were dying out. 'Communal and historic feasts declined to extinction; and once public celebrations became increasingly private.' More individualistic forms of organisation arose to replace the ailing social institutions of the village or the *quartier*. In Provence the *chambrées* of the *bourg* increasingly became identified with different political groupings, and in the 1880s they often turned themselves into more specialised *cercles des travailleurs* or *sociétés républicaines*, where officials were elected, minutes kept and speakers invited. Social life was becoming more compartmentalised, more open to outsiders and increasingly centered on the café rather than the *chambrée*.[4]

A broadly similar process of change was at work in the major urban centres. Traditionally, in the city sociability had been determined by close neighbours or by the guild, and often the two influences were combined because of the tendency of members of certain trades to live and work in the same streets. The decline of the guild system obviously dealt a serious blow to urban social life. Philosophers and sociologists like Durkheim regretted the disappearance of trade associations where men had gathered together 'principally for the pleasure of living together, for finding outside of oneself distractions from fatigue and boredom, to create an intimacy less restrained than the family and less extensive than the city'. Comte had earlier added his voice to the chorus of concern to insist that 'ritual and feasts were things men could not do without and [he] proposed elaborate institutions to provide them'. Historians also noted the waning of traditional sociability; this theme became something of an obsession with Michelet, who complained about the unsociability of the later nineteenth century and called for a return to a warm, gregarious and anti-individualistic society based on the spirit of *amitié*. Georges Duveau, in his classic history of the social life of workers under the Second Empire, also felt that 'popular festivity no longer had the abandoned and assertive air of the earlier part of the century'.[5]

In the larger cities established patterns of festivity and amusement were beginning to give way under the impact of economic disruption, immigration and mass politics. In Paris, for example, the famous Shrovetide Carnival, which had formerly been a flamboyant, uproarious affair with men dressing as women and enormous amounts of food and drink on offer, was cleaned up and infused with patriotic fervour. Huge floats proclaiming the virtues of good citizenship and advertising new consumer goods replaced the spontaneous frenzy of the old street parades, which had usually involved the daubing of passers-by, preferably well-to-do women, with a substance looking like excrement (normally mustard or melted chocolate). During the later nineteenth century the authorities increasingly condemned such practices in the name of decency and good order. The crowds were no longer asked to participate in Carnival and were provided with an edifying spectacle instead. The festival queen elected by the municipality was now a seemly and virtuous daughter of the Republic who bore little or no resemblance to the libidinous, foul-mouthed washerwomen who had formerly presided over the excesses of Carnival. Modern public festivals to celebrate Republican values tended to degenerate into commercial-cum-chauvinist parades where 'Liberty was a lifeless abstraction piously invoked in speeches' and little remained of the old sociability of the street, the *quartier* and the city.[6]

So much for a short history of sociability. Such changes may at first appear to have little connection with the rise of modern sport, and it is certainly the case that the two phenomena have never before been properly related. Both, however, are part and parcel of the rise of mass culture. On occasions social commentators have observed that sports clubs along with other modern leisure institutions fulfil age-old social functions, or that the only contemporary equivalent to the tumultuous festivals of traditional urban life is mass spectator sport. Odd hints have been thrown out, but there has been no explicit investigation of these important lines of continuity. Yet the modernisation of physical culture and the triumph of the café as 'the preferred context' for social life offers an excellent illustration of the close relationship of sport and sociability in this century.

The back room of the local café became the social centre for the thousands of clubs formed in France around the late nineteenth and early twentieth centuries. Specialisation and the collapse of the old leisure pursuits did not mean that sociability was dead but only that it was taking new forms. Changes in the laws restricting the licensing of drinking places, falling prices of alcohol and, most importantly, the consequences of the changes in sociability outlined above combined to give a huge boost to social drinking in the *belle époque*. 'Not counting the city of Paris, there were almost 357,000 *débits de boissons* in France in 1880; by 1900 the figure was well over 435,000. At the turn of the century France had by far the most drinking places of any country in the world.' A fair number of these cafés were used by sportsmen as places in which to hold meetings and to celebrate or drown their sorrows after a game. To this day there is a *Café des Sports* in almost every small town, and the larger ones are still full of bars decorated with the colours, trophies and photographs of teams that patronise the establishment.[7]

Some early temperance enthusiasts had seen the practice of sport as a potential antidote to alcoholism, but they soon indignantly noted that games appeared to stimulate rather than discourage the consumption of drink. Advertisements often explicitly linked drinking with games by showing sporting stars consuming a particular apéritif or endorsing the virtues of a certain type of beer. So important was the custom provided by thirsty sportsmen that café-owners frequently became honorary members of a number of different clubs in order to increase their custom. The Cyclo-Club du XXe Siècle, for example, had sixty active members and 'a dozen honorary ones, all of whom were café-owners or innkeepers in the vicinity of Lyon'. When it came to sport, French café-owners had a good deal in common with the English publicans of the mid-nineteenth century who, when they were forbidden to hold brutal sports, 'showed their customary resilience in the face of social change: they organised or subsidised spectator sports, and annexed cricket grounds or sports clubs to their premises'.[8]

For café-owners the French equivalent of village cricket is a game of *boule* or *jeu provençale*. It is hardly a coincidence that the various modern forms of the game have developed at roughly the same pace as the triumph of the new commercial drinking outlet. Like the café, the game of *boule* underwent a marked transformation from the later nineteenth century onwards. It was at this time that the rules were standardised and the first proper associations formed. Tradition has it that *pétanque*, a variant requiring no special pitch and allegedly deriving its name from the pigeon-toed stance of the players (*pieds tanqués*), was first played in Provence around 1910. Both *pétanque* and *jeu provençale*, which requires a smooth pitch and involves throwing the *boule* considerable distances, were formalised around the First World War, and in 1922 a Fédération Nationale de Boulistes was formed. What had formerly been a casual game soon became an organised sport, with local, regional and national competitions involving up to 150,000 licensed players by the mid-thirties. In parts of the north and west of France skittles was similarly transformed at about the same time. Traditionally, there had been an enormous variety of skittle games in different parts of France. At Revin in the Ardennes games were still organised by the captains of youth as part of the annual celebrations until the early twentieth century. In the villages of the Ariège 'the game of skittles was the only form of Sunday amusement' before the First World War. *Quilles à neuf*, or ninepins, was especially popular in the south-west, where a large tournament was sponsored by the municipality of Dax in 1898. Thereafter, annual competitions attracted players from all over the south-west. In the inter-war period a commercial traveller from Pau started a national competition with large prizes donated by the town-council and by the *Petite Gironde*, which gave extensive publicity to the new sport.[9]

Both *boule* and *quilles* are essentially sociable, café-based activities. In fact, organising local matches is often an important task of a café-owner, who stands to make considerable sums from the drinking associated with the game. In Peyranne, the village in the Vaucluse studied in the early 1950s by Laurence Wylie, men still congregated in the café on Saturday night to play *boule* in the square outside, which the *cafetier* would illuminate at his own expense. Play would start about ten o'clock in the evening and often go on until the early hours, with groups of players breaking off regularly to consume the round of drinks which whoever lost a game had to buy. The game was woven into the wider pattern of male sociability at the heart of which lay the café. The game was taken seriously and competition was fierce but this did not detract from the sociable side of the sport which, as Wylie observed, was of crucial importance to all concerned: 'the wit, the sarcasm, the insults, the oaths, the logic, the experimental demonstration, and the ability to dramatise a situation give the game its essential interest. Spectators will ignore a game played by men who are physically skilled but who are unable to dramatise their game, and they will gather round a game played by men who do not play very well but who are witty, dramatic, shrewd in their ability to outsmart their opponents'. The area outside the café where the game is played becomes an extension of the café itself, with players and spectators drifting in and out discussing the pros and cons of a particular shot. Should a player 'fire' his *boule* (*tirer*) hoping to knock those of the rival team out of the way, or should he try to roll it up close to the jack (*pointer*) by taking full advantage of the intervening humps and hollows? Important shots might be discussed in this fashion for a quarter of an hour or so. Spectators join in and the opposition try to play off rivalries and grievances in the other team. In the end the crucial *boule* is thrown and the crowd troop back indoors to discuss the outcome and drink *pastis*.[10]

Café-centred games like *boule* are, of course, classic examples of activities in which sociability plays an integral part. Is it then legitimate to suggest that the large number of private clubs set up to promote other types of sport during the Third Republic also had a significant role in the general re-modelling of social life that was taking place? As a leading authority on male behaviour observed, '. . . sport provides an opportunity in countless cultures for the weaving of and participation in the web of male affiliation'. Sports clubs not only offered men enjoyable forms of exertion and emulation through which they could define and develop the qualities of masculinity they admired, they also provided, in the club bar, a new forum where males could meet for comradeship, conversation and revelry amongst their own sex. Sport may well have been a very important channel through which male friendships were forged and maintained at a time when traditional forms of sociability were in serious decline. The contention here is not that sport was purely a social institution but only that we should take more seriously the term 'amical' which so many clubs inserted into their statutes. Displays of physical prowess and group loyalty on the field were complemented by the drinking, story-telling, singing and gambling that took place in the club-house or café afterwards. Some joined clubs primarily for the social opportunities they offered, for what sociologists might call 'the rituals of male bonding'. Being 'a sport' was never simply a bodily inclination; a 'sport' enjoyed a joke, bought 'his round' and participated to the full in the friendly *badinage* of male society.[11]

Field sports have traditionally provided a useful means of creating strong ties of personal affection and loyalty amongst men. In France the frequent use of the term *ami de chasse* testifies to the continued importance attached to friendship in field sports. The very idea of hunting conjured up images of close-knit male groups with almost tribal loyalties. Long after the need to hunt had passed and even in the knowledge that game was very scarce, a large number of men were still prepared to put themselves to considerable inconvenience and no little expense in order to enjoy the intense sensation of the kill and the comradeship that surrounded it. Some affluent urban sportsman loved nothing more than to forgo the sophistication of the capital for a few days to 'go back to nature', living the 'simple life' on the land with a few good friends. 'When we get together', remarks a Norman gentleman in one of Maupassant's stories, 'we talk in patois, we live think and act as Normans, real earthy Normans more like peasants than our own farmers.' Rituals of sporting hospitality played a central role in the life of the upper-class male, who frequently attached great importance to feeling at one with his peers. Shooting parties of 'gens de bon ton' were less solemn, less stiff affairs than they were made out to be.[12]

Great importance was attached to the taking of meals in common. In this sense field sports fitted into the cult of gastronomy, which became an elaborate form of bourgeois culture during the nineteenth century. Those misguided few who joined shooting clubs or went hunting in an effort to work off the effects of over-eating were in for a shock; as much, perhaps more, appears to have been consumed by sportsmen during their play as in the course of business lunches. Long alfresco meals were popular and provided a favourite theme for cartoonists, who loved to depict the somnolent *partie de chasse* stretched out amidst open picnic baskets and empty bottles of wine surrounded by their bemused and restive hounds. Long lunches, however, were nothing in comparison to the long dinners which were held after the day's sport. Books of sporting memoirs abound with tales of eating and drinking late into the night. A good conversationalist was indispensable on such occasions. Some sportsmen were invited to hunt or shoot solely for their gifts as raconteurs. Story-telling at dinner was a cherished male ritual. Hunting anecdotes are legion, many of them tall stories polished and exaggerated over generations, part of an oral tradition of private entertainment justly celebrated by short story writers like Maupassant. 'It was the end of dinner on the first day of the hunting season . . . ' begins one tale, while in another a crippled old gentleman invites a party of sportsmen to his estate so that he can sit 'at the table for three hours at a time telling hunting stories'.[13]

Not much was shot during shooting parties of this kind but there was constant chatter amongst the sportsmen, swearing when they missed a shot, making bets to see who would shoot the next piece, indulging in boasts and counter-boasts, jibes and ripostes punctuated by gales of laughter and the frantic barking of untrained dogs. All this was too much for the visiting English sportsman more accustomed to the relatively discreet behaviour of gentry shooting parties. 'Nature has not been bountiful to our vivacious neighbours in sporting genius', remarked one sardonic British observer; the Frenchman was 'all noise and banter, talking of what he has done or will do, now engaging in some hoarse refrain . . . their shouting at the dogs is a continued annoyance, enough to rouse the game even out of the game bag.' What does not seem to have occurred to this polite English visitor was that sociability itself was probably the primary objective. The shooting of game in quantity certainly cannot have been the main purpose of such gatherings. As the same author notes of shooting on common land, the sporting vocabulary of those taking part in itself reflected the prevailing shortage of game: 'rendered into plain words *beaucoup* means one, a *masse* means two and the superlative *une confusion* means three'. The intense resentment of the shooting permit harboured by the peasantry may have stemmed as much from a sense of exclusion from an enjoyable social experience as from dislike of the urban bourgeoisie or a desire to supplement the family diet.[14]

Friendship had a rather different but no less important place in the officially constituted, private *société de chasse*. The lengthy traditional rituals were perforce cut short, and sociability became subject to the dictates of the train timetable more than before; sportsmen probably became more status-conscious and some certainly used the sport as a form of social and professional advancement; but the importance of sociability in itself was not diminished. Perhaps sporting friendships became less free or spontaneous but there is little serious evidence to suggest that field sports ceased to be the warm, gregarious occasions they always had been. If anything, it might be argued that these sports became rather more sociable as time passed with the influx of a large number of sportsmen more concerned with the social advantages conferred by arms than the actual bearing of them. In fact, all of the new clubs which sprang up at the end of the nineteenth century devoted to modern sports were quick to develop as social institutions. The reorganisation of leisure on a private basis led to a change but not to a decline in the role of sociability as an element in recreation.

La chasse clearly had an important place in the *mores* of the upper-class male, but the social appeal of the sport obviously spread beyond this privileged group. As we saw in our detailed study of field sports, shooting was a more democratic activity in France than in England. Although the urban bourgeoisie were the most prominent social group involved, the sport was beginning to be enjoyed by a growing number of shopkeepers, office-workers and skilled craftsmen, and by the more affluent members of village society. To such people shooting offered not only a good country walk and fresh air, but also the prospect of periodic bouts of social indulgence. In a letter to the *Moniteur de la Côte d'Or* setting out his reasons for refusing to let communal land to an upper-middle-class shooting club, the mayor of a small Burgundian village claimed that such a policy would be socially undesirable, as shooting parties on communal land were one of the most important means by which the local people kept in touch with 'les petits bourgeois du canton'.[15]

A look at some of the shooting clubs set up in the department of the Gard in the later nineteenth century confirms this impression. The Cercle de Saint Hubert at Sauve was composed of 'a small group of friends and sportsmen' meeting on the first and second floors of a local café – mostly minor professional people, shopkeepers and small landowners. Three groups of three brothers made up almost a third of the entire membership. These sportsmen all knew each other well either as kin or as close neighbours. In such cases it is pointless to try to distinguish the social from the sporting aspects of the club; both formed part of a wider masculine culture which embraced hunting, drinking and even dancing. Consider the example of the Cercle Agricole at Saint-Gilles, whose members returned from a shooting trip one evening singing, shouting and dancing the *farandole*; they roamed in and out of several cafés, followed by a piper and shouting 'Long live the King' when they met a Republican. The political bias of these sportsmen – if indeed they were genuine royalists – was probably less important than the drunken jollity of the occasion. Attending a meeting of the commune's shooting club in the village of Peyranne over half a century later, Laurence Wylie noted how quickly specifically sporting questions were submerged in a torrent of argument and abuse which was later smoothed out in the course of a few drinks in the café. The club members and the other clientele all laughed heartily when a report appeared in the Vaucluse section of a Marseille newspaper to the effect that the meeting had been conducted 'in an atmosphere of complete calm and courtesy'.[16]

There were other sports, of course, in which sociability – rowdy or otherwise – played a prominent part. Cycling clubs, with their ambiguous mingling of competitive exercise and casual recreation, were important in this respect. By and large these clubs were composed of men in their twenties and thirties who sought pleasant social intercourse with their fellows, suitably lubricated by regular bouts of eating, drinking and entertainment. A glance at the annual calendar of events of an ordinary club will confirm these basic social priorities. The Véloce Club Barentinois, founded in 1904 in a small industrial town of 6000 inhabitants near Rouen, was probably fairly typical. The Barentin club had its familiar tricolour sash worn by the club champion and boasted a local *notable* as its honorary president. In fact, the only peculiarity of the club is the existence of an unusually detailed account of its social activities in the form of a pamphlet published by one of the founder members on the occasion of its half centenary. We know, for instance, that prospective members were required to produce 'serious references' from two existing members; we know also that the club set considerable store by its friendly relations with the local firemen, with whom it shared a grand annual banquet. The club went to great pains to prevent new members from joining just in order to enjoy this occasion without having paid the full subscription. The social life of VC Barentinois was synchronised to fit in with other popular celebrations such as Bastille Day, and each Christmas from 1905 to 1939 the club organised a fund-raising concert to which the local factory orphans were admitted free. In such ways were provincial sports clubs integrated into the recreational life of small town society.[17]

Most sports clubs were fond of arranging away games and in some cases there seems little doubt that the prime motive lay in the exchange of hospitality rather than in the improvement of standards of play. Again, it was the cycling clubs which were most notorious for promoting these social contacts. An account of one such trip organised by the Véloce Club de Tours describes how the club resolved to make contact with an old cyclist living in a small town some twenty miles away. Far from organising a race to their distination, most of the members of the club were not prepared to cycle even a part of the distance. Instead, they put their bicycles on the train, alighted near the town and rode the last half-mile or so to the town square. Here they were welcomed in fraternal republican style by the mayor and his assistant, 'the worthy schoolmaster'. A huge lunch for two hundred was arranged and, as if to complete the Clochemerle atmosphere perfectly, the day was brought to a convivial close with the singing of *La vieille cloche de mon village*. This tendency to turn cycling into a predominantly social and gastronomic activity was the source of endless jibes from more serious sportsmen. Some riders, like 'the Pure Pleasure Pedallers' of Lower Normandy, even enforced a speed limit to eradicate competitiveness once and for all.[18]

Often, local celebrations brought together the village band and the sports club in a festival of some kind. A large number of musical societies were formed during the later nineteenth century, when music, like dancing and other forms of traditional recreation, was ceasing to be considered a communal activity integral to the world of work. Musical societies were made up of individuals who liked to make music but who could no longer find a traditional outlet for their enthusiasm, just as sports clubs provided exercise no longer available in other forms. The band, the firemen and the village sports club often came together on public holidays to parade in front of the local populace. But while new musical or sporting societies certainly took a regular part in these small celebrations, in the main they went their own way. The old ties of sociability were not forgotten, they were rather transformed into private relationships based on mutual interests. Just as the mixing and mating of the sexes through dancing ceased to be organised on a communal basis, so sports became increasingly independent of communal life while continuing to fulfil some of the functions associated with them in pre-industrial society.[19]

This continuing male exclusiveness manifests itself clearly in the attitude of sportsmen to sportswomen. Despite the self-evident lack of athleticism involved in the activities of a good many clubs, women continued to be excluded from membership. Wives or girl friends were invited to ladies' nights in the same way that the Masonic lodges would offer token appreciation to the women in the lives of their members by holding a special annual dinner or arranging excursions by rail or short boat trips. But on the level of day-to-day club contact women made very little headway in sport. Even in the cycling clubs devoted to gentle touring, there were rarely more than a handful of women members. Most cycling clubs simply refused to accept women. Perhaps on an individual or family basis the bicycle did help women to realise the ideal of shared recreation which many feminists hoped for, but in general it seems as if the role of the bicycle in the emancipation of women was mainly symbolic. A recent historian of European youth has even gone so far as to suggest that participation in sport specifically ensured 'the separation of boys from the world of women during the critical transition from childhood to adulthood'. Whilst such theoretical notions must remain speculative, there is no doubt that adult men consciously sought to use sport, especially game-shooting, as a means of escaping the suffocating tedium of the bourgeois household, where they were sometimes ill at ease, feeling unable to talk freely or to have a few drinks without setting a bad example to their children or scandalising their respectable wives. 'If you don't hunt, what on earth do you do with your Sundays?' was apparently a common conversational gambit in male society.[20]

On the institutional level, women made little impact on sport partly because men did not wish them to. As late as the 1930s serious sportswomen were few and far between. Even when they had ceased to promote vigorous physical exercise, sports clubs remained important places where men met together as men. Over a period of forty years or so it seems that, in many clubs, a process of gradual ossification took place. Unless a club took steps to maintain a steady supply of keen young recruits there was an inevitable tendency for it to degenerate into a social rather than a sporting institution. This criticism was made of the famous Racing Club in the 1920s, and there are plenty of other instances of schisms between active elements and non-active ones. The famous rugby club L'Aviron Bayonnais was formed in the 1890s by keen young oarsmen who found that their previous club had become the haunt of older men who wanted to spend most of their time organising musical soirées or gently drifting down the river.[21]

Clubs such as these evolved into gerontocracies ruled by immovable officials who tended to regard the club almost as if it were their own property. In some cases it actually was. Men stayed on long after they had any active interest in sport purely to enjoy the companionship of their ageing comrades. This development is confirmed by an analysis of twenty-two clubs receiving a subsidy from the city of Paris in 1922. Of those examined, eight had been founded before 1900. These had an average membership of 413 but of this number only 90 were present for municipal inspection. The clubs founded after 1900 had a smaller average membership (152) but a participation ratio almost three times that of the older clubs. In the case of the Barentin club discussed earlier, a president, who had first taken office in 1927, was re-elected in 1954. The Union Cycliste d'Angers, founded in 1885, still had the same treasurer over forty years later. The club captain and secretary were mere youngsters by comparison; they had only held their offices for twenty-five years apiece.[22]

The gymnastic and shooting clubs provide the most dramatic illustration of the tendency for clubs to become dominated by non-active elements. Of the sixty clubs in the Association de la Seine in 1888, each had an average of thirty-three active members and about forty non-active ones. Moreover, these averages concealed wide variations, and certain clubs were heavily dominated by social members. L'Ancienne Lorraine, for example, one of the oldest established clubs in Paris, had only 91 active members out of a total membership of 479. The accounts of several clubs reveal that more was spent on the provision of social facilities and entertainment than on gymnastics itself. In 1908 the accounts of La Sentinelle revealed that only 500 francs had been spent on sporting activity and that 1200 francs went towards the cost of receptions and other social functions to mark the twenty-fifth anniversary of the club. Commenting on a request for a subsidy for La Libérale, a councillor in Paris pointed out that 'the sums spent on gymnastics are insignificant . . . the chief expenses are those concerned with travelling to competitions, holding dances, feasts and concerts'.[23]

Besides acting as drinking clubs, sports organisations also performed other functions. Agulhon has noted 'the plasticity' of the club as a social institution with roles which varied according to the traditions of the particular activity undertaken and the age and class of those attracted to membership. Many a sports club also doubled as an informal youth club. After all, the young had occupied an extremely important place in earlier forms of festivity. Traditional village life had given those between the age of puberty and marriage a major role in recreation. With the collapse of the formal institutions of juvenile sociability – the captains of youth, the groups of 'penitents' and the militia – sport provided an important element of continuity. This has emerged in the analysis of the suppressed festive element in gymnastics. There can be little doubt that a night at 'the club' provided a marvellous opportunity for a youngster to indulge some of his adolescent high spirits. At a time when the formal institution of 'youth' as a special age-category with its own rights and traditions was everywhere in decline, it seems reasonable to surmise that sports clubs helped young males retain something of their former sense of identity. We have seen that sport offered the young compensatory rituals of violence; perhaps it also provided alternative forms of sociability? Within the team itself there was 'a human society which was far better regulated than the outside world in terms of communal solidarity and friendship'.[24]

The middle-class cycling clubs of the eighties and nineties certainly operated in this fashion by allowing the well brought up boy the chance to let himself go. The atmosphere in these early clubs was probably a good deal more riotous and light-hearted than the brief reports of their proceedings in the press would suggest. Members were frequently still in their teens and the older officials sometimes had difficulty in controlling them. A short play published in the *Almanach de la Vélocipédie Illustrée* for 1884 suggests as much. The play, entitled *Une Séance au Vélo-Club d'Y.Z.*' describes the abortive attempts of the president to call to order the club's twenty members, who are busy playing dominoes or billiards or simply drinking and talking in the back room of a café. Each time the secretary tries to discuss serious business, he is howled down by some and utterly ignored by others. When the president complains about this behaviour, he is abused and ridiculed by the rest. The meeting breaks up in chaos as he walks out in disgust, muttering 'shouting, yelling, roaring and nothing decided: that's our night's work'. How many other instances of similar behaviour there have been must remain a matter of speculation. What is not in doubt is that the Church and the Republican youth clubs consciously sought to use the appeal of sport to the lower-class youth as a means of involving him in the wider society and affiliations of Catholicism or the state – a theme which will be examined in more detail later.[25]

Spectator sports, too, came to have a significant place in the social lives of the young. According to at least one shrewd contemporary, spectator sport was becoming a 'fête facile' in which the young found an alternative to rowdy festivals of the past. At a big football or rugby match the young supporter could lose himself in 'the cheerful mediocrity' of the crowd. Besides providing the opportunity to participate in the playful hooliganism of the terraces, which we have already examined, spectator sport offered the young ready-made allegiances based on a natural sense of territorial loyalty. The noisy group behaviour of the young fans was the closest which modernising communities, especially the larger urban ones, came to re-creating the communal loyalties of the traditional village. As the author of a recent work on the history of festivity points out, 'the balls, the fairs, the carnivals and the Mardi Gras have virtually all disappeared . . . only rugby, football and racing remain . . . the authorities have lost the habit of looking after the amusement of the young'. It was only in those areas where bullrunning survived that youths could still 'blood' themselves in the traditional way by executing dangerous movements in full view of the older members of the community. Elsewhere, young men had to restrict themselves either to excellence in modern sports or to approval of it in others as part of their claim to membership of the male clan.[26]

Sports, therefore, have had a hand in the wider transformation of social life which produced the club-based sociability of the period roughly spanned by the Third Republic. Jean Prévost put it neatly in 1925 when he wrote that 'isolated individuals . . . are guaranteed by their role in the team a sense of forgetfulness . . . the team alone offers security which it reinforces in the solidarity of play'. Turning to the social life of sportsmen off the pitch, he observed that 'the love of food which formerly sprang naturally from exercise, lives on in idleness to cause obesity and illness. We all have seen formerly slim players standing on the touch line who are already the shape of the oval ball and will eventually look like the round one'. Group loyalty and good fun lay at the heart of modern club sport. Those who played together stayed together. From the frolics of youth to the quieter pleasures of old age, sport filled an important role in male culture. Just as other strongly masculine institutions have persisted, so the spread of rugby clubs in the Languedoc or of cycling clubs in the Nord gives an indication of 'how male society has evolved' and helps 'clarify the mechanisms that assure the longevity of this very flexible institution' (the all male group). And yet it would be prudent to end on a note of caution. The modern club is as much a product of a particular epoch as its forerunners were. There are signs that the impact of television, the family car and women's liberation, among other things, are weakening the private male club as a natural unit of sporting and sociable activity. Between 1950 and 1968 the share of café-going in the average leisure budget dropped from 40 per cent to 26·4 per cent, although overall family expenditure on leisure increased by around 250 per cent. Men either cannot or do not want to slip off to the café or the club as often as they used to. The future of the club is in doubt; it remains to be seen whether the male group will cling as tenaciously to its privileges and adjust itself as adeptly in the last quarter of the twentieth century as it did in the first.[27]

9　Sport and Status

What was the role of social class in sport? Did the sociability of the club-house provide an arena free from discrimination where a man could cross the class divide and establish bonds of friendship with fellow sportsmen? Or was it rather the case that good fellowship tended to be confined to those of broadly similar status? Instead of helping to break down class barriers, perhaps sport actually confirmed and added a new subtlety to social divisions. The fact that a great many sportsmen were sensitive to questions of status has already emerged in the preceding case-studies of individual sports. What have not yet been discussed are the general issues of prestige and popularity in sport. What strains were imposed by the rapid democratising of hitherto restricted activities, and how did conflicts arise between the followers of different sports or amongst devotees of the same sport?

The most sensible method of splitting up sporting activity according to social status is to divide sports into two basic categories: élite and popular. This was the common distinction used by contemporaries and still provides a more realistic and flexible framework than arbitrary occupational or ideological categories. Admittedly, by the 1930s it was not uncommon to refer to *sport bourgeois* and *sport travailliste*, but before then the terms had little or no meaning for the majority of sportsmen. Regarding the later nineteenth century, when the modern pattern of physical recreation came into existence, the simple distinction between 'the masses' and 'the classes' provides the best way into what is in fact a complex issue. In essence, there were three kinds of sporting activity: those sports played only by the rich; those played mainly by the poor; and those which began as élite sports – game-shooting, cycling, rugby, even athletics – but which spread rapidly in the late nineteenth and early twentieth centuries. Not surprisingly, it was in the latter category that social conflict was most evident. Where certain games remained the preserve of groups broadly similar in wealth and status there was relatively little friction, for obvious reasons. But where mass production and increased leisure began to permit wider participation, class antagonisms of one kind or another were bound to find their way into sport.

It would be quite misleading to imply that social conflict in leisure was unknown prior to the nineteenth century. This was not so; the notion of a harmonious unquestioned hierarchy is clearly a myth in leisure as in other forms of social life. Class friction normally arose between young peasants and apprentices or clerks in the nearby towns. Here the habitual violence of many traditional sports was tinged with an element of class antagonism. The better-off urban apprentices would organise their own games, often followed by a dance. In Provence this occasionally led to fights between those who danced to the sound of the violin (the town youth) and those who could not afford such luxury and had to make do with the drum (the peasant lads). In other words, it is probably misleading to assume too readily a complete integration of non-noble youth in group amusements before the onset of modern leisure activity. As we saw, the formalisation of traditional sociability in the earlier part of the nineteenth century did bring with it a more pronounced division between bourgeois life and ordinary life. These differences were to become more marked as the nineteenth century progressed, though they have been partly undermined by the insidious influence of mass leisure in the twentieth century.[1]

As a general rule, before the onset of modernisation conflicts between the various social groups were less common than they later became because leisure pursuits were so much more rigidly stratified. Before the Revolution non-nobles were forbidden to fence or to hunt anything other than the smallest of game which the upper classes regarded as pests. There was no question of the lower classes joining in the costly organised sports like real tennis. Villagers had their traditional games, as we have seen, often involving fighting or brutality to animals. In addition to these activities there were a host of traditional competitive amusements – village sports like sack-races or egg-and-spoon races, climbing the greasy pole or catching the slippery pig, apple-bobbing, wrestling, running and throwing, skittles and quoits. Unlike the English gentry, many of whom seem to have retained a certain fondness for these games until midway through the nineteenth century, the French *notables* rarely consented to become involved in such vulgar goings-on except perhaps in Brittany, where some of the poorer nobles had stayed closer to local tradition than elsewhere. The same was true of dancing. Huge communal dances where partners moved with slow, simple steps were a feature of life in almost all rural communities until the later nineteenth century, but, as with sports, the privileged evolved their own forms of dancing which involved complex movements requiring the services of a dancing master; 'dancing lessons were part of a gentleman's education as much as fencing lessons were'.[2]

Fencing, in fact, provides an excellent point of departure for a social analysis of modern French sport. An entirely noble sport under the Bourbons, it became increasingly the preferred indoor exercise of the upper bourgeoisie in the course of the nineteenth century. There was no question of fencing, in which the French believed themselves to excel, falling into decline during the nineteenth century. There were always a large number of bourgeois aspirants to the art who were prepared to pay considerable sums to get the best instruction available. Although many provincial fencing masters found it hard to make ends meet, the famous Parisian teachers were at a premium and a few were rumoured to make as much as a hundred thousand francs a year. The early years of the Third Republic saw a veritable influx of new recruits to the select fencing clubs. Deputies wanted to learn how to fence so that they would be prepared, if called upon, to fight a duel. Duelling, an under-researched activity, kept an important place in the *mores* of the social and political élite until the inter-war years. The laws of libel made it particularly important for journalists to have some duelling skill, and in effect this meant skill with the *épée*, the light rapier which became the established duelling sword in the nineteenth century. *Le Figaro* set up its own *salle d'armes* in keeping with its reputation as a socially superior newspaper. While young aristocrats performed below, the clerks from the paper could watch and applaud the complex attacks, parries and ripostes.

Skill in fencing was part of the examination for the top military and naval schools as well as for the prestigious Polytechnique. *Lycées* encouraged the practice of fencing in their efforts to instil patriotism, but the top clubs continued to be dominated by the nobility. The Cercle Hoche, founded in 1900 in Paris had the Duc Decazes as its president and was equipped with a luxurious bathroom, a restaurant, a billiard room and a garden. When the members were not engaged in fencing they organised other sporting amusements typical of the gentleman's club. Private prize-fights were laid on, and on one occasion at least a clandestine cockfight was arranged between the president and the Crown Prince of Belgium. In the south the Fédération d'Escrime du Sud-Est was comprised of fifteen clubs, all of which were run by persons described by the authorities as 'distinctly reactionary'.

The nobility and the upper bourgeoisie favoured fencing for their sons instead of shooting, as being more suitable for potential cavalry officers. In fact, Baron de Coubertin, a great enthusiast, spent many years in the vain attempt to get the Olympic Committee to agree to award medals for the sport of fencing on horseback. As late as 1930 a bitter exchange took place in the Chamber of Deputies over a proposal to cut back army expenditure on fencing masters for officer cadets. The old élite of birth and the new Republican governing strata – politicians, lawyers, men of letters, doctors and professors – rallied round to maintain the old traditions. Fencing was ceasing to be an upper-class amusement pure and simple, wrote the author of an article in the *Annuaire des sports* in 1923, although the president of the Fédération Française d'Escrime was a count. Poincaré had made a point of urging middle-class youth to take up the sport which, it was said, was as much a part of a good education as a knowledge of Latin and Greek. Bourgeois infiltration of a formerly noble preserve and the institutionalising of the sport in the élite educational system provide an interesting instance of limited social integration within the ruling classes.[3]

More exclusive still was hunting. Of all the noble sports of the *ancien régime*, hunting remained the least accessible and consequently the most prestigious. Arguably, this is still the case. The *chasse à courre* required not only the resources to buy and maintain several good hunting horses, it also called for equestrian skills which could only be acquired by careful training, preferably in childhood. As we saw in the earlier case-study of the sport, there were invariably more wealthy aspirants than there were places in good packs. Nobles were very reluctant to sacrifice control of their local hunt, even if family funds were low and a valuable saving could be made. Hunting was simply part of the noble style of life, a stately aristocratic progress through 'their' forests, a visible reminder to the peasants of the superior status that even the detested democracy of the Republic could not expunge.

The glittering world of the great hunts drew the rich like bees around a honeypot. An illuminating example of the appeal of the sport is provided by the marked interest shown in the office of *lieutenant de la louveterie*, a master of hounds appointed to each area by the government to keep down the number of wolves. While this may have been an important task under the Bourbons, by the later nineteenth century the office was of purely honorific value. Outside of the Dordogne and the wildest parts of Brittany there were no wolves at all, and yet the competition for the title remained keen. Under the Third Republic the local nobility often feigned indifference to the appointee, who was frequently a bourgeois supporter of very moderate Republicanism. Occasionally these appointments became a pure farce; the job was doled out to quite unsuitable persons purely to gratify their desire for social prestige. In the Pas-de-Calais the local forest inspector complained bitterly to the prefect of 'the systematic inertia of Monsieur Leroy', the *lieutenant de la louveterie*, in the matter of pest control. Leroy, the director of a large coal-exporting firm in Calais, had long since ceased to chase foxes or take the duties of the post at all seriously. He simply wanted a title.[4]

On the whole, however, hunting remained too difficult and too expensive to suffer seriously from the problem of large-scale bourgeois infiltration. Of course, the same constraints did not apply to shooting. As we saw earlier, there was an enormous increase in the number of middle-class men taking up shooting during the second half of the nineteenth century. Game-shooting offered the aspiring young businessman the chance to make the acquaintance of older men in more established positions. Snobbery was an integral part of sport at this level. The practice of game-shooting in a good club was quite simply a mark of social distinction, one of the subtle ways in which status was defined and consolidated. Dressed in shooting gear, armed and ready, the sportsman could 'lift up his head and set himself apart from passers-by'; his appearance and his right to bear arms were the outward signs of 'the gulf separating the sportsman from the mass of humanity'. Shooting carried with it an aura of danger and lent a touch of heroism to the safe existence of the merchant or the solicitor. The townsman could play the country squire for a few hours, patronising the rustics and indulging in a little conspicuous consumption to impress his neighbours. Earlier in the century *nouveaux-riches* cockneys had made similar social capital from shooting by choosing 'the most circuitous way out of town, passing through a long train of populous thoroughfares *en route* for the field'.[5]

The upper classes resented the way that the sport was being socially devalued by the bourgeoisie who 'invaded their land' by train and 'massacred their game' with expensive modern guns. The development of shooting clubs enabled middle-class men to afford to shoot game which was beyond the means of the lesser nobility. Many would no doubt have agreed with an aristocratic critic who felt that the shareholders in such clubs were like those young men who were too poor or too calculating to take a mistress of their own, and therefore made arrangements to share the costs amongst others in need of her services. Game-shooting came to be considered somewhat *déclassé* for the nobility, some of whom thought that the term 'chasseur' should not be accorded to 'this bunch of smartly dressed gents who spend their Sundays sitting on comfortable little stools waiting for game to be driven in front of the guns'. The Prince de Monaco pressed home this attack on the practice of *battue* shooting, and, by implication, on the new breed of sportsman, with an article in *Le Figaro* in 1906, which he followed up with a more detailed critique in the specialist press describing the *battue* as 'a degenerate custom, the product of riches and snobbery'. Jean Renoir made a similar point in the famous shooting scene from his film *La Règle du jeu*.[6]

Bickering between the middle and upper classes declined in the inter-war years. The reason for this new understanding lay in the massive increase in the numbers of those involved in the sport. Familiarity with firearms learned in the trenches, the collapse in the real cost of the permit through inflation, the increase in mobility and more adventurous attitudes to leisure on the part of the urban *petite bourgeoisie* all contributed to a tripling in the number of permit-holders between the outbreak of the First World War and the early 1930s. Everyone agreed, even the poorer sportsman, that there were too many guns after too little game. But this is where agreement stopped. The rich demanded that the price of the permit be raised substantially; nobles and bourgeois ceased to feud and joined forces in the face of a common threat from the masses. Costly clubs and associations were formed to fence off land and to see that it was properly guarded. The right to guard private sporting land became a key issue between those with substantial landed interests and those who demanded 'free shooting everywhere for everyone'; the former denounced the latter as 'bolshevik-tainted demagogues', while neo-Jacobins on the Left accused the rich of attacking the free-born Frenchman's right to exercise arms. Sporting issues were inevitably drawn into the wider political arena as the challenge from below reached its climax in the mid-thirties. The world of game-shooting was most sharply divided at the point when it appeared to have become most democratic.[7]

Horse-racing was another sport which attracted both the rich and famous and the lower classes. But there were important differences. Racing was a spectacle rather than a participant sport and as such it could accommodate a wider range of social groups than field sports. Owners and fashionable race-goers were spatially segregated from the mass of punters. High standards of dress and an invitation system kept undesirable elements out of the exclusive enclosure. Considered primarily as a participant activity, horse-racing was run by a closed élite made up of some of the oldest families in France supplemented by a small number of exceptionally rich bourgeois. The apogee of the racing world was the Jockey Club, founded in 1833 to improve French bloodstock and standards of racing. However, its social prestige outstripped its sporting importance in the later nineteenth century. To many members, or would-be members, of the Jockey Club, its ostensible function soon became incidental to its chief purpose, which was to provide introductions for the already high-born to visiting heads of state, important ambassadors and famous families. The Jockey Club represented the pinnacle of social aspiration for generations of rich men. Significantly, Proust modelled Swann partly on Charles Haas, the son of a rich stockbroker and a hero of the Franco-Prussian

War, who, apart from the Rothschilds, was the only Jew to be admitted to the Jockey Club. The Jockey Club, in fact, provides an instructive exception to the general pattern of *rapprochement* between the élites of birth and wealth which emerged in the course of the Third Republic. As time passed it actually became harder to get in. Between 1849 and 1870 the Club admitted an average of twenty-two new members per year; between 1870 and 1914 this figure fell to seven per year and slumped even further during the inter-war years to two per year. Membership of France's most famous club became a family possession passed on from father to son. Hostility to the Republic and the increasing intervention of the state in the world of racing meant that the Jockey Club became more and more a place for great nobles to congregate and less of a sporting club in the accepted sense of the term.[8]

The Jockey Club could afford to be an exception because of the wealth of its members. Most élite clubs became less exclusive and increasingly made little or no distinction between the upper bourgeoisie and members of the nobility. This emerged clearly in our earlier analysis of the introduction of English sports into France. The ideal of the Baron de Coubertin and other upper-class advocates of athletic sports was the creation of a mixed élite of birth and wealth, 'an open bourgeoisie in which every well brought up young man would have his place', as the brother of France's first international rugby captain described it. Barriers between the upper and middle classes were to be broken down on the playing fields in imitation of the achievements of the English public schools. The Racing Club de France, the founding club for athletic sports, and its rival, the Stade Français, soon established an enviable social *cachet* in Paris. Membership of the Racing Club rose from around 250 in 1891 to over a thousand in 1904. By the middle of the inter-war years the number of 'Racingmen' had risen to five thousand, although critics claimed that the average turn-out on the track was little over thirty. The products of the best Paris schools often gravitated towards Racing or Stade or to one of the other exclusive sports clubs like the anglophile Standard Athletic Club as part of a natural social progression. These clubs at first limited themselves to the athletic sports – running and rugby were the respective summer and winter favourites – but as they became larger and better established they tended to branch out into other, less competitive forms of physical recreation. Swimming pools and large club-houses with lavish social facilities were built. The Racing Club eventually purchased a golf-course within easy reach of the capital.[9]

The point made here is that many of these exclusive clubs had social functions which extended well beyond fostering the health and business efficiency of the fortunate few. Some clubs had an important role in courtship. Although, on the whole, clubs of all kinds tended to segregate men from women to preserve male supremacy, there were areas where a carefully supervised mingling of the sexes was not only permitted but actively encouraged. The game of tennis played a central role here. Tennis was the only modern sport in which the sexes could meet easily, and mixed doubles was a unique and useful form of introduction which figured prominently in the social experience of middle-class teenagers from the turn of the century onwards. Mothers were beginning to take their daughters to tennis parties, 'just as they had formerly escorted them to the ball'. Tennis courts could be marked out in the spacious gardens of the rich in the English fashion. Private tennis parties were arranged to which suitable young men and women would be invited for tennis followed by tea on the lawn. There is a charming account of one such experience in the life of the young Marcel Proust, whose family inhabited exactly that stratum of the upper middle class which so favoured the sport and the anglophile *snobbisme* associated with it. Reminiscing much later with his servant Céleste, Proust recalled the manner in which he had met and fallen in love with the beautiful young Jeanne Pouquet (the future Princess Radziwill): 'When we went to play tennis, in the morning, I took lots of sandwiches and all sorts of little cakes. I couldn't do enough to please her. I bought her presents and flowers . . . I loved watching her hair fly when she was playing tennis. The other boys were jealous of my pretty speeches and sometimes got their own back by hitting the ball into my boxes of *petits fours*.' However, sporting prowess rather than precocious genius made the greater impact on the young lady, and Proust added somewhat wistfully, 'Of course, I couldn't shine in the same way they could'.[10]

Tennis soon supplanted other nascent garden-based games for young ladies, such as badminton or croquet. The tennis sections of the Racing Club or the Stade Français, the lawns of the exclusive Ile de Puteaux club set on an island in the Seine alongside the fashionable Bois de Boulogne, or the courts of the Villa Primrose in Bordeaux quickly established themselves as venues for polite courtship. In these clubs and their imitators the status of prospective members was carefully screened in an attempt to ensure that the 'right sort' of boy met the 'right sort' of girl. Veto and recommendation systems restricted social adventurers. The Tennis Club de Lyon, for example, founded in 1900, charged an annual subscription of one hundred francs. Once accepted, however, for only an extra fifty francs the whole of the family could join, thereby ensuring that athletic young men would be accompanied by their eligible female relatives. Commenting on the social composition of the Tennis Club de Lyon, the authorities noted that it counted among its members some of the most distinguished names in the city, many of whom came from the old silk families. Simone de Beauvoir, dutiful daughter of a Paris advocate, recalled that tennis was really the only form of exercise permissible to well-bred young women in the early twentieth century. Cycling was thought to give too many opportunities for escaping the constant surveillance necessary to preserve a girl's reputation. Tennis was less dangerous in this respect and could be played at home, in a club or during summer holidays at fashionable resorts. The fine sand or clay courts of the Riviera soon became almost as familiar to top tennis players as the lawns of Wimbledon.

It was, therefore, entirely appropriate that the first French tennis player to achieve world renown was a woman, Suzanne Lenglen, who won the French national championship in 1914 at the age of fifteen. She went on to win Wimbledon each year from 1919 to 1925, when she dropped only four games in the entire championship, after which she turned professional for a fee rumoured to be over a hundred thousand dollars. She had come a long way in the dozen or so years since the young Jacques-Henri Lartigue, later to become one of the world's most celebrated photographers, captured her marvellous blend of grace and athleticism during training sessions supervised by her father. Significantly, Suzanne's mother was worried in case her daughter became too involved in competitive sport and forgot the real purpose of the ladies game: to stay fit, feminine and to find a man. Suzanne Lenglen grew up in the new world of jolly middle-class adventure, in which young men experimented with cameras, motor-cars and aeroplanes while their sisters practised forehand and backhand returns of serve. Lenglen's male counterpart was Jean Borotra, 'the bounding Basque', a graduate of the Polytechnique and subsequently to become a minister of sport under the Vichy government. With Lacoste, Cochet and Brugnon, he formed the 'Four Musketeers' who captured the Davis Cup and several Wimbledon titles between the wars. Although a precursor of contemporary 'gamesmanship' when at play – a master of all the tricks, clowning, stalling, tantrums and crowd-baiting – when he was off the court he was the epitome of the charming, well-bred Frenchman: the *bourgeois-gentilhomme* in fact, a model for the middle-class young man and in consequence a suitable object for well-bred female admiration. The Roland-Garros stadium, the French Wimbledon, was built predictably close to the Racing Club and the Auteuil and Longchamp race-courses, forming with them a tight-knit concentration of élite entertainment in the heart of the most exclusive part of the city. Throughout the thirties tennis was the only sport in which women played an important part as spectators and of these the majority were well-to-do society ladies.[11]

Not all upper- and middle-class sports were as successful in stemming the tide of democracy. Shooting, as we have already seen, was deeply divided along broadly class lines: the wealthy gun versus the *petit chasseur* in his commune. Rowing was another activity favoured by the well-to-do, who found it difficult and embarrassing to keep the masses at bay. Rowing as a recreation was popular with Parisians. Even the most cursory glance at the social content of Impressionist painting attests to that. Zola's *Au bonheur des dames*, published in 1883, gives an excellent picture of water sports on the Marne on Sundays. A group of students and a rival gang of drapers' assistants race each other, exchanging insults as they go. A fight amongst those left on the bank breaks out, recalling 'the old hatred between students and shop assistants' and their competition for the limited pool of easy women.[12]

This was hardly the most favourable atmosphere for the dissemination of the ideals of 'fair play' and 'self-government'. Yet upper-class reformers persisted in their efforts to introduce the recreational institutions of Eton and Harrow into polite Parisian society. It seems as if they met with some success, for the author of a guide to sport in Paris published in 1889 noted that competitive rowing was becoming a rather more dignified activity. Senior civil servants and titled people placed themselves at the head of the new clubs which sprang up along the banks of the Seine and the Marne. Coubertin was a great admirer of rowing, which he had observed in the English public schools, and he took a leading part in encouraging the sport among affluent young men in the 1880s. The Joinville Boat Club, founded in 1880, charged four hundred francs entrance fee and a further three hundred a year thereafter, and took as its motto that 'one can be an oarsman and remain a gentleman'. The anglophile oarsmen from the top *lycées*, the universities and the professions were most anxious to distinguish themselves from *hoi polloi*. The new clubs with their expensive skiffs permitted 'one to take to the water without having to mix with vulgar people who, hiring old rowing boats, go off on Sundays and Mondays – especially Mondays – to visit the various clubs and bars that cluster along the banks of the Seine and the Marne'. Not surprisingly, fashionable rowing clubs had their catchpenny imitators: 'dish water sailors', as the Goncourt brothers contemptuously called them, 'who seek social distinction through boating'. Raymond Benoit, an engineer from Lyon, was a classic example. He founded a sailing club in Lyon, making himself president for life and nominating his son as successor on his death. He limited membership to twenty, and tried to persuade the cream of Lyon society to join. 'This man is socially ambitious', a police report on the club observed; he was using sport 'to climb out of the class in which he was born.'[13]

Sumptuary distinctions were important in all sports where status was at stake. Expensive uniforms or fashionable sportswear proclaimed to the world that the wearer belonged to a select club for the leisured and affluent. In fact, if certain forms of dress had not been useful for purely practical reasons, status-conscious sportsmen would probably have had to invent them. This actually happened during the bicycle boom of the 1890s. As soon as the bicycle became more popular the cycling gentleman felt the need to distinguish himself at a glance from a member of the lower classes taking the same form of exercise. 'Immediately, a host of dressmakers got to work to devise an outfit which was both expensive and sophisticated enough to make it crystal clear that the wearer was not the kind of person who needed to work for a living.' Members of early cycling clubs were frequently required to wear special Norfolk jackets and caps bearing club insignia. The Touring Club de France went so far as to specify a completely new uniform which was obligatory dress for all official excursions. As we saw, middle-class men taking up game-shooting did the same. Only those members of the country gentry who were already well-known in the locality could afford to dress in their old tweeds and boots. In some cases the image created by the clothes became an end in itself. This was especially true of affluent socialites during the twenties and thirties, when casual leisure-wear became increasingly fashionable. 'I know many of my contemporaries', wrote the author of a book aimed at the young bourgeois male, 'who pretend to take up a particular sport only in order to be able to wear the uniform.'[14]

From what little we know of working-class recreation it does not appear that within its own social hierarchy a noticeably more open or less status-conscious attitude prevailed. There was a hierarchy of skill, income and status within the urban masses which was no less real or rigid than that which operated in society as a whole. In a city like Marseille, where the working class was basically divided into the indigenous population which dominated the skilled trades and the immigrant workers who were forced into the unskilled ones, there appears to have been very little mixing on a recreational level. Segregation operated on a social as well as on an occupational basis. 'The native Marseillais working in the exclusive trades avoided contact with strangers . . . both his favourite forms of recreation, the *cercle* and the *cabanon*, were closed to outsiders. The *cercle* was a social club which maintained a meeting place where members gathered in the evening . . . the *cabanon* was a small fishing cabin on the sea, usually owned in common by several workers.' The *cercle* and the *cabanon* could be joined by invitation only, 'and such invitations were very rare'. Moreover, it seems as if problems of integration were not significantly eased by the passage of time. A survey of the social life of workers in Saint-Etienne in the period 1890 to 1914 shows that 'different categories of workers did indeed form separate and identifiable entities' and that 'a total mixing in all aspects of life did not occur'. The three main working-class groups – ribbon weavers, armourers and miners – rarely shared leisure activities together.[15]

Similar distinctions emerged in the gymnastics movement.

Before the popularity of football and cycle-racing in the twentieth century, the organised competitive activity which came closest to being a thoroughly working-class sport was gymnastics. The covert festive quality of this modern form of martial acrobatics has already been analysed, but its social significance requires further discussion. Although gymnastics played so prominent a role in the life of lower-class young men, it never became a mass phenomenon in the way that modern football has done. To some degree this was because commercialisation was strongly discouraged. The lack of a competitive spectator dimension to gymnastics (excluding occasional public displays) limited its appeal as a form of entertainment for an undifferentiated national audience. But this was only part of the explanation. The social structure of the sport also had a major role to play in discouraging the spread of gymnastics to the youth of France as a whole. It must be remembered that gymnastics was seen by many as a means of social control, as a way in which lower-class youth might be imbued with a proper respect for the *patrie* and, by implication, for the status quo. In order to be a gymnast it was necessary to join a club. Joining a club meant acceptance of a set of rules and implied obedience to the officials of the organisation. This in turn entailed acceptance of the dominant role of middle-class sponsors and of the day-to-day authority of young men who had been singled out by their elders for positions of special responsibility within the club. These considerations imply that only the more respectable elements of working-class youth would tend either to seek membership or to be accepted as members. Minimum standards of dress and behaviour were laid down. Such requirements meant, in effect, that boys from fairly stable homes with regular work formed the great majority of active members, whilst the prospective *lumpenproletariat* were left to hang around the street corners, drifting early into heavy drinking and sometimes turning to crime.

In this instance the division between 'respectable' and 'unrespectable' elements seems to have operated through leisure in much the same way that it did in Victorian Britain, where more research on this theme has been carried out. The point here is that a simple distinction between middle- and working-class activities – a vulgar class analysis – is too rigid to be of much value. A more sophisticated social profile of gymnastics requires distinctions to be drawn between the various groups of lower-class youth on the one hand, and between the participants and the organisers on the other. An interesting feature of the sport was the absence of the younger members of the bourgeoisie from a movement which attracted a substantial number of middle-aged doctors, lawyers and merchants as officials or honorary members. The explanation for this discrepancy is fairly obvious. The sons of the bourgeoisie were not expected to join in the activities of their social inferiors; gymnastics was considered more appropriate for the future private than for the potential officer. Indeed, the few sons of *notables* who did join gymnastic clubs in the chauvinistic surge of the mid 1880s were soon forced to leave 'because of their social prestige in the locality'.[16]

On the other hand, it was thought proper and patriotic for affluent older men to encourage the sons of the honest poor in exercises which were believed conducive to military revival and social stability. It was for such reasons that solid members of the bourgeoisie were prepared to sponsor clubs which they may have been reluctant to allow their own children to join. So high a premium was placed on cultivating disinterested patriotism amongst French youth that some form of state decoration was the usual reward for this type of community service. Medal-hunting proved an ulterior motive for many officials. In a lengthy survey of the state of gymnastics in Paris in 1901, a councillor remarked that a good number of the less active clubs seemed to have been formed primarily to get a *légion d'honneur* for their patrons. Gym clubs, therefore, were frequently more complex in class terms than they appeared to be. Different social groups were drawn together for a variety of reasons which defy the crude categorising of the sport as 'bourgeois' or 'proletarian'.[17]

More detailed evidence of the nature of social stratification in sport can be found in an analysis of the composition of the many cycling clubs founded around the turn of the century. Cycling was eagerly espoused by those in the lower middle classes for whom it represented a healthy, outdoor recreation as opposed to the unhealthy alcoholic amusements of the poor. Just as the affluent bourgeois had sought to distinguish himself from the common cyclist, so the respectable clerk or craftsman in his turn tried to use the bicycle to further his quest for a social identity distinct from that of the rest of the masses. A few people with marked social aspirations were perhaps using the sport to test the dictum that 'whoever can copy the bourgeois style of life can become a bourgeois'. Certainly, cycling sometimes provided a member of the lower middle class with an opportunity for contact with a fair range of middle-class occupational groups. A clerk might meet an educated professional man. In Saint-Etienne, for example, the élite of the working class, the armourers, played a notable part in cycling, whereas the miners and weavers, who formed the main occupational groups, were conspicuous by their absence. Sport fostered mixing between occupational groups already close to each other in the social structure but it did not act as a source of upward social mobility *tout court*.[18]

Naturally, the possibilities of social contact varied according to the geographical situation and the type of activity undertaken. A survey of cycling carried out in 1892 lists a large number of private clubs and in many cases gives details of the occupations of their members. Broadly speaking, most clubs fell into one of two categories. First there was the small town club, in which people of a reasonably wide social range were represented, then came the city-based club, which tended to be segregated along recognisable class lines. Whilst a survey of this kind is of little use in ascertaining the degree of working-class upward mobility through sport, as it was not until after the turn of the century that bicycles began to be items of mass consumption, it does provide one or two interesting insights into the relationship between the bourgeoisie and those hovering on its fringes.

In the small town club a fair amount of mixing between the lower middle class and the bourgeoisie proper seems to have taken place. At Montauban the one club in the town was run by a gym teacher (president), a cycle-shop owner (vice-president) and a clerk (secretary), but it had two *notaires* and four *propriétaires* among its members. Likewise, at Pau membership was sufficiently open to include an advocate and a baker in the same club. A cycling club was formed in the small town of Aigues-mortes in the Camargue in 1897 which contained thirty-seven members, including a solicitor, four merchants, three café-owners, three land agents, three students, two teachers, a draper, a chemist, a carpenter, a grocer, a clerk, a saddler, a tobacconist, a baker and a smallholder. The entire gamut of small town society was represented.[19]

In the larger towns there appears to have been less opportunity for making useful contacts as most clubs were more homogeneous in social composition. There were fewer instances of the kind of mixing between the bourgeoisie and the lower middle class which seems to have taken place to some degree in the small town clubs. A mixture of small shopkeepers, office-workers and members of the labour aristocracy formed the nucleus of most cycling clubs formed in Paris in the 1890s. For example, a random selection of Parisian clubs listed in 1892 reveals that eleven out of seventeen members of the Cyclistes de Buttes de Chaumont were clerks of one kind or another and that the other members included a watchmaker, a tailor, an ironmonger, a goldsmith and an engineer. The president of the club, however, was a factory owner and his presence may have provided an added social incentive for membership. Many other clubs were broadly similar in composition. The Véloce Club de Passy listed twenty-three out of its forty-five members as *employés*, and forty-three out of the sixty-five members of the Vélo-Tir Parisien fell into the same occupational category.[20]

Social homogeneity was also a feature of cycling clubs in the larger provincial cities. Weber notes that the membership of the Club Vélocipédique de Bordeaux was solidly bourgeois and included 'five wholesale merchants, three university professors, a doctor, a dentist, a chief engineer, a builder and a shopkeeper'. Likewise, the composition of the Véloce Club Bordelais, the oldest club in France, was exclusive. It is small wonder that when the lower middle classes began to take up the sport they were forced to form their own clubs such as the Vélo-Touriste Bordelais, which was composed entirely of commercial clerks. They in turn would have little or nothing to do with the genuinely popular sports organisations which began to be formed in the later nineties. For instance, office-workers and small businessmen were conspicuously absent from clubs like the Cyclistes Girondins, founded in 1897 and composed mainly of shop assistants and hairdressers. When working men began to take up cycling they showed a marked tendency to form their own organisations rather than risk a rebuff at the hands of an established club. In fact, in the late 1890s clubs with self-explanatory names like Guidon Ouvrier de Corbeil and Pédale Ouvrière were already beginning to be formed, although it was not until the inter-war years that the bicycle was a common possession in working-class homes.[21]

Given the importance attached to questions of status amongst cyclists it comes as no surprise to find that social conflicts within and between clubs were fairly frequent. As early as 1888 some members of the smart Société Vélocipédique Métropolitaine thought that the club was being infiltrated by more popular elements and proposed to raise the entry fees and restrict membership. The new members were naturally opposed to this and each group adopted the political labels of their day: the élitists were known as the *opportunistes* and their younger adversaries as the *radicaux*. Eventually the disgruntled older members left to form the Cercle de la Pédale with the motto 'peu mais bien'; those familiar with modern French slang may feel there is a more obvious explanation for the schism, but the adoption of the word 'pédale' to mean homosexual appears to be too recent a usage to permit this ingenious theory. The members of the Cercle de la Pédale in all probability left the parent club on the grounds of snobbery rather than out of a need to escape their heterosexual fellows.[22]

Minor social skirmishes of this type were quite frequent in the 1890s. One form in which bourgeois indignation made itself felt was through complaints about the overcrowding of the roads. Though it may seem laughable by the standards of today, this was regarded as a real problem by certain contemporaries. The spread of the bicycle in the *fin-de-siècle* meant that the roads were considerably busier than they had been in the halcyon days of the pioneers. Baroncelli's handbook for Parisian cyclists, *Guide des environs de Paris*, went through seventeen editions between 1884 and 1894. A survey of cyclists leaving Paris on a Sunday morning in the summer of 1893 counted 5573, and numbers rose vertiginously in the following years. This expansion set in motion a process of friction between the established cyclist and the numerous newcomers, who thronged favoured spots and reduced the social value of the sport. A correspondent to the *Revue du Touring Club* fulminated against the spread of the bicycle in no uncertain terms: 'The bicycle is charming but there are too many cyclists . . . it breaks my heart to see this treasure [the bicycle] wasted, available to everyone. It should be reserved for the intelligent who alone know how to enjoy what it offers . . . For goodness sake! leave nature to the true tourist, and do not transport people out of their normal sphere. In the end they will be happier that way'.[23]

Similarly, after the takeover of the sport by the lower middle classes in the 1890s, there was some resentment of the infiltration of industrial workers and apprentices. The fashion cycle was set in motion with its inevitable social consequences. The hostility of the lower-middle-class cyclist towards his working-class counterpart came to the surface after 1900, if a report in the *Revue Sportive* is to be trusted. The article in question gave an account of an unpleasant scene involving the Union Cycliste de Batignolles, a club composed of office-workers, who refused to sit at the same table as a group of workmen against whom they had been competing. This isolated incident may not in itself be of much significance, but the comment of the journalist reporting the matter to the effect that such breaches of fraternal behaviour were not rare is worthy of note.[24]

Conflicts of a corresponding kind took place in other sports. It is no exaggeration to say that the well-bred young anglophiles of the eighties and nineties contemplated with undisguised horror the rapid democratising of their activities and the prospect of socially mixed clubs. An influential sporting journal of the period noted that the intermingling of the classes would cause all sorts of problems that it was simply more sensible to avoid in the first place. The ideals of liberty, equality and fraternity should be kept firmly where they belonged: on public monuments and on the backs of coins. Efforts to merge clubs in order to improve facilities or cut costs were rarely successful unless the clubs concerned were made up of broadly similar groups of people. When the Union Sportive de Carcassonne, composed 'almost exclusively of the sons of the bourgeoisie', joined forces with the Etoile Sportive Carcassonnaise, a club formed by 'a handful of clerks and working men', conflicts broke out almost immediately. Both clubs were soon reorganised along more socially cohesive lines. A further example of the difficulty involved in crossing the social barriers through sport is provided by the Bordeaux Université Club which merged with the famous rugby side Stade Bordelais in order to be able to use Stade's facilities. The linking of the two clubs turned out to be a temporary affair because the students, mostly from upper-middle-class homes, were unwilling to rub shoulders with 'a fair number of clerks, *employés*, shop assistants and commercial travellers'.[25]

Clearly, incidents of this kind, though undeniably significant, should not be taken as typical or representative of the average experience of most sportsmen. To point out the extent to which questions of status permeated sport is not to suggest that class conflict was the dominant feature of sporting life. That would be as simplistic as the outlook of those social engineers who blithely believed that class differences could all be sorted out on the playing fields, or as the doctrinaire conception of the communist sports movement of the 1920s which saw sport as an instrument in the class struggle and condemned every non-communist club as 'bourgeois'.

As a whole, the 1920s and 1930s saw a significant growth in participation in a wide variety of leisure activities formerly restricted to the rich which in many respects prefigured the post-war pattern of affluent hedonism, the celebrated 'new' France. Although in the thirties the workers certainly lacked the necessary material basis for a life of leisure, the two-week paid holiday was won in 1936. Hours of work were reduced, the 'weekend' entered the vocabulary of daily life and the young in particular showed themselves determined to explore their own country to a far greater extent than their city-bound parents had done. Clearly, it would be wrong to exaggerate the convergence of middle-class and working-class styles of relaxation, but the similarities – a new love of the outdoor life and of physical exercise – are worthy of note. A recent survey of youth movements in France in the 1930s shifts our attention away from the over-publicised reactions of Parisian students and steers us towards an examination of the leisure activities of the Catholic youth clubs (with around 200,000 members), the scouts and the numerous burgeoning juvenile associations which all shared 'a certain romanticised attitude to communal life'. The seeds of the camping craze of the fifties and the peculiar mixture of exercise, primitivism and conviviality of the Club Méditerranée may have their origins in the thirties. Until recently we have been too engrossed by the momentous political events of the thirties to notice the silent changes that were taking place. In addition to the greater amount of free time, there was the spread of the motor-cycle, which permitted the better-off worker to imitate the new mobility of the middle-class car owner. There was a substantial programme of public building inaugurated by the Popular Front government to improve leisure facilities such as public swimming pools, football pitches and athletics tracks. Excursion tickets to the Riviera, skiing trips and even aeroplane rides were laid on in an effort to break down social barriers in leisure. These disparate influences – more time and resources, more sophisticated requirements and attitudes – revealed the makings of a new style of leisure activity in which class distinctions, though always present, would be less obtrusive than before.[26]

But this is to run a little ahead of the story. Historians love to find the origins of one pattern of events in an earlier period in which we formerly thought quite different relationships held sway. So it is in this case. There is no escaping the fact that during the thirties political and social divisions were particularly marked. Despite a few early indications of class convergence in mass leisure, it remains true that new forms of sporting activity did not significantly alter established patterns of social behaviour. In the main, sports clubs did not act as channels for social mobility or improved understanding between broad status groups, apart from the closer links that were sometimes forged between birth and wealth. Real class barriers could not be bridged by sport, which was more important as a means of consolidating prestige than as a method of acquiring it. All footballers were equal but some were more equal than others. Whilst vulgarisation was a general feature of recreation, social distinction remained an integral part of sport. To French sportsmen as to Frenchmen as a whole, fraternity was an elusive goal more easily realised within classes than between them.

Sport and Politics: Ideology and Recruitment

Advocates of competitive exercise, particularly before 1914, were fond of remarking that sport and politics were opposites and should not be mixed. The view that sport represented a pure and uncorrupted form of activity and an end in itself came to be an article of faith amongst the athletic fraternity. Yet could it be that the sportsman doth protest too much? Perhaps the very vehemence of the denial of political motivation should encourage the social historian to look more closely into the matter. If sport had really been as detached from political life as its protagonists claimed would it have been necessary to make the point over and over again? Predictably, the real state of affairs was rather different from this idealised posture of neutrality and non-involvement in the more contentious areas of national life.

The degree to which sport impinged on 'politics' depends largely on how the latter term is defined. If politics is understood in the narrow sense of democratic elections and the formation of governments then admittedly the connections prove to be tenuous. State involvement in sport was limited to smallish subsidies for private clubs before the leisure programme of the Popular Front got under way in the mid-1930s. But if we choose a broader definition which takes into account the dissemination of political ideas and the recruitment of support for bodies with strong ideological convictions such as the Church, then sport undoubtedly had a significant role to play. Sports were of considerable importance in spreading the cult of nationalism amongst French youth around the turn of the century; the value of sport in the recruitment of the young was a lesson soon learned by Church and state alike, and games were increasingly drawn into this area of conflict in the decade preceding the First

World War. During the inter-war years sport became more involved in the dissension between employers and workers, with both groups sponsoring their own clubs and competitions. Political parties started their own sports sections, whilst right-wing activists made use of sport for overtly reactionary purposes – a trend which culminated in the adoption of a compulsory sports programme by the Vichy government to promote the ideals of the National Revolution.

Several of the most important political influences on the development of sports in the later nineteenth century have been mentioned in previous chapters. The defeat of France in 1870 had administered a salutary shock to those who had come to take French hegemony in Europe for granted. The humiliation of Sedan provoked an impassioned debate on how the manifest deficiencies in French military power might be remedied. Important political figures like Gambetta and Jules Simon partly blamed the lack of proper physical and military training in schools and advocated obligatory periods of exercise and firearms training in order to beat the Prussians at their own game. Paul Déroulède, the violently chauvinist ex-soldier and propagandist of French military resurgence, was put in charge of a committee to investigate physical and military training in schools. It was under the influence of the extreme patriotic reaction of the 1870s that a good many of the early gymnastic clubs were founded. These were often associated with shooting clubs, to which the older members graduated after military service.[1]

As one might expect, the nationalist lobby were more interested in encouraging sporting activities with obvious military application than in encouraging a wide variety of exercise as an end in itself. Gymnastics were the most natural outlet for the type of strength and discipline admired by those who espoused the cause of *revanche*. English sports were dismissed as frivolous novelties. This ensured that it would be German team gymnastics, rather than the more graceful Swedish style of exercise designed to improve posture and agility, which dominated the Union des Sociétés Françaises de Gymnastique, which had as its motto 'Faites-moi des hommes, nous en ferons des soldats!'. At first the new government of moderate Republicans co-operated with the strident voices calling for the harnessing of sport to train youth in the arts of war. Elementary schools were asked to form infant drill groups called *bataillons scolaires*. Nine- and ten-year-olds were dressed up in uniforms and paraded around playgrounds like conscripts. With the rise of anti-parliamentary nationalism in the 1880s, and particularly after the challenge to the Republic by General Boulanger, the *bataillons scolaires* were phased out. They had been 'un erreur patriotique' which had proved counter-productive – the sheer ludicrousness of children playing at soldiers often amused rather than impressed onlookers – and which had provided a breeding ground for authoritarianism.[2]

Rather than pursue a policy of militarising boys before their time, Republican educationalists henceforth preferred to encourage general physical training in schools by requiring that there be four periods of gymnastics per week. But little was done in the way of providing equipment or training specialised staff, and as the horrors of the military defeat receded from memory so did the official impetus to promote organised exercise. On the whole the state chose to use its political influence through the offer of subsidies and moral support to various approved private bodies such as the gymnastic union, the Union des Sociétés de Tir en France and the Union des Sociétés d'Education Physique et de Préparation Militaire de France. These latter two bodies were founded in the mid-1880s when the movement for *revanche* was at its height. Republican governments had to be careful not to alienate useful pressure groups and sporting associations unnecessarily, thereby adding a potentially dangerous weapon to the arsenal of their conservative adversaries. The New Right certainly tried to infiltrate a range of sports movements. It was in a speech praising the spirit of discipline to be found in the gymnastic and shooting clubs that Déroulède first made a clear allusion to the incoherence of the parliamentary system. The Ligue des Patriotes, a mass nationalist organisation aimed at strengthening the French army, was founded at a meeting of the gymnastic clubs of the Seine, and many ordinary people apparently thought that the two organisations were one and the same. A sizeable number of the leading officials involved in gymnastics and shooting openly supported Boulanger and encouraged their members to join in demonstrations sympathetic to the General's plans for military and constitutional reform.[3]

The influence of the defeat of 1870 apart, there were other forces in late nineteenth-century France favouring the cause of competitive physical exercise. This period saw not only the recrudescence of militarism in France, it also witnessed the growth of racial nationalism. The writings of Charles Darwin and Herbert Spencer were crudely transposed into a social theory which asserted that man was not one species but a number of competing species (or races) locked together in a life or death struggle for domination. Social Darwinism appeared to legitimate the competitive ethic and placed great emphasis on the proper physical and mental adaptation of man to his environment. As society became more mechanised and sedentary, there was a genuine, if far-fetched, apprehension that within a few generations men would begin to lose the full use of their limbs and become totally cerebral creatures. Sport was the best means of avoiding the creation of a purely intellectual man and of assuring the future of the race noted the editor of a survey of the spread of sports amongst men of letters.[4]

Linked to such widely-felt fears was a growing interest in theories of race, and the belief that the French were in the grip of a process of degeneration which only a systematic programme of physical training could reverse. Some claimed that the French aristocracy had been fatally weakened by inter-marriage with the Italian nobility, whilst others stressed the effects of the Napoleonic wars in depleting the peasant stock of France. Social Darwinism encouraged influential conservative thinkers like Hippolyte Taine to conclude that the 'recent French defeat was a natural evolutionary outcome of the detestable French Revolution', whilst Gobineau predictably saw the whole episode in terms of racial weakness and as a vindication of his own ideas. France would inevitably succumb to conquest unless firm action was taken to halt racial decline. Therefore, the forces which encouraged population growth also frequently encouraged the practice of sport.[5]

So far we have concentrated our attention on those who were primarily concerned about the declining power and prestige of France within the continent of Europe. However, there were others who took a wider view of the role of France in the world and who advocated the cause of athletic sports as an integral part of the great imperial adventure of the late nineteenth century. The special contribution of Coubertin and Grousset has already been examined in an earlier chapter. Here we need only reiterate that English sports appeared to foster exactly those virtues which had helped the English élite in the conquest of a vast colonial empire. Rather than see France persevere in a fruitless war with Germany of the kind advocated by the nationalistic supporters of gymnastics, those who favoured the cause of English sports in the *lycée* or college looked to Africa and Asia as the primary outlet for French energies. The rhetoric of Empire with its stress on adaptability and endurance found an echo in the language of sporting innovators like Georges de Saint-Clair, an early secretary of the national athletics association, who claimed that games created men 'who know how to will, to dare, to venture, organise, govern and be governed'. These views were shared by Father Didon, principal of the Dominican College at Arceuil, one of the first among French schools to introduce games for its students. When Father Didon visited Eton in the late 1890s, he remarked that 'boys who learned to command in games were learning to command in the Indies'. Whereas leaders of the gymnastics movement were primarily concerned with the training of soldiers and rarely took their eyes off the Rhine, many of those who gave money or lent the prestige of their names to clubs practising English sports did so in the belief that team games produced just that blend of initiative and co-operation which would help France expand her overseas possessions. The leading athletic journals of the nineties made frequent and explicit references to the role of sport in the promotion of imperial endeavour. In the course of the 1880s 'France absorbed Tunisia, took over most of Indo-China, got a foothold in Madagascar, and moved out into the Sahara from bases along the coast'. Popular sporting papers like *La Vie au Grand Air* divided their attention equally between the Empire and the stadium, with reports of rugby matches juxtaposed with photographs of natives recently brought into the beneficent ambit of French commerce and culture.[6]

The mixture of militarism, Social Darwinism and imperialism produced a potent and bellicose set of values in the sporting community on the eve of the First World War. 'Agathon's' famous survey of élite Parisian youth carried out in 1913 laid great emphasis on the role of sport in producing 'a spirit of solidarity, a feeling of communal activity where each individual is prepared to make sacrifices. On the other hand sports also encourage endurance, sang-froid, military virtues and sustain the war-like feelings of the young'. 'La guerre . . . c'est sport pour le vrai', remarked a contributor to the volume, and the author of a lengthy book on the technique of rugby published around the same time was even more specific: 'The struggle which these two fifteens take part in is a battleground in miniature; to win you have to be both physically and morally prepared; you have to be strong, resolute and dedicated to the colours you defend and to the ideals they represent . . . In the battle some will die, some will fall in the struggle but others will continue to fight for the flag.' If this seems excessive then consider the following extract from the popular daily sports paper *L'Auto* dated 3 August 1914:

> Mes p'tits gars! Mes p'tits gars chéris! Mes p'tits gars français! Listen to me! For fourteen years *L'Auto* has come out every day and has never given you bad advice, eh? Well then, just listen!
> The Prussians are a bunch of bastards . . . dirty square heads, mindless sheep without the slightest initiative and ready for the slaughter . . . You've got to get them this time, those dirty bastards. Believe me, a Frenchman could never bow down before a German.
> This is the big match that you have to play and you must use every trick that you've learned in sport . . . But beware! When your bayonet is at their heart and they beg for mercy, don't give in. Run them through! Let's have done with these evil imbeciles who for the last forty-four years have stopped us from living, loving, breathing and being happy.
> . . . No more of these sauerkraut men, no more pickpockets, no more tin Gods twirling their moustaches and claiming that Germany is attacked. No more Kaiser! No more Agadir! No more bloodsuckers! No more nightmates! No more bastards!

Here endeth the lesson according to Henri Desgrange, founder of the Tour de France and editor of a sports paper with an annual circulation of over forty-three million by 1914.[7]

Whether the idea was propagated through the more restrained channels of upper-middle-class sporting literature or through the sub-Barrèsian rhetoric of the mass press, sport became closely linked in the minds of many with the concept of a 'national revival' which would re-establish French hegemony in Europe. Despite Coubertin's appeals for fair play and international harmony, sporting competitions between nations tended to be viewed in narrowly nationalistic terms. At first the French government was rather slow to exploit the patriotic potential of sport, and when the Olympics came to Paris in 1900 on the initiative of their founder, Pierre de Coubertin, they were officially treated as a mere sideshow to the World Exhibition. Facilities were very poor with the discus and hammer throwers having to compete amongst the trees of the Bois de Boulogne! However, when the Games returned to France in 1924 with 44 countries fielding 5,533 athletes, a proper stadium was built and the state took a close interest in the proceedings. Although sports facilities were still very limited in France as a whole, money was made available for the Olympics as a matter of national prestige. International sport was turning into a 'war without weapons' in the service of a rapacious patriotism.[8]

Despite the fact that many agreed in general terms on the role of sport in the promotion of nationalism, there were deep divisions over the efforts of the Catholic Church to capitalise on the new vogue for exercise by founding a large number of youth clubs or *patronages*, in which sport had an important place. With the disestablishment of the Church in 1905 these organisations became more numerous and more active. As a result the conflict between the Catholic Right and the supporters of the Republic continued until the outbreak of the war. Even the Union Sacrée could not prevent a prefect in 1918 from recommending that a sports club be refused a subsidy because 'it is clearly under clerical control'. Indeed, a study of the sectarian conflict within sport during the pre-war decade adds a useful dimension to the contention of a recent historian that 'it is wrong . . . to assume that after 1905 religious disagreements ceased to be a major divisive force'.[9]

A prime object of official concern during the period 1905 to 1914 was the phenomenal success of the Catholic sports and gymnastics organisation, the Fédération Gymnastique et Sportive des Patronages de France (FGSPF). In November 1905 there were only 72 clubs in this organisation but less than nine years later there were 1763. With approximately 180,000 active members, the FGSPF on the eve of the First World War was as strong as the state-sponsored gymnastics body, which had 350,000 members, about half of whom were non-active. The dramatic growth of sport within the Church was part of a deliberate campaign to increase the appeal of Catholicism to the adolescent. The institutional basis for rapid growth already existed in the form of the parish-run study circles for the young which were now transformed into modern youth clubs. Bible study was abandoned for all but the most intelligent and pious, and a muscular christianity was encouraged instead. The Church made great play of its patriotism and at the same time warned the state that it would henceforth tolerate no further interference in its affairs. As the bishop of Bayonne told a large assembly of Catholic athletes, 'you will declare war on those who make war against God'.[10]

The efforts of the Church in this field were considerably assisted by gifts of land and money from sympathetic Catholic *notables*, who not infrequently played an active part in these organisations themselves. In Angers, for example, the clerical party founded the Union Sportive et Gymnastique d'Anjou. The president was a retired colonel, 'one of the *notables* of the reactionary party'; other important figures included a cavalry officer who had resigned from the army after writing an insulting letter to the minister of war and who was living off his private income. There were three counts on the committee and a wine merchant 'in the commercial grip of clerical bankers'. In Ambérieu a similar state of affairs prevailed, with the Catholic club run by a conservative local nobleman, the Comte de Tricaud, whilst in Saint-Pol a prominent Camelot du Roi, Monsieur de Valicourt, was in charge of operations. Ambitious Catholic activists soon realised that sport provided a valuable key to the closed world of the younger worker and began to found clubs specifically designed to attract the adolescent.[11]

But, in general, clubs were based on the parish unit and were run by priests themselves. This was particularly true of the west of France, where there was a high level of commitment to the clerical cause at the grass-roots. It was in the west that sport was most sharply polarised into the clerical and anti-clerical camps. The old established divisions in the Vendée, for instance, were clearly expressed in recreational terms. As a former state teacher in the department of Deux-Sèvres recalled, 'the inhabitants followed two parallel paths: two schools, two bands, two libraries and two sports clubs'. Small towns and villages frequently ran two clubs where they could scarcely support one. In the west the church clubs played a notable part in the processions and rituals of Catholicism. When the local bishop arrived for the annual confirmation service they marched in a guard of honour at the head of the procession in their resplendent costumes, banging their drums and blowing their bugles in symbolic defiance of the secular authorities. In comparison with such spectacular celebrations, remarked a local teacher, the Republicans' parades in the west were feeble indeed.[12]

In some cases, clerical marches of this kind led to confrontation with the Republican authorities. On the most comic local level, for instance, there was the case of the conflict between a clerical lawyer, the president of a local Catholic gymnastics club, and the anti-clerical mayor of the village of Saint-Jean-de-Bonnefonds in the department of the Loire. Both men thoroughly detested each other, and when the mayor capriciously used his authority to forbid a public display and parade by the club, the lawyer decided to take his revenge. He planned to hold a procession without the mayor's permission and, in the classic tradition of the charivari, to dress up some dummies to look like several of the local Republican dignitaries, mount them on donkeys and drive them through the main street. The mayor got wind of the plan just in time and some donkeys suitably attired were in fact found near where the march had been due to start. Both sides then contented themselves with a few well-chosen insults, and the whole affair passed off without further ado. Obviously, too much importance can be attached to one incident of this kind, although the fact that a special report on it was filed by the security police tells us something of the significance which the authorities were beginning to attach to the politicising of sport.[13]

During the first decade of the century there was considerable apprehension amongst anti-clericals over the remarkable success of the Church as a recreational institution; some went so far as to suggest that sport had saved the Church, and others claimed that it was primarily sport which was responsible for the fact that in the years following the disestablishment the Church had succeeded not only in holding its own against the state but had attracted into its ambit youths who would otherwise have been indifferent to religion. A special report from the Seine-et-Marne in 1908 noted that the new social institutions created by the Church in that area were numerous and varied, but that those which had enjoyed the most dramatic success were the sports clubs. A report of the same year from the Nord observed that until around 1900 the Church had taken very little interest in sports of any kind, but that the arrival of a militant bishop coinciding with the disestablishment had led to the setting up of forty clubs in Lille alone.[14]

From the beginning the state kept a close watch over all recreational bodies associated with the Catholic Church. For example, in the 1890s the author of an authoritative work on Church–state relations has noted the close surveillance of church activities. In the Meurthe-et-Moselle this included the submitting of a report on the activities of a cycling group called the Chevaliers Cyclistes de la Croix. In Lyon the authorities were similarly watchful of the political sympathies of sports clubs. In the dossiers which were kept on all private bodies, in accordance with the Law of Associations (1901), there is usually a brief remark on the political complexion of the club. Most clubs are recorded as having 'opinions republicaines modérées' but a fair number were described as being 'clerical' or 'reactionary' in their political views.[15]

More important than this policy of surveillance, however, was the strategy of counter-attraction. From the 1890s onwards an important, though until recently neglected, aspect of Church–state rivalry centered on the battle between the curé's club and the youth organisations run by lay teachers, the *patronages scolaires* or *petites amicales*. 'Between 1894 and 1904 over six thousand primary schools in France established youth clubs for their graduates' and 'according to the Ministry of Public Instruction they had seven hundred thousand members by 1914'. They constituted the largest section of the Republican youth movement and, in the words of an activist from the south-west, were designed to stop 'religious and reactionary *patronages* . . . seizing our pupils when they come out of school and seeking to destroy that which we have sought to raise in their minds'.[16]

Those who ran the *petits-A's* soon learned that uplifting educational activities were less popular than vigorous games and excursions. In addition to keeping young men and women out of the hands of the Catholics, officials wanted to provide them with respectable amusements by which 'boys might be drawn away from the hurly-burly of the streets to the regulated competition of the playing field'. Sports of all kinds had a major place in the life of these clubs. Competitions and leagues were organised. After the war football became the major attraction and a national championship was run for the first time in 1929, with basketball, cross-country, athletics, fencing, skiing, tennis and swimming following suit. The *petits-A's* were united into the newly created Union Française des Oeuvres Laïques d'Education Physique, which ran almost 5000 clubs with more than 310,000 members by 1939.

In addition to supporting the work of the *patronages scolaires*, Republican politicians took special care to foster good relations with the three thousand or so patriotic gymnastic, shooting and military preparation clubs outside the ambit of the Church. Take, for example, the case of the Union des Sociétés Françaises de Gymnastique. President Loubet attended their annual gathering, the *fête fédérale*, during each of the seven years of his presidency, and this tradition of government representation at the highest level continued throughout the period. In 1909, for example, the minister of war was present to address the gymnasts who had assembled at Angers under the aegis of the distillery magnate André Cointreau. Here, amid thousands of gymnasts from all over France, an elaborate Republican ritual was enacted with one distinguished speaker after another coming to the podium to salute the *patrie*, the politicians and the organisers of the event. The proceedings were begun by the president of the Union, Charles Cazalet, who addressed the minister and the audience in the following terms:

> The gymnasts of the Union, in the name of whom I have the honour of speaking, would be most ungrateful if they did not publically thank the Republican government and particularly thank you yourself, who have never ceased to offer us all kinds of encouragement; you know that all our efforts are bent towards the improvement of the race and the preparation of our youth to serve as effectively as possible in the ranks of the army which we regard with such affection and of which we say in the words of the poet: 'J'ai fait de ta grandeur, ma plus belle espérance!'.

Monsieur Cointreau then added his contribution, promising that if France or the state were ever in danger they had only to make the appropriate gesture and the youth of the Union would spring to their defence. 'Vive la France! Vive la Patrie! Vive la

République!' One patriotic speech followed another, each echoing the same Republican sentiments, until the final ceremony when the faithful were awarded their state decorations. Three *officiers de la légion d'honneur* were bestowed on the most influential figures, twelve *officiers d'instruction publique* were granted, forty-three *officiers de l'académie*, eighteen *chevaliers de mérite agricole*, two *officiers du Nicham-Iftikhar*, thirty *médailles d'argent*, grand module, fifteen *citations et lettres de félicitations*. It is small wonder that these gatherings soon earned the reputation of being little more than a means by which the Republican faithful were recompensed for their work in keeping the young loyal to the government and the army.[17]

In this climate of sectarianism little proper co-operation between sporting bodies on a truly national basis was possible. For a while France had two international football teams, until the Catholics finally got control of a single united league in 1913. In the case of gymnastics, co-operation proved impossible. The state was firmly against the USFG joining with the Catholic gymnasts in the face of the growing German threat. When pressed on the issue of the professed political neutrality of the non-Catholic gymnastics organisation, its leader remarked with a casuistical skill worthy of the Jesuits that 'political neutrality should not be confused with political indifference'. To be a Republican was not to be involved in politics but merely to accept in a patriotic spirit the existing political arrangements.[18]

Trouble flared up between the Catholic and non-Catholic bodies on several occasions during the pre-war period. The mayor of the frontier town of Nancy invited both factions to attend a great patriotic rally intended to impress the Germans in 1909, but the prefect intervened to ban the event lest there be any violence between the large groups of mutually antagonistic sportsmen. In 1911 there was a series of street brawls in Roanne when the assembled Catholics tried to march through the town. Members of the Action Française invaded the sub-prefecture, and in classic Republican fashion a local teacher replied by pelting the Catholics with stones from his window as they passed his house. It was only through the Union Sacrée of the war that these conflicts subsided. With the ending of the war and the election of a partially clerical government in 1920 there was little basis for continuing the conflict. The FGSPF in fact became the first Catholic body to be officially recognised, and its annual gathering was presided over by Millerand and Marshal Foch in 1921. There was sometimes *détente* at a local level too. In Monségur, a *bastide* of 1300 inhabitants in the Gironde, the pre-war *amical laïque* and church *patronage* joined forces to end sectarianism in sport by forming one club, the Sporting Club Monségurais.[19]

Although the forces of nationalism and clericalism continued to make themselves felt in sport during the inter-war period, there was an increasing tendency in the 1920s for sports to become involved in conflicts between employers and unions or in the wider struggle between conservatism and socialism. Prior to 1914 it was the role of the Catholic clubs in sport which proved to be the most contentious issue, whereas after the war attention came to be focused on the efforts of industrialists, agitators and party politicians to exploit sport. The *Annuaire des Sports* of 1922 lamented the fact that 'despite the law, which forbids all political or religious discussions, the parties are more or less openly infiltrating sporting associations'.[20]

Clearly, the use of sport to indoctrinate the young with staunchly nationalistic values before 1914 had carried with it strong overtones of the need for greater social control of the lower classes. A significant body of opinion had in principle encouraged the practice of sport on the grounds that it led to more social mixing, lessened class tension and helped maintain social stability. Under the title *Régénération sociale sur la pelouse*, one sanguine sportsman had argued that through a common interest in games 'the rich would be stripped of their contempt or indifference for the worker, whilst the poor would rid themselves of the envy and the hate of the upper classes which makes them on occasion savage and vicious'. Another hopeful sporting theorist of the early twentieth century promised that sport would be 'a social educator', promoting a 'veritable equality' between men transcending the boundaries of class.[21]

Whilst there had been an undoubted element of social engineering in the thinking of late nineteenth-century propagandists of sport, there had been relatively little explicit use of sport as a means of raising or lowering the consciousness of the urban working classes. Neither employers nor unions took much interest in the opportunities it offered for propaganda. A socialist sports federation was founded in 1908, the Fédération Sportive du Travail (FST), but initially entry was restricted to those who were already party members and, apart from the odd article in *L'Humanité*, little attempt was made to woo the young worker through sport. Employers were only marginally more active in this field. Around the end of the century the large department stores and banks began to subsidise clubs for their staff. For instance, the Grands Magasins du Louvre formed a shooting club in 1885 called Halte-là! and started a cycling club in 1896. But, with the exception of occasional patriotic or recreational initiatives for the shop-worker or clerk, not much else was done.

This situation was transformed during and after the First World War. Football was becoming popular amongst provincial workers before 1914 but the garrison matches which were arranged to keep the troops happy helped to spread it even further. In addition, the granting of the eight-hour day in 1919 and the increasing trend towards Saturday half-day ('la semaine anglaise') meant that a far greater number of working men were now in a position to indulge their new sporting interests. Several surveys carried out in the early 1920s to find out how their leisure was being used all come to the conclusion that sport was more popular than 'culture' with the working classes. While these social changes were taking place, industrial conflict, which had been partially suspended for the duration of the war, once again loomed large on the horizon. There were a series of long and bitter strikes in the early 1920s. These tensions were further aggravated by the schism in the Socialist party resulting in the emergence of the French Communist party as a separate political force dedicated to class war.[22]

It was in this context of industrial strife and changing leisure patterns that a number of the larger firms began to take a serious interest in recreational programmes for their workers. A survey of these new forms of paternalism carried out by the Ministry of Labour in 1921 and 1922 noted, for example, that Peugeot had acquired extensive playing fields adjacent to all four of their factories, that Michelin workers had a sports complex with a large swimming pool, and that other famous names like Renault, Schneider and even the champagne firm of Pommery all laid on sporting facilities of one kind or another. If France was not yet 'a land fit for heroes to live in', it was at least becoming a place where the proletariat could play. Obviously, employers believed that corporate sports encouraged a sense of *esprit de corps* amongst the workforce and provided an alternative to left-wing politics or the consumption of alcohol as a leisure activity. 'I am a firm advocate of sport', confessed André Citroën, 'I do my best to encourage it and expect the best results from it amongst my workers.' Just in case there was any doubt as to what such 'results' were expected to be, the author of the article in which Citroën was cited quoted approvingly from the works of 'a prominent foreign industrialist', who claimed that 'any young worker who dons the garb of an athlete soon considers himself a gentleman and rejects all anarchistic notions'. Ernest Mercier, France's leading industrial manager and technocrat, founded a workers' sports magazine *Le Muscle* in the interests of national efficiency and social peace.[23]

Naïve though these ideas were, sports certainly proved to be the most popular of the recreational initiatives of the *patronat*. Film shows, talks and visits to museums smacked too much of bourgeois condescension and class manipulation, but sport appeared to be free of such associations. As a result, corporate clubs devoted to a wide range of sports sprang up throughout France during the twenties and thirties. An inquiry carried out in 1935 showed that out of eighty-five factories in the survey eighty had their own sports facilities. Interestingly, in contrast to other ventures like libraries or allotments, most of the sports clubs tended to be run either wholly or partly by the workers themselves. Although it seems clear in retrospect that many of these corporate clubs were relatively independent of the board-room and probably derived part of their popularity with employees from that fact, there was still a good deal of understandable anxiety on the Left about the very existence of such clubs. The communist *Sport Ouvrier* warned its readers that 'the ruling class seeks to infiltrate the habits, styles of life and thought of its adversaries without their knowing it' and that corporate sports 'will undermine the critical spirit and foster a climate of discipline and respect vis à vis bourgeois chaos and its institutions'.[24]

Diatribes of this kind were the stock in trade of *Sport Ouvrier* and were by no means directed only at conservative opponents. After the schism between the communist and socialist elements within the FST at the annual congress held in 1923 at Montreuil, a propaganda war broke out. By a narrow majority of 126 to 111 the delegates at the conference had voted to leave the reformist Socialist Workers Sports International based in Lucerne and affiliate themselves to the new Red Sport International run from Moscow. The socialists walked out of the FST to set up their own organisation, the Union des Sociétés Sportives et Gymniques du Travail. Reliable figures are hard to come by but one estimate gave the communists eighty-five of the ninety clubs in the department of the Seine with about an equal share of a rather smaller number in the provinces. *Sport Ouvrier* harangued the socialist organisation from the start, branding them as 'enemies of the proletariat and capitalist collaborators', whilst denouncing socialism in more general terms as 'the opium of the people, the last rampart of the bourgeoisie'. For their part, the socialists called the communists 'the valets of Moscow', which provoked the response that it was better to act for the Third International than to 'serve as an agent of the counter-revolutionary government press'.[25]

This endless round of abuse left little time for sport. It is small wonder that the communists in particular had very limited success in their mission to exploit sport for the purpose of proletarian revolution. At first they blamed 'administrative mistakes or errors of theory' for their apparent lack of appeal to the young worker, but by 1926 they were forced to admit to having 'concentrated too narrowly on politics. Our organisation should be more broadly based and our propaganda more concerned with sport itself.' With this end in view they set up a 'propaganda commission' and established a bulletin aimed at 'bourgeois' clubs. Whether such bureaucratic proliferation had any impact on recruitment is difficult to say, as the paper ceased to appear on a regular basis shortly afterwards. The Tardieu government of 1930–32 did its best to suppress the FST, but it re-emerged in a slightly strengthened position with 115 member clubs in the Paris area representing about 9000 sportsmen and 80 clubs in the provinces with about 5000 members. The breach between the communists and the socialists was finally healed in 1934. Sport, therefore, was one of the first areas in which the new spirit of compromise, tolerance and solidarity between the parties of the Left made itself felt. The Fédération Sportive et Gymnique du Travail (FSGT), as the new union of socialist and communist sportsmen was called, grew rapidly during the Popular Front era. In 1935 it numbered 732 clubs with 42,706 members, and by 1938 this figure had risen to the impressive total of 1687 clubs with 102,694 members. In other words, the spread of specifically working-class socialist sports clubs was roughly commensurate with the general growth in other working-class institutions such as trades unions during these years.[26]

It was no coincidence that this expansion of sporting activity took place at the same time as the advent of France's first socialist government. In addition to its primary tasks of disbanding the fascist leagues and dealing with the problems of recession and unemployment, the Communist-backed coalition of Radicals and Socialists led by Léon Blum was pushed into more immediate social reforms by the strikes and factory occupations of June 1936. The success of the Left in the election had prompted demonstrations of mass elation in many major industrial centres and demands for the forty-hour week and an increase in wages. These were granted by the employers in the Matignon agreements, and their capitulation gave a further boost to an already festive atmosphere in the occupied factories. The Blum government followed up this popular impulse by offering cheap holiday travel and announcing a major construction programme to improve sports facilities, together with other measures to encourage wider participation in physical recreation.

'Sport for all' was the brainchild of Léo Lagrange, a young socialist lawyer who was made junior minister for leisure and sports in the Blum government. The creation of this new post meant that full official recognition had at last been given to a huge and hitherto neglected area of social life. Right-wing critics mocked the 'ministry of idleness', but its origins lay in the old High Commission for Physical Education and Sports set up after the First World War on staunch nationalist grounds. The difference between the two bodies lay in the greater powers accorded to the new minister and the greater emphasis given to the enjoyment of leisure regardless of class. The new ministry was more effective than the old commission, which had been run by minor politicians and which was first attached to the war ministry, then to the education ministry and finally to the health ministry. These constant moves reflected the ambiguity in the official mind over the status and role of sports. This administrative confusion combined with tight budgets meant that the commission had relatively little impact. So France in the mid-thirties was still desperately short of municipal sports facilities such as playing fields and swimming pools.[27]

The building of new facilities became the chief Socialist and Communist objective in their leisure programme. A pilot scheme was started in three departments – the Aude, the Loiret and the Meurthe-et-Moselle – to provide 50 per cent state backing for the provision of amenities for sport and recreation. Nearly 2 million francs were granted to 290 communes in the Loiret alone during the 2 years of the experiment. Plans to extend the programme to a further twenty-nine departments had to be cut back because of financial constraints. Nevertheless, about 400 separate projects were under way by the end of 1937, and 25 million francs had been spent on sports in 1936 alone. In addition, official encouragement to participate in organised physical activity was provided by the new *brevet sportif populaire*. This certificate was designed to reward youngsters who wanted to acquire basic skills – running, jumping, throwing, climbing and swimming – and it seems to have been a great success. In 1937, 600,000 boys and girls took the test either through their schools or clubs and 420,000 passed.[28]

Behind these initiatives lay the deeper fear that if the liberal democracies failed to involve themselves in new forms of popular culture, the extra-parliamentary Right would manipulate sport for its own ends. Hitler's 'Strength through Joy' movement and Mussolini's 'Dopolavoro' programme 'to solve the problem of the workers' leisure' had made a considerable impact on fascist sympathisers and Republicans alike. The fact that the German sports programme reached its climax with the Olympic Games of 1936 at the very moment that the Popular Front came to power gave added prominence to the issue. To men like Lagrange it seemed vitally important to show that it was not only the radical Right which advocated mass physical exercise and sports. During the 1930s fascist intellectuals like Drieu de la Rochelle had gone so far as to suggest that 'the physical reform of man must be our immediate enterprise'. 'French fascist writers were calling for "a revolution of the body", a multiplication of athletic teams, scouting groups, hiking associations, youth hostels and sports stadiums.' Shortly after being appointed, Lagrange voiced his concern about these developments in a radio interview: 'We have heard all too often that a democratic country by its very nature is incapable of creating a vast sports and leisure organisation. Our ambition is to show the fundamental error of that view.' Jean Zay, the talented young education minister, who like Lagrange was later to become a fatal victim of the German occupation, recalled in his prison notebooks that for Lagrange 'sport was the driving force of French vitality, the welfare of the race'.[29]

Such sentiments were, of course, so commonplace that they were virtually clichés. What is interesting here is that the vocabulary of racial health and national resurgence so beloved of the Right was now also being used by the Left. All the same, this similarity in vocabulary concealed important differences between the two sides, not only in their political philosophies but in their attitudes towards the segregation of sporting activity according to income and social background. Lagrange and his supporters particularly sought to break down the class barriers which prevented working people from playing games like tennis or from taking up winter sports. Efforts were made to interest young workers in climbing mountains or sailing boats. Skiing was popularised and the 'trains de neige' leaving Paris for the Alps during the Christmas holidays became a familiar sight. The young could stay in youth hostels and rent equipment cheaply, thereby combining sport with holiday-making in a way that has since become extremely popular. There can be little doubt that these imaginative enterprises helped to lend the Popular Front some of the mystique with which it has subsequently been endowed in the mind of the urban workforce. Léon Blum certainly took pride in such achievements, as he revealed in his defence during his trial at Riom in 1942, when he was accused of having undermined the French nation. His literary gifts were particularly in evidence when he recalled the feeling of physical liberation and the simple enjoyment of the open air associated with the summer of '36:

> I did not often leave my office, . . . but each time that I did, crossing the wide Parisian suburbs I saw the roads thronged with old cars, motor-bikes, tandems with working class couples in matching pullovers as if to show that the idea of leisure evoked in them too a simple and natural sense of style. All this gave me the feeling that, despite everything, I had helped embellish and illuminate lives that were otherwise dark and difficult. It was not just that these people had been removed from the pubs or that there were new facilities for a

full family life. It was that they now had a sense of the future, a sense of hope.[30]

Rhetoric apart, the summer of 1936 was a turning point. For the first time the recreational activities of the working class, whether in the form of holidays or sports, received official sanction and support. With this in mind it is perhaps ironical that, in the sphere of recreation at least, the 'hope' Blum spoke of was in part fulfilled by the very institution that had placed him on trial: the Vichy government. Vichy took up the cause of sport with a vengeance. A supporter of the new regime remarked that too little had been done to encourage sport before 1940, with the result that during the thirties youths took to political activism of the wrong sort and to street-fighting when they should have been working out their natural aggression on the sports field. Sporting bodies were purged of politically unreliable elements, and a new timetable was introduced into the schools which prescribed nine hours a week of physical education and sport. Students were expected to spend three afternoons a week playing games. Borotra, the athletic tennis player who had thrilled Wimbledon in the twenties, was placed in charge of the programme, which was meant to produce a sense of discipline and group loyalty in French youth. A pamphlet written for young rural workers stated these objectives explicitly: 'In sport you are preparing your apprenticeship for full social life . . . if you are obedient and respect the rules of the game on the pitch, then you will behave similarly when you are not at play'.[31]

The intense propaganda in favour of the active rather than the contemplative life, the obsession with the need for 'roots', the decadence of urban life and the importance of traditional values were all combined in the drive to revive the French nation through sport. The words of Marshal Foch were quoted time and again: '40,000 people watching a few youngsters playing sport; I'd far rather see the opposite.' The emphasis placed on pious, obedient citizenship and patriotism has unmistakeable echoes of the earlier writings of social catholicism. The Vichy administration did not slavishly copy the sporting programme of the Third Reich, rather it provided an opportunity for more conservative reformers to try out some of their ideas. The potential of sport as a source of social cohesion had been a strand in conservative thinking on leisure all along, and as late as 1939 these ideas were still being actively canvassed. A substantial investigation of the impact of paid holidays post 1936 by a social catholic from Toulouse emphasised the opportunity presented by sports and holidays 'for putting back the *joie de vivre* that the class struggle had taken out'. New recreational ventures, he went on, 'will provide the chance for frequent encounters with other social strata . . . through popular leisure we can proceed to a better form of social organisation'. Some of these ideas find expression in a tendentious handbook, *Jeunesse qui vit*, published in 1942, which describes the marriage of a printing worker to a young typist. The book explains how to have a good time and be happy, and is full of references to the joys of sailing boats, hill-walking and playing games. This couple and their friends are dedicated to a life of good, clean fun and hard work. They resolve to reform France through a programme of muscular Christianity centered on the idea that 'the past is past'.[32]

Leaving out clerical and nationalist sentiment, the concept of good and active citizenship advocated in *Jeunesse qui vit* bears a marked resemblance to the preference for the outdoor life displayed by the propagandists of the Popular Front. In fact, despite their endless tirades against the Left, Vichy politicians took over a good deal from their detested predecessors. The *brevet sportif* was retained in altered form, and the same dislike of professionalism and spectator sport which animated socialist reformers found its echo in the more reactionary puritanism of Pétain and his followers. This surprising degree of similarity in the actual content of the sports policies of the Popular Front and the Vichy government reflects a common preoccupation with the formation of character through sport. Whether they grew up to be good socialists and trade unionists or staunch Catholic nationalists, the young were expected to be loyal, cheerful, active and obedient. Increasingly, governments of the Left and of the Right came to see sport as playing an important part in this process. The twentieth century saw the emergence of mass society, and games seemed to offer an excellent opportunity for moulding the masses.

Of course, we are talking here of how reformers and politicians sought to take advantage of the new popularity of sports; this is not the same thing as analysing the actual impact of recreational propaganda on ordinary participants. How much notice did they take of the ideological sauce served up with their sport? Only a careful investigation of each activity could provide a full answer to this question, although the detailed analysis of gymnastics in an earlier chapter certainly suggested that there was a significant gap between the intentions of those who enthusiastically directed operations from above and the actual effect that they had on those below. The resistance of the rank and file to the various forms of political propaganda that they encountered in play is hard to document, but the following two examples, drawn from very different social contexts, are suggestive. Apparently, the readers of *Sport Ouvrier*, the fiercely politicised communist paper, often exhibited either ignorance of or resistance to the proletarian doctrine of sport. 'There are still many', complained an indignant militant, 'who firmly believe in the bourgeois doctrine of the neutrality of sport.' Perhaps the author of a later article came rather nearer to a balanced estimate of the paper's appeal to Parisian workers when he upbraided his comrades for buying the paper primarily to see their names in print. Likewise, a survey of the bourgeois students of the *grandes écoles* carried out in 1930 reported a similarly negative attitude towards the values which those directing their activities sought to impart to the élite of French youth: 'What do the young think of sport? They don't think anything very much. It's fun, that's all. The sporting theories devised by arthritic old men leave them cold. They don't play sport for the good of the race or in the interests of national defence. They play it for its own sake.'[33]

Although these fragments of evidence are little more than straws in the wind, they serve to make the point that as far as sport was concerned the influence of political ideas was probably always tempered by the more athletic priorities of the young. Sport in France struck a balance between the didactic and the ludic from the late nineteenth century onwards, and this relationship between pleasure-seeking and social purpose has persisted, with the balance tilting one way or the other depending on the particular group in power. This brings us back to our point of departure. While it has been proved beyond doubt that a wide range of individuals and groups sought to harness sports for their differing political purposes, it is doubtful whether any of them were completely successful. Political control through sport was easy in principle but difficult in practice.

11   Conclusion

In his classic essay on the play element in culture, *Homo Ludens*, Huizinga noted that 'contests of skill, strength and perseverance have always occupied an important place in every culture either in connection with ritual or simply for fun or festivity'. Ever since the ancient Greeks men have channelled their playful instincts in competitive directions in order to display their prowess. Yet, sports should not in consequence be seen as 'fixed unchanging entities that have always existed in their present form and will always continue to do so'. Both the form and the content of these manifestations of the ludic drive have evolved in step with wider changes in living conditions and social attitudes. In particular, the upheaval in the economic and social structure of Europe that took place in the course of the later nineteenth century helped to dissolve traditions of popular recreation that had grown up over the centuries. No branch of sporting activity was untouched by the overall process of modernisation. New sports like cycling were produced by technological progress, whilst older games were recast to fit the rhythms of an industrialising society. Even traditional country sports were transformed and infiltrated by new social groups.[1]

The main differences between modern sports and their antecedents lay in the degree of organisation, specialisation and competition involved. Changing rhythms of work and rapid technological advances in communications and manufacturing facilitated the emergence of forms of physical activity that were both more intense and more complex than their predecessors. Those who had been brought up in the communal traditions of rural sports, where little or no distinction was made between real athletic achievements and popular revels like apple-bobbing and blindman's buff, found the seriousness and discipline of modern sports more than they could comprehend. Sports were removed from their casual, local context and became standardised national games with sophisticated rules and hordes of supporters. Football was no longer a village game in which the youths of adjoining parishes worked off their frustrations in the manner of a public affray; it became an ordered activity in which violent behaviour and local patriotism were reduced to manageable proportions. Skill was increasingly substituted for strength, and a more generalised belief in the value of competition replaced the narrow focus of communal rivalry that had dominated sports in the past. This revolution in recreation was first visible in Britain, where economic and social change had been most rapid, but between 1880 and 1900 other modernising economies began to follow suit. By the turn of the century each society had begun to develop its own specialisms and most advanced countries shared enough common sporting interests to give rise to a series of international competitions, of which the Olympic Games, founded by a Frenchman in 1896, is the most famous.

The *belle époque*, the period from the mid-1890s to the outbreak of war in 1914, was the crucial phase in the transformation of leisure activity, and particularly sport, in French society. As economic growth in France had on the whole tended to be slower than in Britain or Germany there is a temptation to assume that France remained overwhelmingly traditional. One of the objects of this study has been to show that France was decisively modernised during the *belle époque*, whilst still doing justice to those elements of French physical recreation that remained in part traditional. Although regional influences continued to be important in French leisure (as the detailed examination of bull-fighting and cockfighting revealed), they too were subject to the wider forces of commercialisation and social change. The status and popularity of indigenous village games fell sharply with the spread of the bicycle and the gymnastics movement and with the introduction of rugby and association football. Folklorists believe that it was during the decade preceding the outbreak of the war that traditional rural sports went into irreversible decline, a decline which the disruption and reorientation of youth in the First World War served to intensify. In the 1920s millions of young Frenchmen took up organised competitive exercise in private clubs set up for the purpose. The old *fête populaire* was finished for the young.

Sport became an integral part of modern culture during this era. As early as 1901 journalists were confidently predicting that historians of the future would have to include a couple of chapters on the bicycle and on athletic sports if they hoped to do justice to the changing character of daily life in France around the turn of the century. The spread of sport 'was one of the most memorable features of the late nineteenth century,' recalled an informed contemporary. In 'Agathon's' famous pre-war survey, Parisian students played the new sports with the same gusto with which they received garbled Bergsonism or intuitively took up the call of the National Revival. With its cult of gratuitous effort, sport was not only a rejection of the sterile, cerebral academic tradition but a denial of strictly utilitarian or materialistic values as well. In sport, the young bourgeois in search of a new code of ethics imbibed a belief in competition not as a means to an end but as an end in itself. Sports mirrored and intensified the pace and pressure of modern capitalism, providing a means of working off the aggression it generated and of refining the qualities it required. These developments were noted by contemporary intellectuals who had predictably ambivalent attitudes to the phenomenon. 'After having unduly neglected exercise in the past we are now in danger of going too far in the opposite direction', complained one critic; others went even further and accused sport of trivialising social life, infantilising the masses and encouraging an anti-intellectualism among the sons of the bourgeoisie. Even Barrès bemoaned the mindlessness of his own athletically-inclined young nationalists, but Jean Giraudoux strongly defended sport as 'the art by which man liberates himself from himself'.[2]

Contemporaries who lived through this period of the modification of existing sports and the introduction of new ones could not help commenting on the swiftness and scope of the process. The author of a book of sporting memoirs published in 1904 noted that as far as non-traditional sports were concerned 'fifty years ago there were few persons, a very small number really, who took an active interest in sports; these individuals were all from a privileged social background and formed themselves into a kind of aristocratic élite, whereas these days a host of people drawn from a broad cross-section of society take an interest themselves either by playing or by becoming loyal and often passionate followers of certain spectator sports'. All the same, the spread of modern sports throughout society was by no means a steady or simple story, and careful distinctions need to be made concerning the timing and extent of the involvement of the various major occupational groups. Only a small minority of Frenchmen at first took an active part in sport. Gymnastics admittedly found a sizeable lower-class following and by 1914 football teams were becoming fairly commonplace in industrial suburbs, but it was not until the twenties that modern sport became an integral element in popular culture. During the late nineteenth and early twentieth centuries it was the bourgeoisie who blazed the trail. With a few prominent exceptions, the nobility tended to restrict itself to hunting, and in the 1880s it was the affluent young man from a commercial or professional family who took up cycling or played English team sports, often doing so whilst still a schoolboy or student. Indeed, playing new sports came to be seen as a necessary outlet for the *lycéen* oppressed by the dismal academic routine. But from the mid-nineties onwards a noticeable change took place. The lower middle classes arrived on the scene in force. Many a young lawyer must have contemplated with some apprehension the hordes of clerks, shopkeepers and skilled craftsmen who bought themselves bicycles and shooting permits or began to play the games that had formerly been the preserve of the privileged.[3]

Before 1914 adult manual workers who were interested in sports mostly confined themselves to following cycle races or the local football team as a spectator. The majority of factory workers put in long hours at tiring jobs, and most of the peasants worked even harder. What they wanted was relaxation and entertainment rather than vigorous physical exercise for its own sake. Spectator sport offered them the sense of collective identity and conviviality that had formerly been associated with the *fête*. Fuelled by the popular press and eagerly taken up by the radio, which became a common household object during the thirties, spectator sport acquired an almost religious aura for the thousands who were devoted to it. Figures like the Pelissier brothers in cycling and the boxer Carpentier were idolised with no less fanaticism than the new stars of Hollywood. Although problems of population concentration prevented France from developing as successful a commercial football league as

England, professionalism was recognised in rugby (the thirteen-a-side game got under way in the thirties) and in football, too. The current vogue for live broadcasts of important games goes back to the Popular Front era. Nowadays radios have been replaced by colour televisions, but cafés are still regularly transformed from noisy drinking places into hushed neon-lit stadia in miniature for a big match. The usual babble of voices subsides. All that is heard above the agitated sound of the commentary is the intermittent groan, oath or cheer according to the fortunes of the favoured side. Football, cycling and rugby provide mass entertainment for the relatively undifferentiated audience of the New France. The enjoyment of spectator sports now takes its place alongside the family car and the annual holiday in the vision of the 'good life' to which so many aspire. The convergence of leisure interests that has become so much a feature of 'the affluent society' in France, as elsewhere, is nowhere more evident than in the rise of sport as a passive masculine preoccupation between the wars.

Participation, however, was a rather more complex matter. Those who took an active part in sport usually joined a private club of some kind. The club was the fundamental unit of amateur sport. As social institutions clubs may have encouraged some mixing between men of varying ages, but men of different classes did not mingle so easily. Considerable variations certainly existed between the small town clubs, which were relatively heterogenous, and the clubs in the big cities, which tended to be more clearly differentiated along class lines. Sport could provide channels of upward mobility to the determined individual, but in the main it reinforced existing social divisions. Simply because a large number of men played the same games there is no reason to believe that the old communality of the *fête* was a feature of the new social life of the club. Mass involvement did not in itself create fraternity. Sport remained stratified as a participant activity after it had ceased to reflect social distinctions very accurately as a spectacle. Manual workers joined leagues where they increasingly had the chance to play against clubs of broadly middle-class composition, but the two strata were rarely found on the same side.

Clubs had a wide range of social functions other than the provision of specialised facilities for certain forms of physical activity. Looking behind the athletic facade of club life, it appears that sports clubs frequently performed social duties formerly associated with craft corporations and the like. Males met together to drink, talk and generally celebrate the virtues of masculinity. They claimed that women were excluded simply because females were physically unsuited to vigorous sports, but this argument also applied to some of the men who were members. The truth is that the enjoyment of male society was a part of the rationale of the sporting life; sports clubs provided a masculine haven where fathers could escape their children and husbands their wives, where male stereotypes of female behaviour might come in for jocular examination and where concrete examples of man's superior physical abilities were ready to hand. Closely connected to this role was the function of the club as an agency for assisting the transition of youths to adulthood. Sports teams formalised the traditional adolescent 'bands' with their 'captains' which had previously been a common feature of village society. Team sports trained adolescents in assertiveness while emphasising the need for group loyalty and co-operation. Clubs channelled violent impulses in socially acceptable directions and legitimised aggression by containing it. Achievements in sport at club level could act as a rite of passage through which a youth's manly prowess was displayed and given proper public recognition without undue injury to the person or damage to property.

Under the Third Republic organised physical exercise was championed by a wide range of political interests, mostly in the Centre and on the Right, and normally for avowedly nationalist ends. All ideologues of sport sought to create more obedient, energetic and resourceful individuals, whatever party or principle they represented. Sport became caught up in the Church–State conflict and was the scene of fierce competition between the two factions for the allegiance of the young after the disestablishment of the Church in 1905. After the First World War it was the parties of the Left who attempted to undermine the efforts of clerics and employers to infiltrate sport. Although the efficacy of sport as an instrument of political propaganda remains in doubt, the evidence of its manipulation for political ends is incontrovertible, culminating in the adoption of physical exercise as a panacea for an ailing France by the forces of Vichy.

Shifting our attention from the ideological dimension to the general distribution and nature of sporting activity in France over the last century, three external influences are evident. First, there is the importance of British sports, especially the winter ball games, which made a greater impact on France than on any other European country. It should be remembered that it was not only association football that the French took from the English: they learned rugby too. Rugby has subsequently gone from strength to strength in France and has a following in the south-west which for sheer fanaticism can only be matched by the Welsh. Second, despite the dramatic impact and subsequent importance of these games, the German influence on physical recreation, both through her example and on account of the resentment and fear she excited, should not be forgotten. France differed markedly from Britain in having two large and powerful gymnastics organisations. Gym only gradually gave way to football as the major group sport. Third, there is the hispanic influence. France was unique among the advanced European countries in permitting bullfighting, which became a leading summer spectator sport in the south of France and enjoyed considerable success in northern cities like Lille and Roubaix, where Flemish traditions, notably cockfighting, had prepared the way.

Although France adopted a good deal of sport from abroad, it is hardly fair to accuse French sport of being purely derivative. In their great cycle races the French achieved an originality and prominence that is beyond dispute. The classic road races provided the kind of mobile spectacle that was peculiarly suited to the dispersed nature of the French sporting public. Those who lived in the numerous small market towns of France and followed sport through the newspapers were able to see top professional sportsmen free of charge as the Tour de France, the Paris–Bordeaux, the Paris–Roubaix or one of the many other classic road races passed through their area. Most towns were too small to be able to subsidise permanent, stadium-based spectator sports – this is why there was no fully professional football league until the early 1930s – but there was fierce competition for the honour of acting as a checkpoint for a great race. Cycle-racing pioneered mass spectator sport in France. It was the first activity of a modern, standardised kind which made an impact in the countryside as well as in the town; it began by providing amusement for the culturally deprived masses of the large cities and ended by penetrating the hitherto closed world of rural entertainment. Cycling was the first spectator sport to accept professionalism, advertising, sponsorship and sensationalism. Between 1890 and 1914 it won universal acceptance in a country renowned for its tenacious regional traditions and must be considered France's first national sport.

All in all, diversity was the single most distinctive feature of sport in France. Despite the swiftness of the general process by which 'massive market interests came to dominate an area of life which until recently was dominated by individuals themselves', the French lived up to Lucien Febvre's dictum and preserved variety in the face of the powerful forces of national uniformity. The range of sports available was probably unparalleled elsewhere in Europe. In the Languedoc you could go to a bullfight in the summer or a rugby match in the winter without leaving the *bourg*; you could sip *pastis* and watch the ancient bat and ball game of *tambourin* in the square of the small towns of the Hérault or go to see the water-jousting tournaments at Sète. If you lived around the Pyrénées there was the marvellously fast and sophisticated Basque game of *pelote*, in which teams of players would send a special ball hurtling at a distant wall from a basket-type racket strapped to their arms. In the Nord you were liable to find a cockfight and a football match taking place on the same day. French sport resembled French society in the importance attached to local tradition, despite the inexorable pressures of commercialisation. Rugby, for example, served to strengthen rather than undermine ancient instincts of local patriotism. In the casual violence of the crowds or the occasional loutish antics of gymnasts there was a hint of the age-old revels of the *fête*; a sense of periodic release, of festive abandon and insubordination still found modified expression in the sports of the Third Republic. Yet, the old traditions of violent play and village rivalry now existed within a framework of growing standardisation, with Frenchmen speaking the same language, reading the same newspapers and often playing the same games. A boy born into the world of the Commune and living out his allotted time until the Second World War could hardly have failed to notice the substitution of the archaic amusements of his father's generation by the new leisure activities of his own. He might have viewed with a certain distaste the rampant commercialism of the modern sportsman and cast his mind back to the unsullied ideals of the heroic amateur age of his youth. But it is more likely that he himself would have been drawn into the web of mass entertainment, with its magazines, films, cars, holidays and sports, almost as completely as his own children, with their athletic idols and Hollywood stars. With the new cult of records and of measuring the merits of one man or machine against another with mathematical precision, the whole apparatus of modern competitive sport established itself in the mind of the common man alongside older traditions of sociability and strong local or regional loyalties. It was precisely this combination of sentiment and science, of parochial ties and cosmopolitan commercialism, which gave the sports of France their distinctive character between the mid-nineteenth and mid-twentieth centuries.[4]

Notes

CHAPTER 1

1. E. Weber, 'Gymnastics and Sports in Fin-de-siècle France: Opium of the Classes?', *American Historical Review*, vol. 76 (February 1971), p. 70; G. Magnane, *Sociologie de sport* (Paris, 1970), p. 45; see also J. Dumazedier and A. Ripert, *Loisir et culture*, vol. 1, *Loisir et la ville* (Paris, 1966), p. 47; J. Walvin, *The People's Game, a Social History of British Football* (London, 1975), p. 2.
2. Dumazedier and Ripert, *Loisir et culture*, vol. 1, p. 47; a useful short summary can be found in N. Anderson, *Work and Leisure* (London, 1961), ch. 1; J. Dumazedier, *Vers une civilisation de loisir* (Paris, 1962) is the best introduction to the problem in France.
3. E. Chapus, *Le Sport à Paris* (Paris, 1854); C. de Caumont, *Le Sport, il y a cinquante ans* (Paris, 1904); A. Faure, *Paris Carême-prenant: du Carnival à Paris au XIXᵉ siècle* (Paris, 1978); P. Lafargue, *Le Droit à la paresse*, ed. M. Dommaget (Paris, 1969), p. 79; E. Weber, *Peasants into Frenchmen: the Modernisation of Rural France* (London, 1977), p. 40; on the character of modern sport see E. Dunning, *The Sociology of Sport: a Selection of Readings* (London, 1971) and A. Guttman, *From Ritual to Record: the Nature of Modern Sports* (New York, 1978).
4. The *fête* has come in for a great deal of historical attention in recent years. The best introduction to its study is probably the special number of *Annales Historiques de la Révolution Française*, no. 221 (1975).
5. There is no adequate recreational survey of France for this period but the position in Britain is clearly set out in R. W. Malcolmson, *Popular Recreations in English Society 1700–1850* (Cambridge, 1973).
6. For a useful short discussion of this transition see M. R. Marrus, 'The Emergence of Leisure', ed. P. N. Stearns (Missouri, 1974), 'Forums in History'.
7. G. Dupeux, *French Society 1789–1970*, trans. P. Wait (London, 1976), especially pp. 157–9.
8. P. Albert, *Histoire générale de la presse française*, vol. III (Paris, 1967), pp. 383–4, 584; T. Zeldin, *France 1848–1945. Intellect, Taste and Anxiety*, vol. II (London, 1977), pp. 552–3, 560–2.

9. Dupeux, *French Society 1789–1970*, pp. 175–6, and A. Daumard, *Les Fortunes Françaises* (Paris, 1973), especially Tables v and vii.
10. Weber, 'Gymnastics and Sports in Fin-de-siècle France', p. 76; M. Spivak, 'Le Développement de l'éducation physique et du sport français de 1852 à 1914', *Revue d'Histoire Moderne et Contemporaine* (January–March 1977), pp. 28–48.

CHAPTER 2

1. J. Kemp, *Hunting and Shooting in Lower Brittany* (London, 1859), p. 27.
2. G. d'Havrincourt, *La Chasse à tir d'aujourd'hui* (Orléans, 1930), pp. 16–17, gives a useful summary of the position before 1870.
3. For the beginnings of peasant shooting see G. Thomin, *Notes sur la chasse dans l'Agenais* (Agen, 1877) and P. Lenglé, *La Chasse pour tous* (Paris, 1909), p. 10.
4. Statistics of permit sales were published in the *Annuaire statistique*. For a more detailed analysis see 'Permis de Chasse, 1876–1889', *Journal de la Société Statistique de Paris* (1890), p. 314; see also *Congrès International de la Chasse* (Paris, 1907), statistical appendices i–iv.
5. C. Adam, *Alphabet des chasses* (Paris, 1859); A. Rossel, *Daumier, émotions de chasse* (Paris, 1973).
6. I. Hope, *Brittany and the Chase* (London, 1853), p. 12.
7. L. Vauzanges, *Les Sociétés françaises de tir* (Paris, 1882) for a comprehensive survey of shooting clubs mostly founded in the 1870s; see also Chapter 3, p. 40.
8. These figures come from the *Annuaire statistique* and from d'Havrincourt, *La Chasse à tir d'aujourd'hui*, p. 6.
9. *Congrès International de la Chasse*, Appendix 4, 'Relevé par département de la population totale (1901) et de la population électorale (1905) et proportion, en 1895 et 1906, du nombre des chasseurs de cette dernière'; *Le Journal des Chasseurs*, 1 May 1894, p. 374; *La Gazette des Sports Illustrés*, 22 October 1882, p. 4.
10. J. P. Samat, *Chasses de Provence* (Marseille, 1896), p. viii.
11. *Congrès Internationale de la Chasse*, Appendix 3, 'Relevé par département du nombre de chasseurs de 1895 à 1906 et progression de ce nombre'; H. de Lacaze, *A propos de chasse dans les Landes de Gascogne* (Mayenne, 1960), p. 15; H. du Blaisel d'Enquin in the journal *L'Eleveur* (1930), cited in d'Havrincourt, *La Chasse à tir d'aujourd'hui*, p. 288.
12. M. Bidault de l'Isle, *Le Chasseur à tir* (Paris, 1912), p. 38.
13. *Le Saint Hubert Club Illustré*. The issues of this journal used for the sampling of the social composition of members are cited in the text.
14. F. Suchaux, *Souvenirs d'un chasseur* (Bar-sur-Aube, 1894), p. 139; F. Devillard, *Souvenirs de chasse* (Moulins, 1911), pp. 14–16.
15. J. Levitre, *Organisation des chasses* (Anet, 1908), p. 33; *La Chasse moderne, encyclopédie du chasseur* (Paris, 1912), p. 69; F. Thévin, *Annuaire générale de la chasse et de ses fournitures* (Saint-Germain-en-Laye, 1912), p. 446.
16. E. Bellecroix, *La Chasse pratique* (Paris, 1886), p. 368; d'Havrincourt, *La Chasse à tir d'aujourd'hui*, p. 6.

17. *Le Chasseur Illustré*, 25 September 1892, p. 307; and *Le Petit Chasseur*, 20 October 1912, p. 666. For a discussion of sociability and shooting see Chapter 8, p. 160.
18. See Chapter 1, pp. 8–9; Dupeux, *French Society 1789–1970*, p. 152.
19. AD Gard, 6M, 1054, L'Union des Chasseurs, 16 August 1892; J. Jacobs, 'A Community of French Workers: Social Life and Labour Conflicts in the Stéphanoise Region, 1890–1914' (unpublished D.Phil. thesis, Oxford University, 1973), p. 85.
20. This brief account of the politics of the *permis de chasse* is taken from the *Congrès Internationale de la Chasse*, pp. 519–28, 602.
21. *La Gazette des Sports*, 1889, p. 545; *La Chasse et les droits des propriétaires*, par 'un propriétaire' (Tarbes, 1879), p. 124; *Le Petit Chasseur*, 16 July 1912, p. 376.
22. Weber, *Peasants into Frenchmen*, p. 249; E. Guillaumin, *La Vie d'un simple*, ed. Stock (Paris, 1957), pp. 145 and 233; P. Yvon, 'Autour du permis de chasse', *Société d'Etudes Folkloriques du Centre-Ouest* (July–August 1975), pp. 5–7.
23. E. Grenadou and A. Prévost, *Grenadou, paysan français* (Paris, 1966), pp. 146–7; L. Waulthier, *Communalisation de la chasse* (Paris, 1908); AD Gard, 6M, 1564, letter dated 12 September 1908.
24. Marquis de Foudras, 'Les Gentilhommes chasseurs', preface to the edition prepared by Musée de la Vénerie (Paris, 1962); La Duchesse d'Uzès, *La Chasse à courre* (Paris, 1912); *Le Saint Hubert*, February 1953, p. 31.
25. C. de Canteleu, *Manuel de la vénerie française* (Paris, 1890), p. 412; *La Gazette des Chasseurs*, 1883, p. 5.
26. B. Chabrol, *Histoire de la vénerie française* (Paris, 1963) gives a useful survey, pp. 47–62.
27. There is an account of this ceremony in *Le Moniteur de la Chasse et des Tirs*, 11 November 1882, p. 1, and in La Duchesse d'Uzès, *La Chasse à courre*, p. 58; de Lacaze, *A propos de chasse dans les Landes de Gascogne*, pp. 21–2. See also Chapter 8, pp. 158–9.
28. For an excellent account of the infiltration of new wealth into hunting in England, see R. Carr, *English Fox-Hunting* (London, 1976), especially pp. 152–6.
29. A. Marx, *En plein air* (Paris, 1887), p. 286; L. Levesque, *La Chasse et la grande propriété en Seine-et-Marne* (Provins, 1891), p. 9; Chabrol, *Histoire de la vénerie française*, p. 63.
30. *Le Sport Gazette*, 1 August 1883, p. 2.
31. P. Caillard in F. G. Aflalo (ed.), *Sport in Europe* (London, 1901), p. 122; *Le Petit Chasseur*, 17 December 1911, p. 10, and 22 June 1913, p. 404; Pearson Phillips, 'Death in the Forest', *Sunday Telegraph Supplement*, 18 February 1979, pp. 20–26, gives a lively and well-illustrated account of stag-hunting around Paris today.

CHAPTER 3

1. J. C. Dixon, 'Prussia, Politics and Physical Education' in P. C. McIntosh (ed.), *Landmarks in the History of Physical Education* (London, 1971), p. 128;

H. Bunle, 'L'Education physique et les sports en France', *Journal de la Société Statistique de Paris* (1922), pp. 135, 138. There may be considerable errors in these figures but they serve to give a general indication of the scale of the phenomenon under discussion.

2. D. Mamoz, *La Gymnastique au XIXe siècle* (Paris, 1891), ch. 1.

3. For an up-to-date discussion of the evolution of gymnastic techniques see J. Ladegaillerie and F. Legrand, *L'Education physique au XIXe et au XXe siècles* (Paris, 1971).

4. Spivak, *Revue de l'Histoire Moderne et Contemporaine* (January–March 1977) especially p. 29.

5. G. Flaubert, *Oeuvres complètes*, ed. Seuil (Paris, 1964), vol. II, p. 262.

6. R. Auget, *Histoire et légende du cirque* (Paris, 1974).

7. Ibid., pp. 49, 127; Simone Bertault, *Piaf* (Penguin: London, 1973), pp. 14–15.

8. Weber, 'Sports and Games in Fin-de-siècle France', p. 73; G. L. Mosse, *The Nationalisation of the Masses* (New York, 1975), pp. 127–136.

9. L. Colland, *La Sentinelle de Reims* (Reims, 1911), p. 10.

10. *Le Moniteur des Bataillons Scolaires* (September–October 1883), p. 11; *Le Gymnaste*, 28 September 1901, p. 237; *La Gazette des Sports Illustrés*, 24 September 1881, p. 1; AD Seine-Inférieure, 4TP, 9.

11. *Le Gymnaste*, 15 January 1883, a commemorative edition for Gambetta; also 15 December 1887, pp. 394, 399, and 14 February 1889, p. 547; *Le Temps*, 6 November 1900; see also Chapter 10, pp. 191–2.

12. *Le Sporting*, 17 July 1880, p. 3; *Con. Mun. PV*, 25 February 1885, p. 150.

13. 'Commission du Budget: bataillons scolaires, gymnastique et jeux scolaires', *Con. Mun. RD*, no. 156 (1889); AN, F17-6912, 6917, 6922, contain depressing surveys by the Ministry of Education on the lack of facilities and local co-operation.

14. D. Mamoz, *De la gymnastique au XIXe siècle*, pp. 139, 222; AD Hérault, 58M, 13.

15. AD Seine-Inférieure, 4TP, 9.

16. *Le Gymnaste*, 20 December 1890, p. 463; J. Jacobs, 'A Community of French Workers', p. 84; 'Rapport de Muzet sur la demande de subventions aux sociétés de gymnastique' *Con. Mun. RD*, no. 31 (1892); G. Picot, *Les Garnis d'ouvriers* (Paris, 1900), p. 11.

17. M. Bahonneau, *La Gymnastique raisonnée à l'usage des employés et des ouvriers* (Angers, 1911).

18. *Le Moniteur de la Gymnastique Scolaire, Hygiénique et Medicale*, 15 January 1869, p. 3.

19. For a biographical sketch see *Dictionnaire de biographie française* (Paris, 1959), vol. 8, p. 6; see also the following editions of *Le Gymnaste*: 15 July 1899, p. 34; 18 November 1899, p. 361; 10 August 1901, p. 118, and the article 'Solidarisme', 1 July 1905, p. 4.

20. *Le Temps*, 16 May 1875, p. 2; *Le Gymnaste*, 1 January 1885, p. 14; *Le Moniteur Officielle de la Gymnastique et de l'Escrime*, 4 August 1886, p. 3; N. Laisné, *Nouvelles Observations sur l'enseignement de la gymnastique* (Paris, 1886), p. 8; Faure, *Paris Carême-prenant*, p. 153.

21. For a short account of the dance see Zeldin, *France 1848–1945*, vol. II, pp. 656–60; also Weber, *Peasants into Frenchmen*, ch. 26; E. Shorter, *The*

Making of the Modern Family (London, 1976), p. 214; AD Gard, 6M 1130 and 1185.

22. For primary evidence of gym clubs functioning in this way see *Le Gymnaste*, 1 January 1885; AD Rhône, 4M 2, 'Projet de fusion des sociétés de gymnastique de la troisième arrondissement'; *Le Revue des Sports*, 26 February 1887, p. 5; *Les Sports Athlétiques*, 20 December 1890, p. 5.
23. AD Hérault, 58M; Zeldin, *France 1848–1945*, vol. II, p. 484; see also Chapter 8, pp. 163–5.
24. *Le Gymnaste*, 10 September 1888, p. 136; 25 November 1899, p. 381; 19 August 1905, p. 199; see also Chapter 10, pp. 209–10.
25. *Encyclopédie générale des sports* (Paris, 1946), pp. 439–444; see also Chapter to pp. 196–8.
26. T. Margadant, 'Primary Schools and Youth Groups in pre-war Paris: Les "Petits-A's"', *Journal of Contemporary History* (April 1978), p. 331.
27. For a more extended discussion of the social role of sports clubs see Chapter 8; for the role of respectability in British leisure see P. Bailey, *Leisure and Class in Victorian England* (London, 1978); H. Cunningham, *The Volunteer Force: a Social and Political History* (London, 1975).

CHAPTER 4

1. M. Pfefferkorn, *Le Football association* (Paris, 1921), p. 278.
2. E. Weber gives an excellent account of the role envisaged for English sports by men like Coubertin in 'Pierre de Coubertin and the Introduction of Organised Sport into France', *Journal of Contemporary History*, vol. V, no. 2 (1970), pp. 3–26.
3. These themes emerge clearly in Coubertin's early works: for example *Souvenirs d'Oxford et de Cambridge* (Paris, 1887), and *L'Education anglaise en France* (Paris, 1889). For an identical contemporary view see L. Latour, *L'Education physique en Angleterre et en France* (Paris, 1891). The standard biography is Y-P. Boulongne, *La Vie et l'oeuvre pédagogique de Pierre de Coubertin* (Ottawa, 1975).
4. Coubertin expresses this view most fully in the opening chapter of *Une campagne de vingt-et-un ans* (Paris, 1909); Coubertin was also a competent historian and the author of a history of the early Third Republic in which his concern over the instability of French social and political institutions is made explicit; R. D. Anderson, 'French Views of the English Public Schools: Some Nineteenth Century Episodes', *History of Education*, vol. 2, no. 2 (June 1973), pp. 159–171.
5. This biographical sketch comes from Weber, 'Coubertin and the Introduction of Sport into France', pp. 10–11; also P. Daryl, *La Renaissance athlétique* (Paris, 1888), a collection of articles written for *Le Temps* by Grousset under a pen-name.
6. For an occupational breakdown of both the Ligue and its rival the USFSA see J. P. Simon, 'Essai sur l'introduction de l'athlétisme en France' (unpublished 'Mémoire pour le diplôme', ENSEPS, 1972).
7. For a more detailed account of the beginnings of the English sports in France, see Weber, 'Gymnastics and Sports in Fin-de-siècle France',

pp. 82–84. Weber's account and my own are based on Georges Bourdon, *La Renaissance athlétique et le Racing Club de France* (Paris, 1906).

8. Ibid., pp. 87–97; Marx, *En plein air*, p. 107.
9. G. Duhamel, *Le Football français, ses débuts* (Paris, 1931) gives a fascinating first-hand account.
10. Ibid., p. 45.
11. There is a good account of Tissié's early efforts to launch sport in Bordeaux in J. Thabault, *Sports et education physique* (Paris, 1972), ch. v, 'Le Docteur Tissié et la Ligue Girondine d'Education Physique'; see also Weber, 'Gymnastics and Sports in Fin-de-siècle France', p. 87.
12. C. Lagarde, *Au pays du roi Henri, pays de beau rugby: cinquante ans à la Section Paloise* (Pau, 1953), p. 15; C. Duhau, *Histoire de l'Aviron Bayonnais, l'époque héroïque* (Bayonne, 1968), p. 22; J. P. Rey, *Tarbes: le rugby en rouge et blanc* (Paris, 1973), pp. 55–6; P. Tissié, *L'Éducation physique* (Bordeaux, 1901), p. xxviii.
13. G. le Roy, *Education physique et gymnastique* (Paris, 1913), pp. 355–8.
14. Zeldin, *France 1848–1945*, vol. ii, p. 688, Graph of Football and Athletics 1919–45; *Almanach du Miroir des Sports*, 1936–7, p. 138.
15. *Le Livre d'Or du Football Club de Rouen, 1899–1969* (Rouen, 1969), p. 9; *Le Sport Amateur*, 20 November 1904, p. 66; *La Revue Olympique*, February 1903, p. 8; M. Soulier, *Le Football gardois* (Nimes, 1969), pp. 117, 151; L'Ecole de Football d'Amiens Athletic Club, *Le Football en Picardie et l'histoire de ses origines* (Amiens, 1948), p. 57.
16. AD Rhône, 4M, Football Club de Lyon, carton 7; Stade Lyonnais, carton 1.
17. Dr P. Voivenal, *Mon beau rugby* (Toulouse, 1962), p. 28; J. Barbat, *Histoire du ballon ovale* (Clermont-Ferrand, 1959), pp. 81–3.
18. Bib. Hist. Coll. Act., 106, carton 00011, undated press cutting; L. de Fleurac, *Les Courses à pieds et les concours athlétiques* (Paris, 1911), p. 44.
19. M. Metjé, *Fondation et vie d'un club: L'Union Sportive Albigeoise 1925–32* (Albi, 1933), p. 40; *Les Sports Populaires*, 20 July 1910.
20. G. Pastre, *Les Boucliers du printemps* (Toulouse, 1967), p. 45.
21. M. Celhay, 'Quand je portais le maillot bleu et blanc', *Société des Sciences, Lettres et Arts de Bayonne* (1975), pp. 405–459; J. Boutain *Un grand club dans une petite cité, L'Union Athlétique de Gujan-Mestras* (Bordeaux,n.d.) was kindly provided by Jacqueline Larrieu; H. Garcia, *La Fabuleuse Histoire de rugby* (Paris, 1973), p. 257.
22. Ibid., pp. 284–92; J. Prat, *Mêlée ouverte* (Paris, 1968) gives a good account of post-war rugby.
23. J. C. Grivot, *Crampons, ballon rond* (Paris, 1970), pp. 25–7; Soulier, *Le Football gardois*, p. 206.
24. *Le Livre d'Or de la Coupe de France* (Paris, 1936), p. xvi; H. Jooris, *De l'enthousiasme au sens des réalités pratiques: contribution à l'étude de l'organisation du football en France* (Lille, 1933); Soulier, *Le Football gardois*.
25. G. Rozet, *Les fêtes du muscle* (Paris, 1912), p. 152; J. Lhermit, *Les Sports pédestres* (Paris, 1911), p. 99; for an interesting account of the life of a semi-professional athlete see E. Anthoine, *Les Sports athlétiques* (Paris, 1913).
26. G. Bénac, *Les Champions dans la coulisse* (Paris, 1963), pp. 84–6; J. Ladoumègue, *Comment j'ai battu deux records du monde* (Paris, 1930).

CHAPTER 5

1. J. Durry, *L'Histoire véridique des géants de la route* (Paris, 1973), pp. 19–23. This work provides an excellent history of the major road races themselves but does not deal with social and commercial questions directly. It is a technical history of the sport.
2. E. Gendry, *Sport vélocipédique, les champions français* (Angers, 1891), p. 22; H. O. Duncan, *Vingt Ans de cyclisme pratique* (Paris, 1896), p. vi; V. Dauphin, *Le Cyclisme en Anjou* (Angers, 1936), p. 42.
3. *Véloce Sport*, 30 April 1885; *La Revue Vélocipédique*, 15 June 1884, estimated that there were around 4000 cyclists in France of which only about 400 were keen competitors.
4. L. Bonneville, *Le Vélo, fils de France* (Paris, 1938), p. 138; *La Revue Vélocipédique*, 25 April 1884; AD Seine-Inférieure, 4TP, 107C, 1.
5. These figures come from the tax returns in the *Annuaire statistique*; Y. Boulinguiez, 'Aspects de la vie quotidienne ouvrière dans le département du Nord à la première moitié du XXe siècle', *La Revue du Nord* (July–September 1972), p. 332; P. Pierrard, *Lille et les Lillois* (Paris, 1967), p. 249.
6. *Cyclette Revue: histoire chronologique du cyclisme*, February 1961.
7. H. Bunle, 'L'Education physique et les sports en France', p. 145; the Fédération Cycliste et Athlétique de France has left no reliable membership figures but Bunle suggests 60,000 in 1911.
8. J. Floch'moan, *La Genèse des sports* (Paris, 1962), p. 122; see also *Le Chasseur Illustré*, 19 November 1893, p. 374.
9. *Con. Mun. RD*, no. 35 (1893).
10. For an account of the spread of the *vélodrome* in Anjou see Dauphin, *Le Cyclisme en Anjou*, p. 32; J. Rennert, *A Hundred Years of Bicycle Posters* (London, 1973), p. 9; Weber, 'Coubertin and the Introduction of Sport into France', p. 18.
11. *Con. Mun. RD*, no. 28, 1895; E. Couratier, *Le Parc des Princes, étude présentée à la Société Historique de Boulogne-Billancourt* (Paris, 1955); M. Viollette (ed.), *Le Cyclisme* (Paris, 1912), p. 125; Bib. Hist. Coll. Act., 106,00009, Cyclisme.
12. *Le Vélo*, 5 February 1895, p. 1; *Les Sports Athlétiques*, 11 March 1893, p. 9.
13. Viollette, *Le Cyclisme*, p. 274.
14. *Con. Mun. RD*, no. 28 (1895); *Con. Mun. PV*, 7 July 1897; *Con. Mun. RD*, no. 8 (1899).
15. M. Martin, *Voyage de Bordeaux à Paris par trois vélocipédistes* (Bordeaux, 1890), p. x; *Revue du Touring Club*, membership figures published annually; M. Leudet (ed.), *Almanach des Sports, 1900–1* (Paris, 1901), p. 97.
16. *Le Vélodrome de Choisy-le-Roi* ('organe indépendante du cyclisme et des intérêts de la banlieue sud de Paris') 4 June 1895, pp. 1–2.
17. L. Baudry de Saunier and C. Terront, *Mémoires de Terront: sa vie, ses performances, son mode d'entraînement* (Paris, 1893), from which the following biographical sketch is taken.
18. *Le Vélo*, 26 March 1894, p. 1; also Durry, *L'Histoire véridique des géants de la route*, p. 43; G. Bénac, *Les Champions dans la coulisse* (Paris, 1963), pp. 9–14, 223–7; *L'Essor*, 27 December 1907.

19. *Le Vie au Grand Air*, 24 December 1899, p. 172.
20. Viollette, *Le Cyclisme*, p. 35; Durry's *L'Histoire véridique des géants de la route* provides an excellent account of these races; also V. Breyer and R. Coquelle, *La Course classique: Bordeaux–Paris* (Paris, 1899).
21. G. Nicholson, *The Great Bike Race* (London, 1977), especially ch. 4; also E. Seidler, *Le Sport et la presse* (Paris, 1964), pp. 37–54.
22. F. Terbeen, *Les Géants de cyclisme sur route* (Paris, 1969), pp. 13–16; A. Chassignon and A. Poirier, *Le Tour de France* (Paris, 1952), p. 14; Nicholson, op. cit., p. 54.
23. Nicholson, op. cit., p. 54 and p. 100; A. Blondin, *Sur le Tour de France* (Paris, 1979), pp. 22–3, an intelligent and elegant interpretative essay.
24. Viollette, *Le Cyclisme*, p. 111; *Le Sport Ouvrier*, 1 August 1926; Nicholson, op. cit., p. 42.
25. Blondin, op. cit., p. 29.
26. R. Barthes, *Mythologies* (Paris, 1957), p. 111; A. Nathan (ed.), *Sport and Society* (London, 1958), p. 31.
27. Seidler, op. cit., p. 73; M. Beaujour and J. Ehrman, *La France contemporaine: textes et documents* (Paris, 1970), p. 244; see also Chapter 10, p. 195 for further proof of Desgrange's chauvinism.
28. R. C. Cobb, *Tour de France* (London, 1976), p. 212, in a review of L. Bodard, *Les plaisirs de l'hexagone*. On the question of the lack of municipal facilities see T. Zeldin, *France, 1848–1945: Ambition, Love and Politics*, vol. 1 (Oxford, 1973), p. 524.
29. G. Thuillier, 'Pour une histoire des gestes en Nivernais au XIXe siècle', *Revue d'Histoire Economique et Sociale* (1973), no. 2, p. 249.
30. Nicholson, op. cit., p. 35.

CHAPTER 6

1. M. Le Grand, *Les Courses de taureaux dans le sud-ouest de la France jusqu'au début du XIXe siècle* (Mont-de-Marsan, 1934), p. 108; *La Nouvelle Revue du Midi*, January 1924, pp. 49–51 and 217–30; M. Martin, *Grande Enquête du journal 'Le Vélo'* (Paris, 1898), p. 78.
2. A. Maureau, *Les Courses de taureaux à Avignon* (Avignon, 1971); *Deb. Parl. Ch. Dep*, 21 June 1884, p. 1429; 'Les Courses de taureaux dans les arènes de Nimes', *La Nouvelle Revue* (September–October 1893), pp. 487–508; *La Gazette des Sports et du Plein Air* (Paris, 1889), p. 588.
3. AD Nord, M.208, 114, letter to the prefect of the Nord dated 5 March 1874 and letter sent by him dated 23 April 1874.
4. P. Pierrard, *La Vie ouvrière à Lille sous le Second Empire* (Paris, 1965), p. 301; A. Desrousseaux, *Moeurs populaires de la Flandre française* vol. 1 (Lille, 1889), p. 116.
5. 'Clic-Clac' (pseud.), *Histoire des courses landaises* (Mont-de-Marsan, 1905), p. 25; A. Lafront, *Histoire de la corrida en France* (Paris, 1977) gives the best account of the development of the sport, especially ch. 3.
6. J. Boulanger and E. Henriot, *Animaux de Sport* (Paris, 1912); A. de Corbie, *Combats de Coqs* (Lille, 1939) offers a short general survey.

7. Maureau, *Les Courses de taureaux à Avignon*, pp. 33–7, and 'Clic-Clac', op. cit., preface.
8. For a brief discussion of emigration from Spain, see R. Carr, *Spain 1808–1939* (London, 1966), p. 413; L. Loubère, *Radicalism in Mediterranean France* (New York, 1974), pp. 104–6; C. Higounet (ed.) *Histoire de l'Aquitaine* (Toulouse, 1971), p. 455.
9. *Deb. Parl. Ch. Dep*, 1897, p. 446; *Toros Revue*, 18 July 1897, p. 1; A. Lafront, *Bibliografía de la prensa taurina francesa, 1887–1961* (Madrid, 1962).
10. P. Rives, *La Corvée de joie* (Paris, 1924), p. 90; *La Revue Cynégétique et sportive*, 1892, p. 171; *Le Coqueleur*, 21 February 1904, p. 1, and *L'Essor*, 26 January 1912, p. 3.
11. J. Boquet, *Lille à la belle époque* (Lille, 1971) is a book of photographs which contains several pictures of cockfights; de Corbie, *Combats de coqs*, p. 58; AD Pas-de-Calais, M. 4669, 2; *Le Coqueleur*, 1 November 1903, p. 2; 15 November 1903, p. 1; 29 November 1903, p. 2; and 10 January 1904, p. 1.
12. Maureau, *Les Courses de taureaux à Avignon*, p. 30; H. de Montherlant, *Les Bestiaires* (Paris, 1926); AD Hérault, Série O (Béziers Arènes 1901–14).
13. *Toros Revue*, 23 October 1898, p. 238; AD Hérault, Série O (Lunel Arènes 1861–1914); AD Gard, 6M, 357.
14. *La Mise à Mort*, 15 May 1893, p. 1; *La Nouvelle Revue*, September–October 1893, p. 496; AD Gard, 6M, 357; Dr. Marc, *L'Aficion et les arènes bitteroises de leurs origines à nos jours* (Béziers, 1959), p. 72; M. Ferrus, *La Corrida à travers les âges à Bordeaux* (Bordeaux, 1925), p. 12.
15. *Le Coqueleur*, 27 November 1904, p. 2, and 4 December 1904, p. 2.
16. *Le Toréro*, 3 September 1899, p. 1; *Toros Revue*, 7 August 1898, p. 116, and 1 December 1897, p. 1.
17. Maureau, *Les Courses de taureaux à Avignon*, p. 23; *Bulletin des Séances de l'Académie de Nîmes*, 1934–6, pp. 123–5.
18. AD Rhône, 7M7, 'Courses de taureaux; difficultés survenues entre messieurs Walbott et Vidal de Marseille' (undated).
19. *Le Toréro*, 29 May 1898, p. 5, and 15 January 1911, p. 1; J. Saint-Paulien, *Histoire de la corrida* (Paris, 1968); R. 'Baranger', *Emma la Caballera* (Paris, 1959).
20. Lafront, *Histoire de la corrida en France*, ch. 7; E. Hemingway, *Death in the afternoon* (London, 1932), p. 246.
21. *Le Toréro*, 14 August 1910, p. 1.
22. Ibid.; *Deb. Parl. Ch. Dep*, 1900, no. 1691, p. 207; P. Maréchal, *L'Évolution de l'opinion publique sur les courses de taureaux* (Paris, 1902).
23. AD Nord, M.208, 113.
24. AD Pas-de-Calais, M.4669, 2.
25. For an example of pro-bullfighting argument, see *Toros Revue*, 18 April 1897, p. 5; also *Le Toréro*, 6 August 1891, p. 1, and 23 August 1891, p. 1; *Deb. Parl. Ch. Dep*, 1897 p. 468–9; J. Milliès-Lacroix, 'Les Origines de la plaza de toros à Dax', *Bulletin de la Société des Amis de Borda* (1974) pp. 213–38, 465–82.
26. V. Petit-Jean, 'Les Combats de coqs dans le nord de la France' (unpublished maîtrise thesis, Paris, 1972) gives information on the present status of the sport.

CHAPTER 7

1. Zeldin, *France 1848–1945*, vol. II, p. 920.
2. L. Chevalier, *Labouring Classes and Dangerous Classes*, trans. F. Jellinek (London, 1973), pp. 422–3; Gautier cited in G. Pillement, *Paris en fête* (Paris, 1972), p. 33.
3. AD Nord, M.208,113 and *Deb. Parl. Ch. Dep*, 1897, p. 465.
4. *Le Toréro*, 24 April 1898, p. 2; also 1 May 1898, p. 1.
5. Desrousseux, *Moeurs populaires de la Flandre française*, vol. I, p. 121; and AD Pas-de-Calais, M.4669-2, letter to the prefect dated 20 February 1894; *Le Petit Chasseur*, 26 November 1911, p. 5.
6. 'Une siècle de corridas bayonnaises, 1852–1952', *La Société de Science, Lettres et Arts de Bayonne*, no. 112 (1966), p. 505; *La Mise à Mort*, 17 July 1893, p. 1; AD Rhone, 7M7, Courses de Taureaux, 3 July 1905.
7. M. van der Meersch, *L'Empreinte du dieu* (Paris, 1951), p. 103.
8. O. Hufton, *The Poor of Eighteenth Century France* (Oxford, 1974), pp. 360–1; T. J. Le Goff and D. M. G. Sutherland, 'The Revolution and the Rural Community in Brittany', *Past and Present* (February 1974), p. 107; M. Agulhon, *Pénitents et francs-maçons de l'ancienne Provence* (Paris, 1968), pp. 62–4.
9. Weber, *Peasants into Frenchmen*, p. 57.
10. R. Thabault, *Education and Change in a Village Community* (London, 1971), p. 164; A. Van Gennep, *Manuel de la folklore française*, vol. I (Paris, 1943), p. 202; C. Seignolle, *Le Berry traditionnel* (Paris, 1969), p. 84.
11. Le Goff and Sutherland, art. cit., p. 107; Souvestre cited in Zeldin, *France, 1848–1945*, vol II, pp. 687–8; Garcia, *Histoire de rugby*, p. 114; C. Tilly, 'The Changing Place of Collective Violence' in P. N. Stearns and D. J. Walkowitz (eds), *Workers in the Industrial Revolution* (New Jersey, 1974), pp. 117–133.
12. Voivenal, *Mon beau rugby*, p. 45; A. Scriven, *Grandes Journées de rugby français* (Toulouse, 1947), p. 25.
13. J. Maieresse, *Football, quand tu nous tiens* (Paris, 1935), pp. 75–6.
14. Garcia, op. cit., pp. 254–7.
15. A. Jauréguy, *Qui veut jouer avec moi?* (Paris, 1939), pp. 116–19; *La Nouvelle Revue du Midi*, 1924, pp. 248–9.
16. J. Gay, *Les Sports et les jeux d'exercice en Anjou* (Angers, 1947), p. 169.
17. *Le Sport Amateur*, 2 June 1905, p. 365; also 15 January 1905, p. 77.
18. *Le Gymnaste*, 6 October 1894, p. 8; also 3 August 1901, p. 105; *Le Figaro*, 3 September 1885; Shorter, *The Making of the Modern Family*, pp. 205–6.
19. *La Cyclette Revue: histoire chronologique du cyclisme*, July–August 1961.
20. R. Ingham (ed.), *Football Hooliganism* (London, 1978) provides a thoughtful review of the problem.
21. Professor Desbonnet, *Les Rois de la lutte* (Paris, 1910), p. 6; P. Pons, *La Lutte et les lutteurs* (Paris, n.d.), pp. 65–7.
22. J. Dauven (ed.), *L'Encyclopédie des sports* (Paris, 1960), pp. 305–6.
23. R. Barthes, *Mythologies*, trans. A. Lavers (London, 1972), pp. 19–23.
24. Dauven (ed.), op. cit., p. 236; L. Hémon, *Battling Malone and Other Stories* (London, 1925), p. 10.
25. *La Boxe et les Boxeurs*, 8 December 1909, p. 1; L. Hémon, op. cit., p. 22.

26. Dauven (ed.), op. cit., p. 141; J. Arlott (ed.), *The Oxford Companion to Sports and Games* (London, 1975), p. 99; S. de Beauvoir, *Memoirs of a Dutiful Daughter* (London, 1963), p. 72.
27. Bénac, *Les Champions dans la coulisse*, pp. 100–105.
28. G. de Maupassant, *Contes et Nouvelles*, ed. A. M. Schmidt, vol. 1 (Paris, 1957), p. 736.
29. Quoted by P. Marsh in R. Ingham (ed.), *Football Hooliganism*, p. 67.
30. L. Tiger, *Men in Groups* (London, 1970), p. 119.
31. H. Zehr, 'The Modernisation of Crime in France and Germany, 1830–1913', *Journal of Social History* (Summer 1975), p. 129; Zeldin, *France, 1848–1945*, vol. ii, p. 916.

CHAPTER 8

1. M. Agulhon's entire work sheds light on the question of sociability, but the most important works are *Pénitents et francs-maçons de l'ancienne Provence* (Paris, 1968), *La République au village* (Paris, 1970) and *Le cercle dans la France bourgeoise 1810–1848: étude d'une mutation de sociabilité* (Paris, 1977); Shorter, *The Making of the Modern Family*, pp. 205–10.
2. Agulhon, *Pénitents et francs-maçons*, pp. 42–63; also L. Roubin, 'Male and Female Space in the Provençal Community' in R. Forster and O. Ranum (eds), *Rural Society in France* (London, 1977), pp. 152–80.
3. Agulhon, *La République au village*, pp. 206–234; also M. Agulhon, 'Une problème d'ethnologie historique: les "chambrées" en Basse-Provence au XIXe siècle' in M. Agulhon (ed.), *Ethnologie et histoire, forces productives et problèmes de transition* (Paris, 1975).
4. Weber, *Peasants into Frenchmen*, p. 397; T. Judt, *Socialism in Provence* (London, 1979), ch. 6, especially pp. 158–166.
5. E. Durkheim, *The Division of Labour*, 2nd ed. (New York, 1964), p. 12; G. Duveau, *La Vie ouvrière sous le Second Empire* (Paris, 1946), p. 487; Zeldin, *France, 1848–1945*, vol. ii, pp. 598, 799–800.
6. Faure, *Paris Carême-prenant, passim*; C. Rearick, 'Festivals in Modern France', *Journal of Contemporary History*, vol. 12 (1977), p. 439.
7. M. R. Marrus, 'Social Drinking in the Belle Epoque', *Journal of Social History*, (Winter 1974), pp. 129–30.
8. J. Jenger, *L'Alcool et le sport* (Seine-et-Oise, 1925), p. 14; AD Rhône, 4M,6; B. Harrison, *Drink and the Victorians* (London, 1971), p. 331.
9. P. Garcin, *Le Jeu de boules* (Mulhouse, 1949), pp. 12–24; C. Plume, *Tout sur la pétanque* (Paris, 1963); H. Tremaud, *Les Français jouent aux quilles* (Paris, 1964) is an excellent history of the game; also G. Ducasse, *Les Quilles de neuf* (Mont-de-Marsan, 1953), pp. 7–22.
10. L. Wylie, *A Village in the Vaucluse* (London, 1951), pp. 250–4.
11. Tiger, *Men in Groups*, p. 123.
12. Maupassant, *Contes et Nouvelles*, vol. 1, p. 204; also M. d'Herbeville, *Messieurs les disciples de Saint Hubert* (Paris, 1905), p. 78.
13. Maupassant, *Contes et Nouvelles*, vol. 1, p. 3 and p. 649.
14. C. Velin, *La Chasse et le gibier dans l'Est* (Epinal, 1888), p. 43, has a superb

comic account of the opening of the season on a *chasse communale*; I. D.
Hope, *Brittany and the Chase* (London, 1853), pp. 7–8.

15. V. Mainfroy, *La Politique d'un paysan à propos du privilège de chasse* (1863),
especially p. 8 (the place of publication is not known).

16. AD Gard, 6M, 1050; Wylie, *A Village in the Vaucluse*, pp. 300–3.

17. C. P. Coutoure, *Cinquante Ans de cyclisme avec le Véloce Club Barentinois* (Le
Havre, 1955).

18. P. Sainmont, *Le Véloce Club de Tours et le doyen des cyclistes de France* (Tours,
1902).

19. Weber, *Peasants into Frenchmen*, ch. 26, especially pp. 450–1.

20. C. de Loris, *La Femme et la bicyclette* (Paris, 1896); also *La Fronde*, 23
December 1897, p. 3, for a feminist viewpoint; J. R. Gillis, *Youth and
History, Tradition and Change in European Age Relations 1770–Present* (New
York, 1974), p. 111; d'Herbeville, *Messieurs les disciples de Saint Hubert*, p. 3.

21. J. H. Adam, 'Loisirs et éducation populaire', *Cahiers de Redressement
Français*, no. 21 (1927), p. 9; Duhau, Histoire de l'Aviron Bayonnais,
pp. 2–7.

22. These figures are based on a table attached to the following document:
'Rapport de L. Bellan au nom de la 4e commission sur la répartition du
crédit affectée aux sociétés d'éducation physique, de tir, de natation et de
sport', *Con. Mun. RD*, no. 128 (1922); Coutoure, *Cinquante Ans de cyclisme
avec le Véloce Club Barentinois*, pp. 14–15; V. Dauphin, *Le Cyclisme en Anjou,
notes et documents* (Angers, 1936), p. 29.

23. *Annuaire illustré des sociétés de gymnastique de l'Association de la Seine* (Paris,
1888), pp. 90–91. Averages calculated from statistics of membership;
L. Colland, *La Sentinelle de Reims* (Reims, 1911), p. 99; *Con. Mun. RD*, no.
164 (1893).

24. Agulhon, *Le Cercle dans la France bourgeoise*, ch. VII, p. 62; J. Prévost,
Plaisirs des sports: essais sur le corps humain (Paris, 1925), p. 120.

25. E. Forestier and F. Gerbert, *Almanach de la vélocipédie illustrée* (Rouen,
1883), pp. 65–76.

26. Pillement, *Paris en fête*, p. 45; M. Mauron, *Les Lampions de la fête* (Paris,
1967), p. 366; see also relevant sections of Chapters 6 and 7.

27. Prévost, *Plaisirs des sports*, p. 33 and p. 121; Roubin, 'Male and Female
Space in the Provençal Community', p. 152; J. Ardagh, *The New France*
(London, 1970), pp. 395–6.

CHAPTER 9

1. For evidence of class conflict in pre-industrial leisure in Provence see
Agulhon, *Pénitents et francs-maçons*, pp. 63–4.

2. Zeldin, *France, 1848–1945*, vol. II, p. 660.

3. *L'Escrime Française*, 9 February 1889; *Les Sports de Nice*, 13 December 1892;
Sport et Santé, 15 January 1930; *La Renaissance: sports, tourisme, et hygiène
sociale*, February 1920; *L'Annuaire des sports* (Paris, 1922), pp. 299–300.
AD Rhône, 4M,5, L'Omnium Lyonnais.

4. See Chapter 2; also AD Pas-de-Calais, M.1389; *La Gazette des Sports*, 1889,
p. 17.

5. *Le Moniteur de la Chasse et des Tirs*, 15 July 1882, p. 1; R. O'Connor, *An Introduction to Field Sports* (London, 1846), p. 83.
6. G. Casella, *Sport et l'avenir* (Paris, 1909), p. 172; d'Herbeville, *Messieurs les disciples de Saint Hubert*, p. 69; *Le Saint Hubert Club Illustré*, 1906, p. 49; C. W. Brooks, 'Jean Renoir', *French Historical Studies* (Fall 1971), p. 281.
7. G. d'Havrincourt, *La Chasse à tir d'aujourd'hui* (Orléans, 1930) especially pp. 20–1; see also Commandant Lansard, *La Chasse des humbles* (Toulouse, 1937).
8. J. A. Roy, *Histoire du Jockey Club* (Paris, 1958), especially p. 141; C. Albaret, *Monsieur Proust*, trans B. Bray (London, 1976), p. 154.
9. G. Bourdon, *La Renaissance athlétique et le Racing Club de France* (Paris, 1906), p. 280; Adam, *Cahiers de Redressement Français*, no. 21 (1927), p. 9; see also Ch. 4.
10. Marx, *En plein air*, p. 193; R. Dieudonné, *Le Parfait Sportif* (Paris, 1924), p. 100, and Albaret, *Monsieur Proust*, p. 182.
11. AD Rhône, 4M,1, Le Tennis Club de Lyon; 'Crafty' (pseud.), *Ançiens et nouveaux sports, Paris sportif* (Paris, 1896), pp. 94–6; Arlott (ed.), *Oxford Companion to Sport and Games*, pp. 75, 547; Jacques-Henri Lartigue, *Diary of a Century* (London, 1978).
12. E. Zola, 'Au bonheur des dames', in *Oeuvres complètes*, ed. H. Mitterand, vol. 4 (Paris, 1967), pp. 816–20.
13. *Le Sporting*, 16 October 1881, p. 1; A. de Saint-Albin, *Les Sports à Paris* (Paris, 1889), p. 40; Goncourts cited in Thabault, *Sports et éducation physique*, p. 156; AD Rhone, 4M,2, Cercle des voiliers de la Saône.
14. 'Crafty', *Ançiens et nouveaux sports*, p. 144; M. Bidault de l'Isle, *Le Chasseur à tir* (Paris, 1912), p. 73; Dieudonné, *Le Parfait Sportif*, p. 24.
15. W. H. Sewell, 'The Working Class of Marseille under the Second Republic' in P. N. Stearns and D. J. Walkowitz (eds), *Workers in the Industrial Revolution* (New Jersey, 1974), p. 92; J. Jacobs, 'A Community of French Workers: Social Life and Labour Conflicts in the Stéphanoise Region, 1890–1914' (unpublished D.Phil thesis, Oxford University, 1973), p. 89.
16. *Le Gymnaste*, 1 December 1884, p. 213; E. Keusch, *Jeux Olympiques et sports athlétiques* (Paris, 1906), p. 9.
17. 'Proposition de H. Galli sur l'instruction militaire', *Con. Mun. RD*, no. 54 (1901).
18. For a British example see R. Q. Gray, 'Styles of Life, the "Labour Aristocracy" and Class Relations in Nineteenth Century Edinburgh', *International Review of Social History* (1973), no. 3, especially pp. 436–441; E. Goblot, *La Barrière et le niveau*, 2nd ed. (Paris, 1967), p. 4; and Jacobs, 'A Community of French Workers', p. 84.
19. A. Chérié, *Annuaire générale illustrée des cyclistes français et étrangers* (Paris, 1892) provides a survey of early clubs listing members' occupations; also AD Gard, 6M,1187, Vélo Club Aiguesmortais.
20. Chérié, op. cit., pp. 51, 57, 61, 222–3, 207–12.
21. Weber, 'Gymnastics and Sports in Fin-de-siècle France', p. 81; Chérié, op. cit., p. 188; also *La Cyclette Revue: histoire chronologique de cyclisme*, August–September 1960. A fair number of corporate clubs were founded

in the nineties but most seem to have been based on large department stores rather than on factories.

22. *Véloce Sport*, 15 March 1888, p. 2.
23. *Le Revue Sportive*, 26 April 1903 – the source of the survey is not indicated. It was claimed that a new survey would be carried out. Unfortunately, this survey, if completed, was never published; *Revue du Touring Club*, December 1895, p. 698.
24. *La Revue Sportive*, 11 June 1903, p. 1.
25. *Les Sports Athlétiques*, 10 January 1890, p. 3; *Almanach du Méridional Sportif*, 1922, p. 17; and Weber, 'Gymnastics and Sports in Fin-de-siècle France', p. 94.
26. A. Coutrot, 'Youth Movements in France in the 1930s', *Journal of Contemporary History* (1970), no. 1, p. 34.

CHAPTER 10

1. See also Chapter 3; for a summary of reactions to the defeat of 1870 see K. A. Swart, *The Sense of Decadence in Nineteenth Century France* (The Hague, 1964), ch. v; also Weber, 'Gymnastics and Sports in Fin-de-siècle France, pp. 74–5.
2. J. Thabault, *Sports et éducation physique*, pp. 95–9; also *Le Moniteur des Bataillons Scolaires*, March 1883.
3. Z. Sternhell, 'Paul Déroulède and the Origins of Modern French Nationalism', *Journal of Contemporary History*, vol. 6, no. 4 (1971), p. 55; see also *Le Gymnaste*, 22 December 1887, p. 394, and 18 August 1887, p. 103.
4. G. Casella, *Sport et l'avenir* (Paris, 1908), p. 12.
5. Swart, op. cit., pp. 124, 137; C. J. H. Hayes, *A Generation of Materialism* (New York, 1941), p. 13; also D. Mamoz, *De la gymnastique en France au XIXe siècle* (Paris, 1891), ch. 1.
6. See also Chapter 4; Weber, 'Sports and Games in Fin-de-siècle France', p. 97; *Les Sports Athlétiques*, 5 January 1895; G. Wright, *France in Modern Times* (Chicago, 1960), p. 311.
7. 'Agathon' (pseud.), *Les Jeunes Gens d'aujourd'hui* (Paris, 1913), pp. 35, 143; J. Dedet, *Le Football rugby* (Paris, n.d.), p. 12; Seidler, *Le Sport et la presse*, pp. 58–9.
8. G. Rozet, *Le Football: sport national et stade communal* (Paris, 1918) emphasises the lack of facilities for representative sport.
9. AD Rhône, 4M, 3, L'Eveil de Lyon; Zeldin, *France 1848–1945*, vol. 1, p. 641.
10. These figures come from H. Bunle, op. cit., pp. 135, 138; AN F7, 13214, prefect of the Landes to the minister of the interior, 8 July 1912.
11. AN F7, 13214: prefect of the Rhone, 21 June 1912; prefect of the Pas-de-Calais, 10 April 1912; unsigned report dated Paris 19 September 1908 on clerical gymnastic clubs in Angers.
12. J. Ozouf, *Nous les maîtres d'école* (Paris, 1967), pp. 29–30, 136.
13. AN F7, 13214, Commissaire spécial, Gare de Saint-Etienne, 8 September 1913.

14. Ibid., Commissariat spécial de Melun, 2 June 1908; untitled and unsigned report on Nord, 27 May 1908.
15. M. Larkin, 'The Church and the French Concordat, 1891–1902', *English Historical Review*, vol. 81 (1966), p. 732; AD Rhône, 4M, cartons 1–11; see also 7M (Tourisme), 1 carton.
16. T. W. Margadant, 'Primary Schools and Youth Groups in Pre-war Paris', *Journal of Contemporary History*, vol. 13, no. 2 (1978), p. 323; Weber, 'Gymnastics and Sports in Fin-de-siècle France', p. 93.
17. H. Brunet, *La XXXVᵉ Fête fédérale de l'Union des Sociétés de Gymnastique de France* (Angers, 1909), pp. 104–10.
18. *Le Gymnaste*, 13 November 1909, p. 783.
19. AN F7, 13214, 'L'Affaire de Nancy and L'Affaire de Roanne': assorted cuttings; Sporting Club Monségurais, *Cinquante-cinq Ans au service de sport* (Marmande, 1976).
20. *L'Annuaire des sports* (Paris, 1922), p. 27.
21. Dr G. Danjou, *Régéneration sociale sur la pelouse* (Pau, 1906), p. 10; C. de Saint-Cyr, *Le Sport, éducateur sociale* (Paris, 1908), p. 16; also P. Didon, *L'Influence morale des sports athlétiques* (Paris, 1897).
22. J. Beaudemoulin, *Enquête sur les loisirs de l'ouvrier français* (Paris, 1924), especially pp. 238–40; P. Rives, *La Corvée de joie* (Paris, 1924), p. 59.
23. *Bulletin du Ministère du Travail*, August–October 1920, pp. 402–9, 509–13; also 1921, pp. 170–6, 309–15; *La Renaissance: sports, tourisme et hygiène sociale*, March 1919, p. 35; Zeldin, *France 1848–1945*, vol. II, p. 1063.
24. G. Etienne, *L'Utilisations des loisirs des travailleurs* (Paris, 1935), pp. 82–3; *Sport Ouvrier*, 5 October 1923 and 6 December 1924.
25. *Le Sport*, 16 April 1934; *Sport Ouvrier*, 15 October 1924.
26. *Sport Ouvrier*, 1 June 1926; *Le Sport*, 16 April 1934; 'FSGT' in *Encyclopédie générale des sports* (Paris, 1946), p. 415.
27. G. Prouteau and E. Raude, *Le Message de Léo Lagrange* (Paris, 1950); P. Marie, *Pour le sport ouvrier* (Paris, 1934) underlines the lack of facilities.
28. G. Barthelemy, *Chapitres du budget de l'Education Nationale relatifs à l'éducation physique, aux sports et aux loisirs; Annexe no. 4438* (Paris, 1939), especially pp. 18, 49.
29. Prouteau and Raude, op. cit., p. 117; R. Soucy, 'The Nature of Fascism in France', *Journal of Contemporary History*, vol. 1, no. 1 (1966), p. 55; G. Lefranc, *Histoire du Front Populaire* (Paris, 1965), pp. 339–40.
30. Ibid.
31. H. Mavit, 'Education physique et sports (Vichy)', *Revue de l'Histoire de la Deuxième Guerre Mondiale*, no. 56 (October 1964), pp. 89–100; R. Haure, *Comment et pourquoi faire du sport* (Bordeaux, 1942), p. 1; A. Frahier, *Sport et vie rurale* (Paris, 1942), pp. 17–20.
32. J. V. Parant, *Le Problème du tourisme populaire* (Toulouse, 1939), p. 207; *Jeunesse qui vit* (Paris, 1942).
33. *Sport Ouvrier*, 5 January 1927; R. Alix, *La Nouvelle Jeunesse* (Paris, 1930), pp. 38–9.

CHAPTER 11

1. J. Huizinga, *Homo Ludens: A Study of the Play Element in Culture*, ed. G. Steiner (London, 1970), p. 221; E. Dunning (ed.), *The Sociology of Sport: A Selection of Readings* (London, 1971), p. xvi.
2. *L'Auto-Vélo*, 5 January 1901, p. 1; Bourdon, *La Renaissance athlétique et le Racing Club de France*, p. 300; 'Agathon', *Les Jeunes Gens d'aujourd'hui*, especially pp. 131–2; Cassella, *Sport et l'avenir*, pp. 51, 260; Zeldin, *France 1848–1945*, vol. II, p. 694.
3. C. de Caumont, *Le Sport, il y a cinquante ans* (Paris, 1904), p. 5.
4. A. Briggs, *Mass Entertainment: The Origins of a Modern Industry* (Adelaide, 1960), p. 28.

Bibliography

A BIBLIOGRAPHICAL NOTE

Sport is not an easy subject for the historian to study at the official level. On a national scale there are few governmental records to consult. The Archives Nationales contain only a couple of cartons of documents on gymnastic education and on political brawls between Republican and clerical sporting organisations. On a departmental level, however, the picture is rather brighter. The prefect liked to keep in touch with private organisations of *all* kinds and after 1901 it became obligatory for private clubs to register themselves with the authorities. Consequently, departmental archives usually contain a number of assorted cartons on sports clubs. Unfortunately, this information often amounts to little more than a copy of the club statutes and a list of members. In some cases the occupations of club members are given and such information has been used extensively in this study. In addition to evidence of club activity, there are sometimes police reports of rowdy behaviour or, in certain areas, of bullfights or cockfights. Six departmental archives were consulted: Hérault, Gard, Rhône, Nord, Pas-de-Calais and Seine-Inférieure (no documents of this kind are extant for the department of the Seine). These six departments were chosen partly because they represented different regions of France and partly in order to include both urban and rural areas. As a whole, governments were not very interested in sport *per se* and official records cannot be considered a major source of information on the subject. The most valuable official sources were the debates and reports of the Paris municipal council. There are only occasional references to sport in the parliamentary debates of the period, although anyone wishing to write a specialised study of field sports would be advised to consult this source.

I was unable to obtain access to the private papers of either national bodies or individual clubs. It appears that virtually nothing exists for the pre-1914 period and only a little more for the inter-war years. 'Professional clubs are generally suspicious of outside inquirers and in addition are singularly unhistorical in their attitude to their own past', comments the author of a recent book on British football. The same seems to be true of France, although further local studies may well uncover some valuable records. Fortunately, there is an abundance of contemporary periodicals and books which go a long way towards making up the archival gap. Broadly speaking, the specialist fortnightly or monthly journals proved to be much more valuable as a source for social history than the daily papers, which were pre-occupied with the results of games. Accordingly, the national press (including *L'Auto*) were sampled primarily for an estimate of their coverage of sports, whereas specialist periodicals were read more systematically.

A   MANUSCRIPT SOURCES

AD Gard	6M, 356–7 (Courses de taureaux)
	6M, 1050–4 and 1185–91 (Cercles et sociétés autorisées)
	6M, 1376, 1382, 1564, 1577 (Chasse).
AD Hérault	58M, 7 (Sociétés de gymnastique autorisées)
	58M, 13 (Sociétés de gymnastique et de tir)
	58M, 52–3 (Montpellier: cercles)
	58M, 72 (Sête: sociétés sportives)
	O, Lunel (Arènes, 1861–1914)
	O, Béziers (Arènes, 1901–14).
AD Nord	M.208, 113 (Courses de taureaux)
	M.208, 114 (Combats de coqs).
AD Pas-de-Calais	M.1389 (Louveterie)
	M.2128 (Courses de vélocipédie)
	M.4669–72 (Combats de coqs)
	1.Z.272 (Sociétés de gymnastique)
	5.Z.201 (Sociétés de tir et divers sociétés).
AD Rhône	4M, 1–14 (Associations-Sports)
	7M7 (Tourisme).
AD Seine-Inférieure	4TP, 107C, 1–9 (Sociétés sportives).
AN	F7, 13214 (Sociétés catholiques: patronages et sociétés sportives).
AN	F17, 6912, 6917, 6922 (L'enseignement de la gymnastique).

B PRINTED SOURCES

(1) PRIMARY SOURCES

(i) Official Publications
Annuaire statistique
Conseil Municipal de la ville de Paris: Procès-verbaux, 1875–1913 and
  Rapports et Documents, 1878–1933.
Conseil Général du département de la Seine: Procès-verbaux, 1875–1919 and
  Rapports et Documents, 1875–1919.
Débats Parlementaires: Chambre des Députés, Procès-verbaux and *Annexes
  (Rapports et Documents)*, 1880–1920.

(ii) Newspapers and Periodicals
L'Action Française, 1909, 1911, 1913, 1923.
L'Auto-Vélo (after 1901, *L'Auto*), 1901–14.
La Boxe et les Boxeurs, 1909–10.
Bibliothèque Historique de la ville de Paris. Collection 'Actualités'.
  (Assorted Press Cuttings). Reference 106,00007–25.
Le Chasseur Illustré, 1892–3.
Le Chasseur Pratique, 1891–2.
Le Coqueleur, 1902–4.
Le Cycliste, 1887–1913.
Education Physique, 1888–90.
L'Escrime Française, 1889–91.
L'Essor, 1907–12.
La France Gymnastique, 1899.
Le Figaro, 1876, 1881, 1886, 1891, 1896, 1901, 1906, 1911.
La Gazette des Chasseurs, 1882–3.
La Gazette des Sports, 1888–93.
La Gazette des Sports et du Plein Air, 1889.
La Gazette des Sports Illustrés, 1882.
Le Gymnaste, 1880–1920.
L'Humanité, Jan.–July 1906, July–Dec. 1908, Jan.–June 1910, July–
  Dec. 1912, Jan.–Mar. 1914.
Les Jeunes: courier du quinzaine du journal 'Le Patronage', 1903–4.
Le Journal des Chasseurs, 1892–4.
La Mise à Mort, 1892–4.
Le Moniteur de la Chasse et des Tirs, 1882–4.
Le Moniteur de la Gymnastique Scolaire, Hygiénique et Médicale, 1868–73.
Le Moniteur des Bataillons Scolaires, 1883.
Le Moniteur Officiel de la Gymnastique et de l'Escrime, 1886.
Le Petit Chasseur, 1908–13.
La Renaissance: sports, tourisme et hygiène sociale, 1919–20.

La Revue Cynégétique et Sportive, 1892.
La Revue des Deux Mondes, 1891–1902.
La Revue des Sports, 1877, 1882, 1887, 1892.
La Revue du Touring Club, 1891–1939.
La Revue Olympique, 1901–9.
La Revue Sportive, 1903.
La Revue Sportive Champenoise, 1903–4.
La Revue Vélocipédique, 1884–5.
La Route: revue illustrée des voyages, du tourisme et des sports, 1909.
Le Saint Hubert Club Illustré, 1906–13.
Le Sport Amateur, 1904–9.
Le Sport Gazette, 1883.
Le Sporting, 1882.
Le Sport Libre, 1900.
Le Sport Ouvrier, 1923–7.
Les Sports Athlétiques, 1890–8.
Les Sports de l'Oise, 1905.
Les Sports de Nice, 1891–5.
Les Sports et la Photographie en Bourgogne, 1889.
Les Sports Populaires, 1908–11.
Les Sports: revue illustrée des sports et du tourisme, 1919–20.
Le Temps, 1873–88, 1893, 1903, 1913.
Le Tireur, 1885–7.
Le Toréo, 1891.
Le Toréo Illustré, 1893.
Le Toréro, 1898–1911.
Toros Revue, 1897–9.
L'Union Patriotique de France, 1888–9.
L'Union Vélocipédique de France, 1906–9.
Le Vélo, 1894–6.
Véloce Sport, 1885–91.
Vélodrôle: journal satirique vélocipédique, 1895.
Le Vélodrome de Choisy-le-Roi, 1895.
La Vie au Grand Air, 1898–9.

(iii) Books, Articles and Pamphlets
L'Action Populaire, no. 208, 1910, 'La Fédération Gymnastique et Sportive des Patronages de France'.
C. Adam, *Alphabet des chasses* (Paris, 1859).
J. H. Adam, 'Loisirs et éducation populaire', *Cahiers de Redressement Français*, no. 21 (1927).
P. Adam, *La Moralité des sports* (Paris, 1907).
'Agathon' (pseud.), *Les Jeunes Gens d'aujourd'hui* (Paris, 1913).
R. Alix, *La Nouvelle Jeunesse* (Paris, 1930).

Almanach de Méridional Sportif (Toulouse, 1922).
Lt.-Col. L. André, *La Tauromachie moderne* (Nimes, 1913).
E. Angersten and G. Eckler, *La Gymnastique de demoiselles* (Paris, 1882).
Annuaire illustré des sociétés de gymnastique de l'Association de la Seine (Paris, 1888).
M. Bahonneau, *La Gymnastique raisonnée à l'usage des employés et des ouvriers* (Angers, 1911).
L. Barron, *Les Jeux* (Paris, 1892).
L. Baudry de Saunier and C. Terront, *Memoires de Terront: sa vie, ses performances, son mode d'entraînement* (Paris, 1893).
A. Bausil and J. Vidal, *Le Rugby catalan* (Perpignan, 1924).
J. Beaudemoulin, *Enquête sur les loisirs de l'ouvrier français* (Paris, 1924).
E. Bellecroix, *La Chasse pratique* (Paris, 1886).
M. Berger, *Pourquoi je suis sportif* (Paris, 1930).
M. Bidault de l'Isle, *Le Chasseur à tir* (Paris, 1912).
Lt.-Col. Blaque-Belair, *Ludus pro patria* (Paris, 1912).
H. Blatin, *Les Courses de taureaux (Espagne et France)* (Paris, 1868).
L. Bonneville, *Le Vélo, fils de France* (Paris, 1938).
J. Boulenger and E. Henriot, *Animaux de Sport* (Paris, 1912).
G. Bourdon, *La Renaissance athlétique et le Racing Club de France* (Paris, 1906).
L. Boussenard, *La Chasse à tir mise à la portée de tous* (Paris, 1886).
V. Breyer and R. Coquelle, *La Course classique: Bordeaux–Paris* (Paris, 1899).
H. Brunet, *La XXXVe Fête fédérale de l'Union des Sociétés de Gymnastique de France: son histoire depuis son origine jusqu'à son apothèse* (Angers, 1909).
H. Bunle, 'L'Éducation physique et les sports en France', *Journal de la Société Statistique de Paris* (May 1922).
Abbé Cadart, *La Gymnastique et les sports dans l'oeuvre de la jeunesse* (Soissons, 1913).
D. Caldine, *Corridas de toros* (Paris, 1900).
G. Casella, *Sport et l'avenir* (Paris, 1909).
R. Cavaillès, *La Taxe sur les vélocipèdes* (Toulouse, 1908).
E. Chapus, *Le Sport à Paris* (Paris, 1854).
La Chasse et les droits des propriétaires, par 'un propriétaire' (Tarbes, 1879).
La Chasse moderne: encyclopédie du chasseur (Paris, 1912).
A. Chérié, *Annuaire générale illustrée des cyclistes français et étrangers* (Paris, 1892).
'Clic-Clac' (pseud.), *Histoire des courses landaises* (Mont-de-Marsan, 1905).
L. Colland, *La Sentinelle de Reims* (Reims, 1911).
Congrès International de la Chasse (Paris, 1907).
M. Cordelier, *Histoire de la Vosgienne, société libre de gymnastique* (Epinal, 1904).

242 *Sport and Society in Modern France*

C. P. Coutoure, *Cinquante Ans de cyclisme avec le Véloce Club Barentinois, 1904–1954* (Le Havre, 1955).
Dr G. Danjou, *Régénération sociale sur la pelouse* (Pau, 1906).
V. Dauphin, *Le Cyclisme en Anjou* (Angers, 1936).
C. de Canteleu, *Manuel de la vénerie française* (Paris, 1890).
C. de Caumont, *Le Sport, il y a cinquante ans* (Paris, 1904).
A. de Corbie, *Combats de coqs* (Lille, 1939).
P. de Coubertin, *Souvenirs d'Oxford et de Cambridge* (Paris, 1887).
P. de Coubertin, *L'Education anglaise en France* (Paris, 1889).
P. de Coubertin, *Une Campagne de vingt-et-un ans* (Paris, 1909).
P. de Coubertin, *Essais de psychologie sportive* (Paris, 1913).
J. Dedet, *Le Football rugby* (Paris, n.d.).
L. de Fleurac, *Les Courses à pied et les concours athlétiques* (Paris, 1911).
G. d'Havrincourt, *La Chasse à tir d'aujourd'hui* (Orleans, 1930).
M. d'Herbeville, *Messieurs les disciples de Saint Hubert* (Paris, 1905).
H. de Lacaze, *A propos de chasse dans les Landes de Gascogne* (Mayenne, 1960).
C. de Loris, *La Femme et la bicyclette* (Paris, 1896).
G. de Maupassant, *Contes et Nouvelles*, ed. A. M. Schmidt, vols i and ii (Paris, 1957).
G. Demeny (ed.), *Le Congrès International de l'Education Physique* (Paris, 1900).
H. de Montherlant, *Les Bestiaires* (Paris, 1926).
G. de Montjou, *Historique des subventions accordées par le département de la Mayenne aux sociétés sportives* (Mayenne, 1924).
P. Déroulède, *De l'éducation militaire* (Paris, 1882).
A. de Saint-Albin, *Les Sports à Paris* (Paris, 1889).
G. de Saint-Clair, *Sports athlétiques, jeux et exercices en plein air* (Paris, 1889).
C. de Saint-Cyr, *Le Sport, éducateur social* (Paris, 1908).
H. Desgrange, *La Tête et les jambes* (Paris, 1895).
A. Desrousseaux, *Moeurs populaires de la Flandre française* (Lille, 1889).
F. Devillard, *Souvenirs de chasse* (Moulins, 1911).
P. Didon, *L'Influence morale des sports athlétiques* (Paris, 1907).
R. Dieudonne, *Le Parfait Sportif* (Paris, 1924).
L. Dubech, *Ou va le sport?* (Paris, 1930).
G. Duhamel, *Le Football français, ses débuts* (Paris, 1931).
H. O. Duncan, *Vingt Ans de cyclisme pratique* (Paris, 1896).
H. O. Duncan and L. Suberbie, *L'Entraînement* (Paris, 1890).
E. Durkheim, *The Division of Labour*, 2nd ed. (New York, 1964). (First published in French in 1902.)
Duchesse d'Uzès, *La Chasse à courre* (Paris, 1912).
R. Fabens, *Les Sports pour tous* (Paris, 1905).
M. Ferrus, *La Corrida à travers les âges à Bordeaux et dans le sud-ouest* (Bordeaux, 1925).

La fête fédérale de gymnastique de Gênève, 18–21 juillet 1891: rapport de l'Association Régionale de Gymnastique de Seine-et-Oise, Seine-et-Marne et Oise (Rouen, 1891).

E. Forestier and F. Gerbert, *Almanach de la vélocipédie illustrée* (Rouen, 1883).

A. Frahier, *Sport et vie rurale* (Paris, 1942).

F. Frayasse and N. G. Tunmer, *Football (association)* (Paris, 1897).

L. Galley, *De la necessité de l'enseignement de la gymnastique dans les villes et dans les campagnes* (Arras, 1882).

P. Garcet de Vauresmont, *Les Sports athlétiques* (Paris, 1912).

E. Gendry, *Sport vélocipédique, les champions français* (Angers, 1891).

P. Grousset, *La Renaissance physique* (Paris, 1901).

E. Guillaumin, *La Vie d'un simple* ed. Stock (Paris, 1957).

Gyp (pseud.), *Sportmanomanie* (Paris, 1898).

G. Hanot, *Pour devenir un bon joueur de football-association* (Paris, 1920).

E. Hemingway, *Death in the Afternoon* (London, 1932).

L. Hémon, *Battling Malone and Other Stories* (London, 1925).

E. Hénard, *Etudes sur la transformation de Paris* (Paris, 1903).

I. Hope, *Brittany and the Chase* (London, 1853).

R. Hue and Dr B. Mothe, *Le parc des sports de Bordeaux-Lescure* (Bordeaux, 1923).

A. Jauréguy, *Qui veut jouer avec moi?* (Paris, 1939).

J. Jenger, *L'Alcool et le sport* (Seine-et-Oise, 1925).

H. Jooris, *De l'enthousiasme au sens de réalités pratiques: contribution à l'étude de l'organisation du football en France* (Lille, 1933).

J. Jusserand, *Les Sports et les jeux d'exercice dans l'ancienne France* (Paris, 1901).

J. Kemp, *Hunting and Shooting in Lower Brittany* (London, 1859).

E. Keusch, *Jeux Olympiques et sports athlétiques* (Paris, 1906).

J. Ladoumègue, *Comment j'ai battu deux records du monde* (Paris, 1930).

N. Laisné, *Nouvelles Observations sur l'enseignement de la gymnastique* (Paris, 1886).

L. Latour, *L'Éducation physique en Angleterre et en France* (Paris, 1891).

E. and G. Lefranc, *Le Syndicalisme devant le problème des loisirs* (Paris, 1937).

P. Lenglé, *La Chasse pour tous* (Paris, 1909).

G. le Roy, *Education physique et gymnastique* (Paris, 1913).

G. Letainturier-Fradin, *L'Activité sportive contient-elle le germe d'une philosophie pratique de la vie?* (Paris, 1913) (Congrès International de Psychologie et de Physiologie Sportive, Lausanne 7–11 May 1913).

M. Leudet (ed.), *Almanach des sports* (Paris, 1901).

J. Levitre, *Organisation des chasses* (Anet, 1908).

J. Lhermit, *Les Sports pédestres* (Paris, 1911).

V. Lopez-Tomayo, *Histoire de la gymnastique moderne* (Paris, 1882).

A. Magendie, *Les Effets moraux de l'éducation physique* (Paris, 1893).

244 *Sport and Society in Modern France*

V. Mainfroy, *La Politique d'un paysan à propos du privilège de chasse* (1863) (no place of publication given).
D. Mamoz, *La Gymnastique au XIXe siècle* (Paris, 1891).
P. Maréchal, *L'Évolution de l'opinion publique sur les courses de taureaux* (Paris, 1902).
P. Marie, *Pour le sport ouvrier* (Paris, 1934).
M. Martin, *Voyage de Bordeaux à Paris par trois vélocipédistes* (Bordeaux, 1890).
M. Martin, *Grande Enquête sportive du journal 'Le Vélo'* (Paris, 1898).
A. Marx, *En plein air* (Paris, 1887).
L. Mazzuchelli and F. Reichel, *Les Sports athlétiques* (Paris, 1911).
C. Meillac, *Les Sports à la mode* (Paris, 1909).
M. Metjé, *Fondation et vie d'un club: L'Union Sportive Albigeoise 1925–32* (Albi, 1933).
Ministère de l'Instruction Publique et des Beaux-arts, *Manuel d'exercices gymnastiques et de jeux scolaires* (Paris, 1892).
Le Musée Social, *Les Espaces libres* (Paris, 1908).
'Les Courses de taureaux dans les arènes de Nîmes', *La Nouvelle Revue*, September–October 1893.
R. O'Connor, *An Introduction to Field Sports in France* (London, 1846).
J. V. Parant, *Le Problème du tourisme populaire* (Toulouse, 1939).
L. Parant, *Les Bataillons scolaires et leur transformation en sections de gymnastique* (Bourg, 1891).
L. Parant, *Les Sociétés de gymnastique dans le département de l'Ain* (Bourg, 1893).
C. A. Payton and E. Reynolds-Ball, *Sport on the Rivieras* (London, 1911)
E. Paz, *Documents pour servir à l'histoire de la gymnastique en France* (Paris, 1881).
Dr L. Petit, *Dix Ans du Touring Club* (Paris, 1904).
M. Pfefferkorn, *Le Football association* (Paris, 1921).
E. Pointié, *Le Football rugby* (Paris, 1905).
J. Prévost, *Plaisirs des sports: essais sur le corps humain* (Paris, 1925).
Le Racing Club de Reims: Annuaire 1908 (Reims, 1908).
J. Raymond-Guasco, *Le Collège d'athlètes* (Paris, 1913).
L. P. Reichel, *La Vélocipédie dans le mouvement athlétique* (Paris, 1892).
P. Rives, *La Corvée de joie* (Paris, 1924).
G. Rozet, *Les Fêtes du muscle* (Paris, 1912).
G. Rozet, *Le Football: sport national et stade communal* (Paris, 1918).
G. Rozet, *Les Sports sur le réseau P.L.M.* (Paris, n.d.).
G. Rozet, *Sous le brassard vert: notes et souvenirs des correspondants de guerre accrédités auprès des armées françaises* (Paris, 1920).
P. Sainmont, *Le Véloce Club de Tours et le doyen des cyclistes de France* (Tours, 1902).
J. Samat, *Chasses de Provence* (Marseille, 1896).

F. Suchaux, *Souvenirs d'un chasseur* (Bar-sur-Aube, 1894).
F. Thévin, *Annuaire générale de la chasse et ses fournitures* (Saint Germain-en-Laye, 1912).
G. Tholin, *Notes sur la chasse dans l'Agenais* (Agen, 1877).
A. Van Gennep, *Manuel de folklore français contemporain* (Paris, 1943).
L. Vauzanges, *Les Sociétés françaises de tir* (Paris, 1882).
C. Velin, *La Chasse et le gibier dans l'est* (Epinal, 1888).
'Vétéran' (pseud.), *La Vélocipédie pour tous* (Paris, 1896).
J. Vidal, *Les Courses de taureaux en Espagne, dans le Midi et à Paris* (Paris, 1889).
M. Viollette (ed.), *Le Cyclisme* (Paris, 1912).
L. Waulthier, *La Communalisation de la chasse* (Paris, 1908).

(2) SECONDARY SOURCES

M. Agulhon, *Pénitents et francs-maçons de l'ancienne Provence* (Paris, 1968).
M. Agulhon, *La République au village* (Paris, 1970).
M. Agulhon, *Le Cercle dans la France bourgeoise, 1810–1848: étude d'une mutation de sociabilité* (Paris, 1977).
C. Albaret, *Monsieur Proust* (London, 1976).
P. Albert, *Histoire générale de la presse française* (Paris, 1967), vol. III.
R. D. Anderson, 'French Views of the English Public Schools: Some Nineteenth Century Episodes', *History of Education*, vol. 2, no. 2 (June 1973).
Annuaire de la Société Historique et Littéraire de Colmar (Colmar, 1962), 'La Colmarienne Société de Gymnastique et des Sports'.
J. Ardagh, *The New France* (London, 1970).
J. Arlott (ed.), *The Oxford Companion to Sports and Games* (London, 1975).
R. Auget, *Histoire et légende du cirque* (Paris, 1974).
P. Bailey, *Leisure and Class in Victorian England* (London, 1978).
R. 'Baranger' (pseud.), *Emma la Caballera* (Paris, 1959).
J. Barbat, *Histoire du ballon ovale* (Clermont-Ferrand, 1959).
R. Barthes, *Mythologies* (Paris, 1957).
M. Beaujour and J. Ehrman, *La France contemporaine: textes et documents* (Paris, 1970).
G. Bénac, *Les Champions dans la coulisse* (Paris, 1963).
S. Bertault, *Piaf* (London, 1973).
A. Blondin, *Sur le Tour de France* (Paris, 1979).
J. Boquet, *Lille à la belle époque* (Lille, 1971).
M. Boulet, *La Signification du sport* (Paris, 1968).
Y. Boulinguiez, 'Aspects de la vie quotidienne dans le département du Nord pendant la première moitié du xxe siècle', *Revue du Nord* (July–September 1972).

Y-P. Boulongne, *La Vie et l'oeuvre pédagogique de Pierre de Coubertin* (Ottawa, 1975).

Y. Brekilien, *La Vie quotidienne des paysans en Bretagne* (Paris, 1966).

A. Briggs, *Mass Entertainment: The Origins of a Modern Industry* (Adelaide, 1960).

C. W. Brooks, 'Jean Renoir', *French Historical Studies* (Fall 1971).

Bulletin of the Society for the Study of Labour History, Spring 1976, 'The Working Class and Leisure: Class Expression and/or Social Control? Report on the Conference held 29 November 1975 at the University of Sussex'.

T. B. Caldwell, 'Le Syndicat des employés du commerce et de l'industrie (1887–1919)', *International Review of Social History*, vol. XI (1966).

R. Carr, *English Fox-Hunting* (London, 1976).

H. Chabalier, 'Les quatres glorieuses de Nîmes', *Le Nouvel Observateur*, 9 June 1973.

B. Chabrol, *Histoire de la vénerie française* (Paris, 1963).

A. Chassignon and A. Poirier, *Le Tour de France* (Paris, 1952).

L. Chevalier, *Labouring Classes and Dangerous Classes*, trans. F. Jellinek (London, 1973).

R. C. Cobb, *Tour de France* (London, 1976).

L. Constant, *Histoire du Stade Aurillaçois, 1904–1972* (Editions du Centre, 1972).

E. Couratier, *Le Parc des Princes, étude présentée à la Société Historique de Boulogne-Billancourt* (Paris, 1955).

A. Coutrot, 'Youth Movements in France in the 1930s', *Journal of Contemporary History*, vol. 1 (1970).

F. Cribier, *La Grande Migration d'été des citadins de France* (Paris, 1969).

M. Crubellier, *Histoire culturelle de la France: XIXᵉ–XXᵉ siècle* (Paris, 1973).

H. Cunningham, *The Volunteer Force, a Social and Political History* (London, 1975).

La Cyclette Revue: histoire chronologique du cyclisme, 1960–1.

J. Dauven (ed.), *L'Encyclopédie des sports* (Paris, 1960).

R. Delannoy, *Coqs de combat et combats de coqs dans le Nord* (Paris, 1948).

R. Demulder, 'Coqueleux et combats de coqs dans le nord de la France', *Revue du Folklore Francais* (January–February 1934).

E. Derancourt, *La Tauromachie en Charente-Inférieure* (Paris, 1933).

L. Desgraves and G. Dupeux, *Bordeaux au XIXᵉ siècle* (Paris, 1969).

M. Diamant-Berger, *Histoire du Tour de France* (Paris, 1959).

G. Ducasse, *Les Quilles de neuf: un sport gascon et son histoire* (Mont-de-Marson, 1953).

C. Duhau, *Histoire de l'Aviron Bayonnais, l'époque héroïque* (Bayonne, 1968).

J. Dumazedier (ed.), *Regards neufs sur le sport* (Paris, 1950).

J. Dumazedier, *Vers une civilisation du loisir* (Paris, 1962).

J. Dumazedier and A. Ripert, *Loisir et culture*, vol. 1, *Loisir et la ville* (Paris, 1966).

E. Dunning (ed.), *The Sociology of Sport: a Selection of Readings* (London, 1971).

G. Dupeux, *French Society 1789–1970*, trans. P. Wait (London, 1976).

J. Durry, *L'Histoire véridique des géants de la route* (Paris, 1973).

G. Duthen and A. Potter, *The Rise of French Rugby* (London, 1961).

G. Duveau, *La Vie ouvrière sous le Second Empire* (Paris, 1946).

L'École de Football d'Amiens Athletic Club, *Le Football en Picardie et l'histoire de ses origines* (Amiens, 1948).

G. Etienne, *L'Utilisation des loisirs des travailleurs* (Paris, 1935).

M. T. Eyquem, *Pierre de Coubertin et l'épopée olympique* (Paris, 1966).

A. Faure, *Paris Carême-prenant: du Carnival à Paris au XIXe siècle* (Paris, 1978).

J. Floch'moan, *Le Genèse des sports* (Paris, 1962).

H. Garcia, *La Fabuleuse histoire de rugby* (Paris, 1973).

G. Gauthey and E. Seidler, *Le Rugby français: encyclopédie du rugby* (Paris 1962).

J. Gay, *Sports et jeux d'exercice en Anjou* (Angers, 1947).

J. R. Gillis, *Youth and History, Tradition and Change in European Age Relations 1770–present* (New York, 1974).

E. Goblot, *La Barrière et le niveau*, 2nd ed. (Paris, 1967).

R. Q. Gray, 'Styles of Life, the "Labour Aristocracy" and Class Relations in Nineteenth Century Edinburgh, *International Review of Social History* (1973), no. 3.

E. Grenadou and A. Prévost, *Grenadou, paysan français* (Paris, 1966).

J. C. Grivot, *Crampons, ballon rond* (Paris, 1970).

A. Guttman, *From Ritual to Record, The Nature of Modern Sports* (New York, 1979).

B. Harrison, 'Religion and Recreation in Nineteenth Century England', *Past and Present*, vol. 38 (1967).

B. Harrison, *Drink and the Victorians* (London, 1971).

B. Harrison, 'Animals and the State in Nineteenth Century England', *English Historical Review*, vol. LXXXVII (October 1973).

J. E. S. Hayward, 'The Official Philosophy of the Third Republic, Léon Bourgeois and Solidarism', *International Review of Social History*, vol. 6 (1961).

J. Hélias, *Le Cheval d'orgeuil* (Paris, 1975).

J. Huizinga, *Homo Ludens: A Study of the Play Element in Culture*, ed. G. Steiner (London, 1970).

R. Ingham (ed.), *Football Hooliganism* (London, 1978).

J. Jacobs, 'A Community of French Workers: Social Life and Labour Conflicts in the Stephanoise Region, 1890–1914' (unpublished D.Phil. thesis, Oxford University, 1973).

Y. Joseleau, 'Le Rôle de l'armée dans l'évolution de l'enseignement

des activités physiques en France au milieu du XIXe siècle à la fin
de la première guerre mondiale (ENSEPS 1972), Mémoire pour le
diplôme.

T. Judt, *Socialism in Provence* (London, 1979).

G. S. Kenyon and J. Loy, *Sport, Culture and Society* (Chicago, 1972).

J. Ladegaillerie and F. Legrand, *L'Éducation physique au XIXe et au XXe
siècles* (Paris, 1971).

A. Lafront, *Bibliografia de la prensa taurina francesa 1887–1961* (Madrid,
1962).

A. Lafront, *Histoire de la corrida en France* (Paris, 1977).

C. Lagarde, *Au pays du roi Henri, pays de beau rugby: cinquante ans à la
Section Paloise* (Pau, 1953).

A. Langlade, *La Gymnastique moderne, ses origines, son intégration, son
actualité* (Paris, 1968).

M. Larkin, 'The Church and the French Concordat, 1891–1902',
English Historical Review, vol. 81 (1966).

J. H. Lartigue, *Diary of a Century* (London, 1978).

J. C. Laurent, *Observations sur la corrida* (Rennes, 1960).

G. Lefranc, *Histoire du Front Populaire* (Paris, 1965).

M. Le Grand, *Les Courses de taureaux dans le sud-ouest de la France
jusqu'au début du XIXe siècle* (Mont-de-Marsan, 1934).

Le Livre d'Or du Football Club de Rouen, 1899–1969 (Rouen, 1969).

L. Loubère, *Radicalism in Mediterranean France* (New York, 1974).

G. Magnane, *Sociologie de sport* (Paris, 1970).

J. Maieresse, *Football, quand tu nous tiens* (Paris, 1935).

R. W. Malcolmson, *Popular Recreations in English Society, 1700–1850*
(Cambridge, 1973).

Dr Marc, *L'Aficion et les arènes bitteroises de leurs origines à nos jours*
(Béziers, 1959).

T. W. Margadant, 'Primary Schools and Youth Groups in Pre-War
Paris', *Journal of Contemporary History*, vol. 13, no. 2 (April 1978).

M. R. Marrus, *The Emergence of Leisure*, ed. P. N. Stearns (Missouri,
1974) in the pamphlet series 'Forums in History'.

M. R. Marrus, 'Social Drinking in the Belle Epoque', *Journal of Social
History* (Winter 1974).

A. Maureau, *Les Courses de taureaux à Avignon* (Avignon, 1971).

A. Maureau, *Un Rapport confidentiel de 1838 sur les courses de taureaux à
Avignon* (Avignon, 1971).

H. Mavit, 'Education physique et sport (Vichy)', *Revue de l'Histoire de la
Deuxième Guerre Mondiale*, no. 56 (October 1964).

P. C. McIntosh, *Sport and Society* (London, 1963).

P. C. McIntosh, *Landmarks in the History of Physical Education* (London,
1971).

H. Meller, *Leisure and the Changing City, 1870–1914* (London, 1976).

Le Monde Nouveau. Numéro spécial, 'La littérature sportive' (Paris, 1924).

G. L. Mosse, *The Nationalisation of the Masses* (New York, 1975).

A. Nathan (ed.), *Sport and Society* (London, 1958).

G. Nicholson, *The Great Bike Race* (London, 1977).

J. Ozouf, *Nous les maîtres d'écoles* (Paris, 1967).

G. Pastre, *Les Boucliers du printemps* (Toulouse, 1967).

V. Petit-Jean, 'Les Combats de coqs dans le nord de la France' (unpublished maîtrise thesis, Paris, 1972).

P. Pierrard, *La Vie ouvrière à Lille sous le Second Empire* (Paris, 1965).

G. Pillement, *Paris en fête* (Paris, 1972).

A. Poitrineau, 'La Fête traditionelle', *Annales Historiques de la Revolution Française*, no. 221 (July–September 1975).

R. Pouillart and J. Williams, *Le Sport et les lettres: le sport dans la littérature française de 1919 à 1925* (Louvain, 1953).

J. Prat, *Mêlée ouverte* (Paris, 1968).

G. Prouteau and E. Raude, *Le Message de Léo Lagrange* (Paris, 1950).

C. Rearick, 'Festivals in Modern France', *Journal of Contemporary History*, vol. 12 (1977).

M. Rebérioux, *La République radicale* (Paris, 1975).

Recherches Internationales à la Lumière du Marxisme, June–July 1965, 'Sport et éducation physique'.

J. Rennert, *A Hundred Years of Bicycle Posters* (London, 1973).

J. P. Rey, *Tarbes, le rugby en rouge et blanc* (Paris, 1973).

J. Richardson, 'Hunting, fishing and "crickett": Anglomanie under the Second Empire', *History Today*, vol. xxi, no. 4 (1971).

R. Rollet, *La Vie quotidienne en Provence au temps de Mistral* (Paris, 1972).

A. Rossel, *Daumier, émotions de chasse* (Paris, 1973).

L. Roubin, *Chambrettes de Provence, une maison d'hommes en méditérranée septentrionale* (Paris, 1970).

L. Roubin, 'Male and Female Space in the Provençal Community' in R. Forster and O. Ranum (eds), *Rural Society in France* (London, 1977).

J. A. Roy, *Histoire du Jockey Club* (Paris, 1958).

J. Saint-Paulien, *Histoire de la corrida* (Paris, 1968).

A. Scriven, *Grandes Journées du rugby français* (Toulouse, 1947).

E. Seidler, *Le Sport et la presse* (Paris, 1964).

C. Seignolle, *Le Berry traditionnel* (Paris, 1969).

W. H. Sewell, 'The Working Class of Marseille under the Second Republic: Social Structure and Political Behaviour', in P. N. Stearns and D. J. Walkowitz (eds), *Workers in the Industrial Revolution* (New Jersey, 1974).

E. Shorter, *The Making of the Modern Family* (London, 1976).

J. P. Simon, *Essai sur l'introduction de l'athlétisme en France* (ENSEPS, 1972), Mémoire pour le diplôme.

R. Soucy, 'The Nature of Fascism in France', *Journal of Contemporary History*, no. 1 (1966).

M. Spivak, 'Le Développement de l'education physique et du sport français, 1852–1914', *Revue d'Histoire Moderne et Contemporaine*, vol. xxiv (January–March 1977).

La Société de Sciences, Lettres et Arts de Bayonne, no. 112 (1966), 'Une siècle de corridas bayonnaises (1852–1952)'.

M. Soulier, *Le Football gardois* (Nimes, 1969).

Sport et développement social au XXᵉ siècle: colloque internationale de la Fédération Sportive du Travail (Paris, 1969).

P. N. Stearns, *European Society in Upheaval*, 2nd ed. (London, 1975).

P. N. Stearns, *Lives of Labour* (London, 1975).

Z. Sternhell, 'Paul Déroulède and the Origins of Modern French Nationalism', *Journal of Contemporary History*, vol. 6, no. 4 (1971).

K. A. Swart, *The Sense of Decadence in Nineteenth Century France* (The Hague, 1964).

F. Terbeen, *Les Géants de cyclisme sur route* (Paris, 1969).

J. Thabault, *Sports et éducation physique* (Paris, 1972).

K. V. Thomas, 'Work and Leisure in Pre-industrial Society, *Past and Present*, vol. 29 (December 1964).

E. P. Thompson, 'Time, Work Discipline and Industrial Capitalism', *Past and Present*, vol. 38 (December 1967).

G. Thuillier, 'Pour une histoire de l'hygiène corporelle. Un exemple régional: Le Nivernais', *Revue d'Histoire Economique et Sociale*, vol. 46, no. 2 (1968).

G. Thuillier, 'Pour une histoire des gestes en Nivernais au XIXᵉ siècle', *Revue d'Histoire Economique et Sociale*, no. 2 (1973).

L. Tiger, *Men in Groups* (London, 1970).

G. A. Tobin, 'The Bicycle Boom of the 1890s: the Development of Private Transportation and the Birth of the Modern Tourist', *Journal of Popular Culture*, vol. 7, no. 4 (1974).

H. Trémaud, *Les Français jouent aux quilles* (Paris, 1964).

A. Varagnac, *Civilisation traditionelle et genres de vie* (Paris, 1948).

P. Vermet, *L'Intervention de l'état dans le sport* (Paris, 1963).

Dr P. Voivenal, *Mon beau rugby* (Toulouse, 1962).

J. Walvin, *The People's Game: a Social History of British Football* (London, 1975).

E. Weber, 'Pierre de Coubertin and the Introduction of Sport into France', *Journal of Contemporary History*, vol. 5, no. 2 (1970).

E. Weber, 'Gymnastics and Sports in Fin-de-siècle France: Opium of the Classes?', *American Historical Review*, vol. 76 (February 1971).

E. Weber, *Peasants into Frenchmen: the Modernisation of Rural France* (London, 1977).

L. Wylie, *A Village in the Vaucluse* (London, 1951).

T. Zeldin, *France 1848–1945*, vol. 1, *Ambition, Love and Politics* (Oxford, 1973), vol. 2, *Intellect, Taste and Anxiety* (Oxford, 1977).

Index